DRESSAGE
WITH MIND, BODY & SOUL

DRESSAGE

WITH MIND, BODY & SOUL

A 21st-Century Approach

to the Science and Spirituality

of Riding and Horse-and-Rider Well-Being

LINDA TELLINGTON-JONES

WITH REBECCA M. DIDIER

Foreword by Ingrid Klimke

TRAFALGAR SQUARE
North Pomfret, Vermont

First published in 2012 by
Trafalgar Square Books
North Pomfret, Vermont 05053

Printed in China

Library of Congress Cataloging-in-Publication Data

Tellington-Jones, Linda.
  Dressage with mind, body & soul : a 21st-century approach to the science and spirituality of riding and horse-and-rider well-being / Linda Tellington-Jones with Rebecca Didier.
     pages cm
     Summary: "Renowned animal behaviorist and horse trainer Linda Tellington-Jones explains how to apply her multi-faceted method, which includes bodywork, groundwork, and under-saddle exercises, to the equestrian sport of dressage"-- Provided by publisher.
  Includes bibliographical references and index.
  ISBN 978-1-57076-426-4 (pbk.)
1. Dressage. 2. Horses--Training. 3. Horses--Psychology. I. Didier, Rebecca, 1977- II. Title. III. Title: Dressage with mind, body, and soul.
  SF309.5.T45 2012
  798.2'3--dc23
                            2012033428

Book design by Carrie Fradkin
Cover design by RM Didier
Typefaces: ITC Veljovic, Avenir

10 9 8 7 6 5 4 3 2 1

DEDICATION

I am dedicating this book to Meggle's Weltall VA, in honor of his enormous heart.

Having the privilege to work with this 18-year-old, 18-hand Hanoverian gelding has given me hope that the courage he demonstrates in developing a new level of trust in humans may inspire other dressage riders to connect with their horses from the heart, and with respect for the incredible gifts horses bring to their lives.

"You wonder why you feel good
when you touch us—
lean into us.
It is because we connect you
to the stars."

—from "Message from the Spirit of the Horse" by Linda Tellington-Jones

CONTENTS

■
■
■
■
■
■
■

RESPECT AND TRUST GO HAND IN HAND AND ARE essential elements in a horse's training, whatever his breed or discipline. The relationship that evolves between a horse and rider depends very much on having respect for and trust in each other—this has been the key to my success and the joy I find in training horses, just as it was integral to my father's work as a rider, trainer, and teacher. My father, Dr. Reiner Klimke, said to me upon giving me the first copy of his seminal *Basic Training of the Young Horse*, "Ingrid, we want to understand the nature of the horse, respect his personality, and be sure not to suppress it at any time during his training. Then we are on the right path."

When asked to give riders one piece of advice, I often say that you must *be patient* and *listen to your horse*. Horses, especially young ones, look for safety—they must know that you, their rider, will guide them and give them the security they seek. The Classical Training Scale is important here, as it gives you and your horse a foundation of training that you can come to rely on.

When a strange situation creates anxiety in your horse, instead of pushing him forward make the circumstances easier for him to handle so he will learn to trust you. Thus, the moment of anxiety passes by and you survive it together without fracturing your relationship. Horses *need* to trust you. In new situations where they falter or spook, it might not be correction that is needed, but reassurance.

Horses also need to know when they've done well and deserve praise, even in the middle of a dressage test. Much has been made of the small pat I sometimes give my horse after a good flying change and many have noticed this in my Olympic dressage test or during the European Championships. But when my horse has listened so well and performed so well, *whenever* that may be, he needs my thanks for that effort.

Trust, reassurance, giving thanks—these are some of the principles that Linda Tellington-Jones outlines in this book. I have known Linda for many years. She visited my father's barn when he was still alive to share her

Ingrid and Linda.

Tellington Method with him and the staff, and she worked with him on several occasions in the years that followed. Linda has also used her *Method* with me and my own horses in Germany and I find that many of her ideals align with my own. Foremost in Linda's technique is the idea of trust—inspiring trust in the horse, nurturing that trust, and helping it evolve into a base so strong that your riding partnership can withstand all manner of challenges from without and within. Linda also recognizes the great value in the Classical Training Scale, and she has creative ways we can subscribe to it in the modern day in order to better serve our horses.

When preparing my event horse FRH Butts Abraxxas for the Olympics in 2008, Linda's *Ear TTouch* and *Mouth TTouch* (around the muzzle and nostrils) applied by me or my groom helped relax him and temper stress related to travel and competition. I have been very impressed with the *Liberty Neck Ring*, which I use with all my horses now. Riding Abraxxas with it has brought me closer to him, made my hands even lighter, and resulted in him listening so very well—it is fantastic! My daughter uses *TTouches* and the *Neck Ring* on her pony, and it is wonderful for me to see how well they work from the viewpoint of a parent and instructor, as well as a rider, trainer, and competitor.

Horses give so much to us. They want to do their best and do things right. They are individuals and need to be treated as such. In the business of horses, of dressage, you have to deal with people and be diplomatic, but most important, if you truly love horses, you have to listen to your heart. Being with horses, in all its ups and downs, should still bring a big smile to your face every day. And it is these joyful resolutions that Linda Tellington-Jones' work, now explored in this book with dressage specifically in mind, can make real for every one of us.

Ingrid Klimke

Winner of Olympic Eventing Team Gold Medals in Beijing, 2008, and London, 2012
Co-author of *The New Basic Training of the Young Horse* and *Cavalletti*
with Dr. Reiner Klimke

PREFACE

THERE ARE A FEW THINGS YOU SHOULD BE AWARE OF AS you begin this book. Firstly, there is a very conscientious use of color in the book's design. This is meant to engage both sides of your brain and provide a means of retaining the information I'm about to present. I hope it adds visual interest to your reading experience while also serving as a useful method of assigning mental and psychological guideposts along your journey as a forever-evolving dressage rider.

Secondly, throughout the book you will see many references to the different facets or "parts" to my *Method*. The Tellington Method is made up of the *Tellington TTouches®*; *Ground Exercises,* consisting of lessons in hand that I call "Dancing with Your Horse," and use of obstacles from the "Playground of Higher Learning"; and *Ridden Work*, which I like to refer to as the "Joy of Riding."

I use (what I think are) "fun" names and acronyms to help you remember the exercises (for instance, a *TTouch* called *Lick of the Cow's Tongue* and a *Ground Exercise* named *Taming the Tiger*) and again to activate both sides of the brain (more on this ahead starting on p. 29). You may think the names and acronyms are a bit odd at first, but I promise you there is research supporting my reasoning for their incorporation. And if they make you smile, so much the better! Smiling can reduce stress and strengthen your connection with your horse. We need to find more reasons to smile in our work with horses (see p. 75).

However, before we get to these cornerstones of my *Method*, I'm going to relate the cornerstones of my *thinking*. I'm inviting you to theorize, alongside me, how we might best deal with the challenges presented to the twenty-first-century rider. And I'm also inviting you to experiment, alongside me, with the myriad options available to us in this day and age, where science *and* spirituality weight the opposite ends of the scale in equal measure, and when we are best advised to observe and absorb *both* in order to attain a state of *balance*—of mental, emotional, and physical equilibrium. This balance is something I feel necessary for both the dressage rider and the dressage horse, and I will explore it in depth beginning on p. 47.

Don't be surprised by what you read in the pages ahead. My goal is to offer you *infinite possibilities* that can make the experience of dressage more joyful and more meaningful for you and your horse. Just wait—you are only just getting started.

Linda Tellington-Jones
Kailua-Kona, Hawaii

NOTE TO THE READER:
HOW TO USE THIS BOOK

I HAVE DIVIDED THIS BOOK INTO TWO PARTS. PART ONE: AN INTRO-
duction to A New Way of Learning and Teaching Dressage is a summary of
theories I have about learning and teaching dressage, as well as a general description of the Tellington Method and how it works. Some of these concepts
may already be familiar to you; others may seem particularly foreign. All provide what I feel are specific ways to clarify the principles of classical teachings
and put them into action. At the same time, they are, perhaps, relatively novel
ideas in how to become a better riding partner to your horse.

Part Two: Dressage and the Tellington Method really broaches the work
I'm known for all over the world, providing specific information as to how it
is applicable in the sport of dressage. It is in this section that I move on from
the broad paint strokes that are the main themes of my work—the concepts
that interweave and connect human and horse, family life and riding life—and
turn your focus to the details.

In Part Two, I provide practical steps to incorporating the Tellington
Method in your everyday interaction with your horse. In addition, you will
find featured profiles of top dressage riders and their horses who I have worked
with during my lifetime. Their stories, their struggles and ultimate triumphs,
can serve to inspire you on your own journey.

In both Part One and Part Two, I make continual references to the different
facets of the Tellington Method: *TTouches*, *Ground Exercises*, and *Ridden
Work* that can be helpful in specific scenarios, such as specialized training
situations, behavioral problem-solving, stress-relief, and day-to-day care and
management. All these *TTouches* and *Exercises* are mentioned in italic in this
book and you can find a short summary of each one—in alphabetical order—
in the *Tellington Method Quick Reference Center* beginning on p. 262. However,
because the sheer bulk of my *Method* with all its techniques in a "how-to"
sense is truly beyond the scope of this book I'd like to suggest you refer to my
previous book *The Ultimate Horse Behavior and Training Book* in order to find
detailed explanations and step-by-step photographic descriptions.

Tellington Training for Horses App

In 2012, I released a fabulous app that can be viewed on your iPhone or iPad. This allows you to have "how-to" *TTouch* guidelines right on your phone or tablet device. The app contains short video clips of various *TTouches*, accompanied by my personal instructions describing how to perform the *TTouches* and what benefits that particular *TTouch* provides. The text included with the app is extensive, explaining how much pressure to use, how to apply the *TTouch*, and which *TTouch* is best suited for specific behavioral, postural, physical, or training issues.

The app includes instructions for *TTouches* and exercises that help with saddling issues; easing soreness in muscles; limiting spookiness; lengthening stride; increasing confidence; lowering pulse and respiration; overcoming resistance; alleviating pain and shock; releasing tension; reducing stumbling; and calming the nervous or frightened horse. The *Tellington Training for Horses App* for your iPhone or iPad can be purchased on iTunes.

I want to make one more particular point before I begin. Many people familiar with my work think that *TTouch* (with double Ts) stands for "Tellington Touch," and for a while, I did try that on for size. However, there were several distinct problems inherent in this treatment. The first is there are many different forms of bodywork that include the word "Touch." The second issue is that *trust* is a major component in my work—in how I have followed my intuition and scientific and spiritual guideposts to nurture my *Method* as it actively evolves each day. Trust is one of the primary goals in the work I do, with both animals and humans: I am earning their trust, one touch at a time! So think of *TTouch* as "Trust Touch," an integral step in improving your relationship with your horse.

Note: Throughout this book, I have referred to the horse as masculine ("he" or "him") and the rider as feminine ("she" or "her"). This is not because I think ill of mares or that I feel men don't, can't, or shouldn't ride. Rather, it is a method of instilling clarity in the prose, and lessening confusion as to subject as we discuss many topics of interest to all of us, whether male or female.

PART ONE

AN INTRODUCTION
TO A NEW WAY OF LEARNING
AND TEACHING DRESSAGE

INTRODUCTION

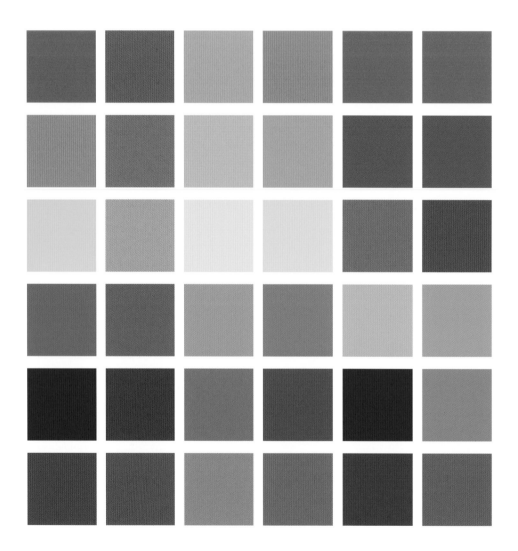

THE ROOTS OF THE TELLINGTON METHOD REACH BACK INTO THE 1960s when my first husband Wentworth Tellington and I established the Pacific Coast Equestrian Research Farm and School of Horsemanship in Badger, California. This center included a nine-month residential training program for riding instructors who, between the years of 1964 and 1974, came from nine countries and 36 states. In those years we also wrote syndicated columns in many horse magazines and mailed our Research Farm Newsletter to 22 countries.

After founding the Tellington Method in 1974, I closed the School of Horsemanship in California and began to travel and teach in Europe, as well as the United States. Since then I have traveled continuously with the intent to share this work. I feel very blessed to have written 19 books published in 13 languages and produced 20 DVDs on how to implement my method, including a video (*TTouch for Dressage*, 1995) featuring Klaus Balkenhol and Nicole Uphoff that was made specifically for the dressage horse and rider and problems they commonly encounter (fig. 1.1).

1.1 I worked with four-time Olympic gold-medal winner Nicole Uphoff and her horses Rembrandt and Day Dream (shown here) in my *TTouch for Dressage* video.

......About My History with Dressage

I have a long history of involvement in dressage. I was a founding member of the California Dressage Society in the 1960s, and I had the good fortune to spend time in California in the early 1970s with Alois Podhajsky, former head of the Spanish Riding School and author of the classic text *My Horses, My Teachers* (Trafalgar Square Books, 1997). At that time he was working with Kyra Downton, who with Kadett, represented the United States at the 1968 Olympic Games in Mexico, where she was the highest-placed US rider and led the dressage team to an eighth-place finish. This

remarkable feat is all the more impressive when you consider that the sixties were a low point in the popularity of dressage in the US: the cavalry had been disbanded and the United States Dressage Federation (USDF) wasn't founded until 1973.

As a young rider I was intrigued by the training methods of French riding master James Fillis, and from his book *Breaking and Riding* (Hurst and Blackett, 1890), discovered the value of flexing the horse at the poll with the plane of the face vertical to create balance. I studied dressage from the classical books and had the good fortune to ride under and learn the art of judging the sport from dressage master Hermann Friedlander. I have worked with some of the top dressage riders in the world, in barns and riding arenas all over the globe (figs. 1.2 and 1.3 A & B).

I have had the honor of riding Grand Prix horses and the joy of performing the movements of the *haute école*, but despite my experiences I know there are others much better equipped to explain the specifics of these movements (figs. 1.4 A & B). My intent is to teach you a new way to *learn* and a new way to *teach*, and therefore, ultimately, to help you assimilate knowledge as you continue your journey as a dressage rider, and increase your ability to use that knowledge in training your horse.

My *Method* applies just as well to teaching a turn-on-the-forehand as it does to one-tempi changes; it is effective for the first-level horse and the Prix St. Georges competitor. It is a new lens through which to view the world of dressage competition and dressage training, and my hope is it will help introduce future generations of happy, contented performers to the highest levels of international acclaim. In this new world I'm imagining, the results in the arena will be only as good as the methods used to attain them, and communion with the horse rewarded as generously as obedience to the bit.

Recent trends in dressage—specifically, competitive dressage—have troubled me greatly, and it has become clear that a new way is needed to offer the potential to reach high levels of performance without sacrificing the well-being of the horse or the integrity of the sport. This book, therefore, is the result of my pondering this issue and struggling with the

1.2 In 2009 and 2011 the Xenophon Society sponsored Tellington Method seminars at Klaus Balkenhol's stable in Rosendahl, Germany. I have worked with Klaus for over 20 years, demonstrating how the Tellington Method can improve dressage performance and overcome resistance while reducing stress in our equine athletes.

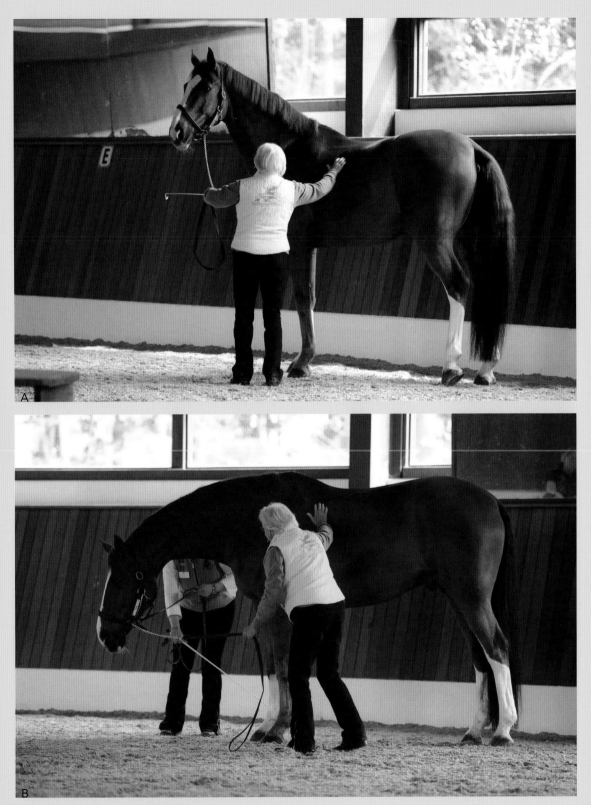

1.3 A & B One of the horses I worked with at the 2011 Xenophon Symposium was Klaus Balkenhol's daughter Anabel's World Equestrian Games team bronze-medal-winning Grand Prix horse, Dablino. This horse is known for his hypersensitivity. He is by nature very high-headed and alert, looking for the next "threat" to appear (A).

   Along with my team of practitioners and Anabel ("Belli"), we worked to get Dablino relaxed and trusting enough to lower his head in front of 240 auditors (B).

1.4 A & B I have had the honor of riding top international Grand Prix horses. Here I adjust my stirrups preparing for a much appreciated and invaluable lesson from Klaus Balkenhol (A) before enjoying piaffe on Garçon who was so light in my hands and responsive to my leg aids (B).

Garçon is the black stallion Klaus was riding when he won his final Grand Prix test before ending his show career so he could concentrate on coaching and training full time.

In 1985 I taught a one-day seminar for riders of the Spanish Riding School at the private stable of Arthur Kottas, head rider there at that time. Just the week before, Arthur had taken in a Thoroughbred jumper who had been sent to him for dressage training. The gelding was tense, and Arthur was interested to know what I would do with the horse.

I demonstrated *TTouches* such as the *Ear TTouch* and *Coiled Python Lift* to instill trust and relaxation, and then I rode the horse. (Note: All the *TTouches, Ground Exercises*, and *Ridden Work* are briefly described in the Tellington Method Quick Reference Center on p. 262. They are explained—and demonstrated—in more detail in my book *The Ultimate Horse Behavior and Training Book*.)

The gelding was high-headed and tense, and to bring the horse into balance I rode with the *Balance Rein* and demonstrated what I call the *Half-Walk*. With raised hands held in a position that I learned from reading about the system used at the Cadre Noir of Saumur, France, I asked the gelding to take steps half as long as an ordinary walk. After six or seven steps in this shortened gait, I lowered my hands and let the reins slide through my fingers. The horse lowered his head and took the reins, lengthening his neck and softening his back. His stride became long and rhythmic.

A retired rider from the Spanish Riding School who was attending the seminar commented, "That shortened walk used to be known as *der Dritte Schritt* ['the third walk']." He said the exercise had been "lost." (Over the years I have used this *Dritte Schritt* with many tense horses, in combination with the *Balance Rein* as just described, with much success.)

The (at that time) recently retired Director of the School, Brigadier General Kurt Albrecht, attended one of my weekend clinics in Austria. I saw him two weeks later at a dressage show he was judging in Vienna and he told me he was "impressed," "excited," and "raving to everyone" about the Tellington Method. I couldn't have been more pleased!

state of today's competitive dressage horses that I have observed in many barns, training facilities, and practice arenas around the world.

.......About Dressage Horses Today

You hardly need a summary of all that has happened in the past decade (or two) to inspire worry and disillusionment both within the dressage world and in those who enjoy it as spectators and aficionados. With the explosion of the online community we have had a constant stream of chatter and debate; we've heard from many sources, from top experts and concerned citizens; we are beginning to understand that "LDR" (low, deep, and round), *Rollkur* (hyper-flexion), and the "blue tongues," "bloody foam," and additional side effects of these and other training methods, are unacceptable, abominable, and some-times—if not most times—cruel.

I've seen *many* unhappy dressage horses being ridden in overflexed positions such as seen with LDR, *despite* the fact that some veterinarians and scientists argue that the horse's airways are compromised in this position (which the Fédération Equestre Internationale—the FEI—recognizes) and that the extreme stress incurred when a flight animal cannot see (which the horse cannot in an overflexed position) is significant and damaging. In addition, there are unresolved questions as to whether such a posture contributes to neurological issues, career-ending injury, and early onset arthritis. I find these horses experience significantly higher incidences of pain—notably in their neck, back, and haunches, all the way down to their hocks and feet—not to mention the mental anguish they suffer, leading to increased (negative) tension throughout their body, and thus further discomfort.

And yet, not nearly enough has been done from the top down to prevent the further dissemination of these techniques. While *Rollkur* (hyperflexion) has now been defined by the FEI as an aggressive form of riding that uses force and thus is an unacceptable training practice, what in my opinion is *the same* abnormal position has been deemed acceptable under the name "LDR."

The proliferation of such training practices is not necessarily the fault of average dressage riders, as many depend upon trainers and professionals far more learned than they are to help them find their way through the maze of dressage theory and the massive body of work that already exists to support it. It is the responsibility of those who both understand how the horse feels and how balanced, beautiful horsemanship can be achieved via *innovative teaching methods*, rather than *coercive training techniques* to provide guidance.

Although I retired from dressage competition in the 1970s, I continue to this day to hone my skills at communicating with horses at all levels of equitation. I have spent some time considering what is different today from yesterday, and what should again be different tomorrow, from today. It is the results of this exploration that I will share in the pages ahead.

.. ....About Something Bigger

This book is meant to be Exhibit A in a new way of learning to ride with brilliance and balance, and to present a method of training that gives your horse as much enjoyment as it gives you—the rider. It is meant to involve both your left and right brain through the thematic use of color and an exploration of the idea of Mind Mapping (see pp. 48 and 55). It is meant to inspire thoughtful criticism of what may now be accepted "norms" in training dressage horses but may not be in the horse's best interest. It is meant to give hope for the years to come to those who, like me, have felt saddened by the state of the sport and perhaps even doubtful that it can be "saved" (for lack of a better word).

I intend to meld what I think of as "hard science"—proven techniques and methods, on the ground and in the saddle, for ensuring the horse's soundness and continued performance—with the spiritual. Spiritual is the "feel," and the belief in something greater existing between you and your horse. You and your horse will become inspiring and inspired competitors, who move as one being.

In the chapters to come, I will talk more about the studies and theories that I find most powerful when working with horses, and I invite you to try these methods for yourself. I'm also going to talk about creating an atmosphere of well-being for your horse, in his stall, his paddock, and the arena; at home and at shows. I'll cover some basic troubleshooting to ensure that your horse is as whole and healthy as he can be as you pursue dressage together.

I also take a look at the Classical Training Scale and offer new ways to interpret its components so that they can work best for you and your horse. Plus, I describe 17 case studies with upper-level dressage horses and how the Tellington Method was shaped to help each of them surmount their issues and improve their performance without the use of forceful techniques, and all the while lessening stress rather than amplifying it.

There are many excellent books about dressage available. They tell you how to train the movements, how to ride a correct test, how to dress, and how to perform. This book is meant to be something else. It is a treatise to all that the sport of dressage has to offer. Truly what I share in this book is the opportunity for you to "be all you can be" in every facet of your life, using the practice of dressage as a means of learning how to visualize your highest potential—for your horse, as well.

How is this possible? Dressage employs both logic and feeling, left brain and right, and if you can use it to improve your understanding of your horse, it will also help you better understand yourself. If each time you mount you

1.5 In this book I offer some of my theories of how we can transform "dressage work" into a "dressage odyssey," making the journey fun for both rider *and* horse. Here I am thoroughly enjoying another ride on Garçon. I had the pleasure of spending a week TTouching this horse at a dressage competition in Stuttgart, Germany, where he and Klaus Balkenhol won the Grand Prix, the Grand Prix Special, and the Freestyle.

are consumed with joy and pleasure at the prospect of the ride before you, your horse will be happier and healthier—and believe it or not, so will the world around you.

I understand if you hesitate here; perhaps you're a bit doubtful that your individual pursuit of an athletic activity can have an impact greater than that of better physical conditioning of you and your horse. While it is easy to see the physiological benefits of a method of systematic training and conditioning such as dressage, it is more difficult to accept that there are positive developments occurring beneath the surface. And even once that is acknowledged, the idea that your horse's mental and emotional well-being, and your own, can have an impact on the world at large, is a bit difficult to get your head around.

But believe it or not, the practice of riding dressage *can* and *will* change how you interact with your family, how you perform at work, and how you address the multitude of challenges the world hands to you every day. It *can* and *will* help your horse live a more fulfilled, mentally curious, social existence.

These are big changes in how to think about the training of dressage horses. Because of the nature of the sport, competition and moving up to "higher levels" will always factor, and there is no reason why performance can't provide an accurate and positive reflection of the work that you and your horse have done together. The act of showing your horse can be noble and can be fun.

In today's dressage arenas, we unfortunately see many individuals who are clearly *not* having fun. We see horses who are miserable, cramped, jabbed, and pushed, and riders who are exhausted by all the cramping, jabbing, and pushing they feel is necessary to get their horse to perform. I don't believe riders want to be cruel to their horse or cause him pain and discomfort. I just feel they don't have a choice—or haven't had a choice, *yet*.

The Tellington Method can offer a choice—in fact, I'll illustrate a number of theories I feel can be used in small or large part to improve the way you train and the way you ride in the dressage arena. You can walk away with only one aspect of my philosophy that speaks to you, but that one piece can be enough to transform your "dressage work" into a "dressage odyssey." That one piece can be all it takes to open up to new ways of communicating. It can be all you need to move up one level (or two!). It can be just the ticket to help you perform consistently and beautifully without relying on force or training devices to attain the scores of which you dare dream (fig. 1.5).

THE CORNERSTONES OF MY THINKING

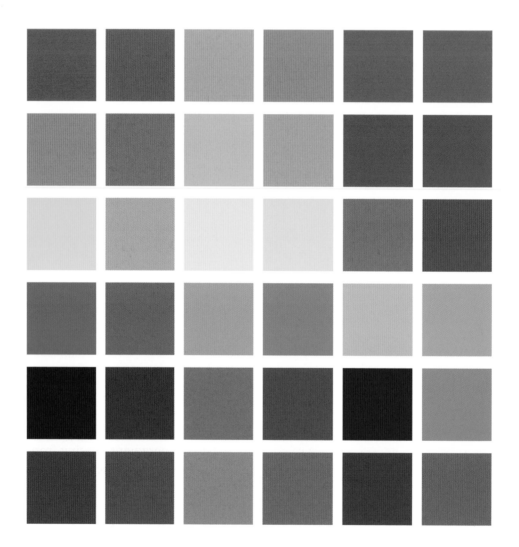

2

......About "Feel"

"Feel." Supposedly, this one little word is what dressage is all about. Four letters. Two consonants. Two vowels. Visually, the word itself is balanced.

We all have some idea, however vague, of what feel is supposed to mean to us as riders. In general, the word "feel" embodies the sense of touch—what our nerve endings take in, absorb, react to when we lay a hand on a warm surface, when we tickle a baby's cheek, when we stroke our horse's neck. This is the tangible side of feel. But we also feel something when we see someone we love after a long separation, when we lose, and when we win.

Though we might think these two types of feel are different, one physical and one emotional, in truth they are *both* emotional, because they are intrinsically linked. The physical sensation of the sun's warm rays on your skin commonly inspires a sense of well-being or happiness, for example. And a cool hard surface might calm an anxious mind. Our inward reactions to outside sensations certainly share commonalities, but they are in a large part affected by our past experiences and individuality—so of course what means one thing to one person means something else entirely to another.

I am going to play with these ideas in this book not because I think you are not familiar with the subject (goodness knows, if one word is overused and over-explicated in the realm of dressage it is feel). But as I travel and do my work—which I have been doing now, all around the world, for almost 50 years—it seems to me that this is the most apparent ingredient missing from today's dressage riders, and I mean at all levels. Yes, of course, mechanics are necessary, important, even integral to the correct and successful pursuit of this higher form of equestrianism, but in the end, without feel, mechanics are just a series of movements and gestures, the horse a puppet and the rider a puppeteer (fig. 2.1).

Feel is closely related to the other necessary element for truly syncopated dressage—where rider and horse move in union, as one creature, harmonious in mind and body and spirit—and that is what I call "heART."

2.1 I feel that today many dressage riders haven't a real sense of what riding with "feel" entails—an intricate interweaving of the physical and emotional sensations inspired by the horse's movement and state of mind. True feel, as is exhibited during a flawless transition or the beautiful pirouette demonstrated here by Ingrid Klimke, involves an intuitive ability to know the horse's actions and reactions as intimately as you know yours, and to move in sync with them as easily as you would your own.

.......About "He*ART*"

I'm an avid reader—my intense travel schedule allows time for reading new material while midair or awaiting transit. I'm also fortunate to be one of "those people" who require less sleep, so during the quiet hours of the morning, between 3:30 and 5:30 a.m., I am finding further inspiration reading books on my iPad.

Those who have visited my website or receive my newsletter are familiar with my recommended reading list, which is forever expanding and changing (for a form of this list modeled specifically for readers of this book, see p. 274). One book that I love, which was published in 2005, is called *The HeART of Nursing*, and was compiled by my good friend and coauthor of my book *TTouch for Healthcare*, M. Cecelia Wendler, RN, CCRN, PhD. Cecelia is a critical care nurse and nursing educator who is devoted to what she calls the "re-humanization" of the nursing profession, and indeed, health care in general.

In *The HeART of Nursing*, Cecelia celebrates centuries of "nursing art" with a modern collection of works (poems, stories, paintings) by nurses who participated in special sessions during the Honor Society of Nursing's biannual convention. Her goal was to demonstrate in this age of technology that health care benefits from self-exploration from a holistic and humanistic point of view. "Nursing art" is an aesthetic representation of a relationship the nurse establishes with her- or himself, and the relationship she or he has with patients and patients' families.

Cecelia uses the term "heART" (with a capital A-R-T) as a device that I find really effective, and therefore I would like to introduce it to you here. I feel it is extremely relevant in the context of dressage. I find it so interesting that we often hear this particular riding discipline referred to as the "art of dressage," and yet, as I've already mentioned, I find it apparent that it has progressively become less and less of a right-brain, or creative activity, and increasingly left-brain and logical (see my discussion of left and right brain, p. 29). In my opinion, this has robbed the sport of its soul: without the idea of dressage as "art" at the core, and without the characteristics that enable us to create art (imagination, vision, empathy, message, feeling, thought, and yes, heart), we are left with a demonstration devoid of meaning and absent personal or social relevance.

I am going to use the term "heART" in this book to encapsulate all that I think must be reinstilled in the sport. It is intended to remind you that the "art of dressage" is indeed an aesthetic representation of your relationship with yourself—as a friend, a parent, a coworker, a career professional, a rider—and with your horse. As a device, I'd like the term to give you a warm, fluttery feeling each time you read it. It is my desire to make you more open to the experience of being "one" with your horse (fig. 2.2). (I take this idea a step further in chapters 5 and 6 where I explain the concepts of *intention* and *heart coherence* and the very real, and scientifically viable, effects they can have on your riding.)

In the course of reading the chapters that follow, I'd like you to feel invigorated by the concept of "heART," perhaps even devoted to its proliferation. When you bring "heART" to your riding and all the work you do with your horse, he will respond with enthusiasm, willingness, and another term I will use again in this book—"sparkle."

.......About the Miraculous and the Divine

Miracles surround us, on a large and small scale. It is on a personal level that we ascertain whether an occurrence qualifies as miraculous. My life has been full of what I consider miracles—from the simple unexpected to the extraordinary. Many of these have had to do with the animals, in yards, pastures, and lakes, on mesas, steppes, and mountaintops, both those in the wild and at home, who have graced my life with their essence.

While the extraordinary is easy to recognize, it is the more commonplace miracles that you must be sure not to take for granted. On many occasions, the most seemingly insignificant of moments can either indicate a tide-change (one small step in a succession of small steps that eventually equal an evolution) or it is, in itself, so integral to progress that your horse learns and performs in an entirely different manner from that moment forward.

Riding a horse is a series of small miracles. It is a miracle that this powerful animal allows you to sit upon his back. It is a miracle he chooses to follow your direction (in most cases), to earn your friendship, your praise, and your loyalty in an intense form of reciprocity seen in few other human-animal relationships. But the miracles don't end there—each time you ask for the most specific of movements, each time you focus on the most subtle of cues, each time you brush your leg against the horse's side and receive a gentle, controlled response, you have experienced a small miracle for which you should be thankful. Remembering to give thanks and express your gratitude for these things should be something you work at daily. I remind myself of this each morning when I rise and each night before I journey into the dream world.

Although whether or not miracles are brought about by divine power may be a point of debate, it is not one that concerns me in this book. Instead, I prefer to acknowledge that events do happen in life that are surprising, inspiring, and in every estimation "good," and in these instances I choose to recognize them as "miraculous." With this attitude as part of your day-to-day existence, an unparalleled relationship with your horse can be the result.

2.2 Riding with "heART," with the idea that *art*—self-expression illustrated in an interesting or beautiful way and capable of inspiring a physical, intellectual, or emotional response from both participants (you and your horse) and onlookers (judges and spectators)—is at the core of your dressage pursuits, and is meant to provide a device to help you "become one" with your horse.

The Miracle of Avignon

In January of 2010, I was visiting my dear friends Frédéric Pignon and Magali Delgado (the world-renowned original stars of the hit equestrian spectacular *Cavalia*) in the South of France. Their 18-year-old dog, Bulle, who was mostly blind and deaf, wandered off and went missing for days. Frédéric and Magali were devastated, and certain that something terrible had befallen their beloved friend.

I have found that some of the ideas espoused by Gregg Braden in his little book *The Secret of the Lost Mode of Prayer* (Hay House, 2006) to be the best way to apply my own ideas of opening my heart and reaching out with love and positive energy from deep within myself in order to find my way through difficult or emotionally trying times. Instead of imagining Bulle experiencing stress, trauma, loneliness, and fear (as it was so easy to do), we all "held" the image of Bulle's safe return, and the joy and gratitude we would feel when we again felt her warmth or stroked her head.

Only a few hours after we began concentrating on changing the feelings we held in our heart, Frédéric and Magali received a phone call. Disoriented and weak, Bulle had been found several miles from home, and was dropped at a veterinarian's office. By a stroke of good fortune, the veterinarian on duty happened to know Frédéric and Magali and recognized their dog. We have come to refer to Bulle's miraculous return as "The Miracle of Avignon." (I've shared more about Frédéric and Magali and their marvelous work with horses on p. 224.)

......About Being Nice to Your Horse…with Boundaries

Now, just because you love your horse, and just because you are nice to him and conscientiously ride with "heART," it doesn't mean you can't establish *safe* and *fair* boundaries. This, I feel, is key to horse training of any sort. On many occasions I have had riders at my clinics who talk to their horse in a way that I feel is inappropriate and ineffective: "Ginger, please do what Mommy wants," or "Lightning, don't push Mommy like that." Horses are not children. They don't sleep in your bed or put their head in your lap. When you really think about it, do you want your horse to act like a child? No, you want him to act like an intelligent, independent being who is capable of taking care of *you* in certain situations, not just vice versa. He has to learn to think for himself in directed ways.

So often riders make the mistake of assuming that in order to be kind, they must allow the horse to do whatever he wants, or make the horse utterly dependent upon them. I feel that this is a trap.

I can't tell you the number of dressage horses I have ridden who, when I've dropped all contact with their mouth, were utterly confused and unable to function. They literally stopped in their tracks or veered every which way. I learned from my first husband Wentworth Tellington the old cavalry test that a horse, once started, should be able to travel on a straight line without support or guidance from the rider, until he is told to turn or stop. I doubt that 80 percent of today's dressage horses can do this, and I feel it should be absolutely fundamental to any kind of horse training, but especially dressage. In the last clinic he taught in the United States before he passed away, dressage Olympian Dr. Reiner Klimke required riders to enter the arena on a loose rein at the trot (fig. 2.3). This exercise was challenging for most of the riders and impossible for several (the *Balance Rein* and *Promise Wrap* helped in these cases—see more about this clinic, at which I worked closely with Dr. Klimke, on p. 21).

We have made dressage horses so dependent on us—on our contact and direction—that they are incapable of thinking for themselves or moving independently of the rider's support and aids. It is of the utmost importance that at the heart of your pursuit of dressage resides mutual respect: not only does the horse respect you, but you respect your horse. Referring to yourself as "Mommy" or "Daddy" is disrespectful. In addition, an attitude such as this exhibits a disconnection from reality. It simply isn't safe to treat a 1,000-pound animal as you would a toy poodle.

The point I must make here is that it doesn't have to be one way or the other, that is, cold and forceful or kind and soft. There are many ways you can set firm and fair boundaries. Beginning on page 82 I'll show you different ways the Tellington Method can help you be just and even-handed with your horse while remaining safe and *always* respectful.

▪▪▪▪▪▪About Science and Spirituality

Depending on where you come from, you are likely to be either swayed by evidence of a *scientific* nature or that of a *spiritual* nature. In other words, many of us are either evolutionists or creationists, with others believing in a hybrid version of the two. In actuality, science and spirituality are about more than test tubes and bible study, they are about the search for *proof* and the search for *meaning*. They are about left brain and right brain. And, it is my feeling—as you will see on the pages ahead—that *both* apply to horsemanship, whichever form (that is, riding discipline) it may take.

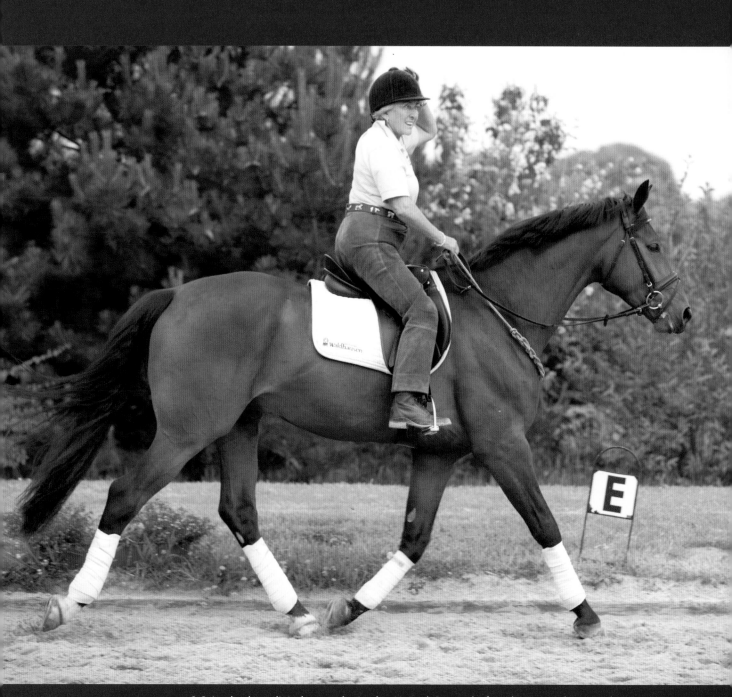

2.3 In the last clinic he taught in the United States before he passed away, dressage Olympian Dr. Reiner Klimke required riders to enter the arena on a loose rein at the trot. It is a good test of whether or not you've provided sufficient "boundaries" for your horse or if he is completely dependent upon your contact and aids for direction and support.

Note: the *Balance Rein* shown here is a Tellington Tool that steadies a horse's mind, enhancing mental as well as physical balance.

In February of 1999, only a few short months before he died, I had the honor of consulting at ringside with seven-time German Olympian Dr. Reiner Klimke as he worked with horses and riders during a four-day symposium at the Los Angeles Equestrian Center (LAEC) in California. We worked with 12 horse-and-rider teams, from First Level to Grand Prix, and spoke to approximately 2,000 auditors each day (fig. 2.4).

It was a distinct pleasure to work with Dr. Klimke. His way of riding and training made the horses happy, and the work I did with *TTouch* bodywork and Tellington Method *Ground Exercises* and *Ridden Work* was magnified through his additions in the saddle or via instruction of the riders.

Our focus over the four days was to develop trust between horse and rider and improve the horse's confidence, as well as promote rhythm and relaxation through generous warm-up and cool-down periods.

"Be nice to your horse," Dr. Klimke told participants, "then you have a right to ask him to work a little." He continuously reminded the riders to "give" with the reins ("release"); touch the horse on the neck with a kind hand; and invite the horse to stretch, use his body, and "be a horse" for a few moments in between exercises.

We both knew that you can't expect a dressage horse to perform in an atmosphere of fear, and this is why our methods dovetailed so well. Whether I was doing a particular *TTouch* or Dr. Klimke was asking for a certain movement, if the horse found it difficult or uncomfortable, Dr. Klimke would stop, give the horse a moment to process, and reapproach. This built the horse's confidence a little more and earned a bit more of his trust.

It was a great privilege to work together with Dr. Klimke in this way, and I believe many of the horse-and-rider partnerships came away from the symposium stronger, happier, and better performing teams.

2.4 In 1999, I had the honor of being a part of a symposium at the Los Angeles Equestrian Center with seven-time Olympian Dr. Reiner Klimke.

2.5 I believe with all my heart that the horse deserves our thanks for all that his species has contributed to ours over time; for his dedicated service; for his willingness to do as we bid; for lessons learned and exercises performed well.

Science has offered great gains in terms of understanding the biomechanics of horse and rider, and it has provided powerful tools in ways to teach animals, and to teach yourself to perform in a certain way, in certain situations.

Spirituality, on the other hand, is the heart of the matter. Without it, there is no life, and no purpose, to what you do. With it, your riding can reach new levels. The science of riding says, "Left rein, left leg, inside seat bone," and the spirituality of it says, "Think forward and up! Think together! Think elevation! Think love! Think fun!"

The science demonstrates *the proof* that through the quantum field, we are all connected (see my discussion of riding with *intention*, p. 60). The spirituality is *the belief in that connection*, and thus the ability to ride with body, heart, mind, and soul in concert with your horse. When the science of riding and the spirituality of riding unite, you get the movement performed as it should be, with brilliance, and again, with "sparkle."

In addition, the spiritual incorporates important aspects of riding that today, I feel, are forgotten or neglected. These include:

- **Thanksgiving:** The horse deserves to be thanked when he performs well, when he does as you bid, when he controls his innate and natural impulses to fight, flee, or freeze (fig. 2.5). This self-control on his part is one of those small miracles I mentioned earlier, and you should not take this one for granted.

- **Tolerance and forgiveness:** With practice, you can learn to tolerate your own learning curve and that of your horse, and to forgive your mistakes and look forward to the next—improved—attempt.

- **Compassion:** The horse is a creature within your power. It is not difficult to make the horse suffer, to choose bits and devices that torment him and coerce him into submission. You need to feel for the horse in order to ride him your best. You need to respect the spur and curb as much as you expect *him* to, and use them with great care, if at all. You need to tune in to your horse and his body so you can tell when he is afraid or when he is hurting. Do not attempt to mask his fear or hurt with quick fixes, but instead seek out the cause of the issue and treat it to ensure the horse's ability to perform confidently and soundly for many years, instead of just a few.

- **Understanding:** You must forever remind yourself that the horse is dependent upon you, not only for food, water, and shelter, but for direction and clear means of communication. If you are incapable of explaining your needs to your horse, then he is incapable of answering in a way that you would find acceptable. By understanding this from the outset, you can

provide a broader base for a mutual relationship, giving it what it needs to grow roots and flourish (fig. 2.6).

You also need to understand yourself. In many instances, horses provide the means to knowing yourself better. This is true regardless of the horse sport you choose to pursue. Horses are a mirror of your emotions: they know when you are stressed, depressed, or confident, and they translate these feelings into movement (elastic and beautiful versus compressed and stinted, for example). In truth, many of you need to see a visual demonstration of your feelings in order to recognize them and deal with them (when they need dealing with). Horses provide this means to understanding yourself.

So many books and DVDs stick to one side or the other of the science and spirituality spectrum. I feel this isn't helpful; it only leaves people inhibited and afraid to venture too far into one territory or another. In this book I intend to meld them inextricably together. And I'd like you to consider whether it ever makes sense to have science without spirituality, and vice versa, since when together, your physical, emotional, and mental performance, and that of your horse, can be so much stronger.

2.6 It is your responsibility to tune in to your horse, both his body and his mind. The Tellington Method provides a means of "tuning in," as I am doing here with Dablino, lowering his head to bring him into "thinking" mode.

THE CORNERSTONES OF THE
TELLINGTON METHOD

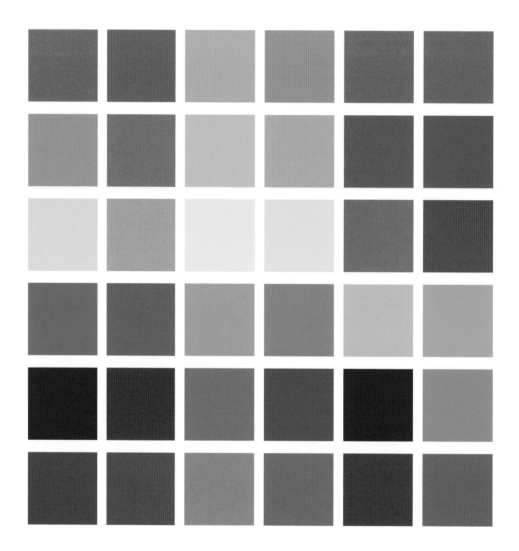

AS A RIDER, HORSE TRAINER, AND ANIMAL BEHAVIORIST, I HAVE BEEN privileged to be part of a revolutionary development in the world of horse training and horsekeeping. After years of riding and teaching, in 1975 the Tellington Method® was conceived. This is a multi-faceted approach to training horses using specialized bodywork known as the *Tellington TTouch®*; *Ground Exercises*—in-hand work I call "Dancing with Your Horse" together with lessons using obstacles known as the "Playground for Higher Learning"— and *Ridden Work*, or the "Joy of Riding." It is now taught by more than 1,000 certified practitioners all over the world, and has changed the lives of tens of thousands of horses—not to mention dogs, cats, other animals (domestic and wild), and even humans (figs. 3.1 A–C).

For years, the Tellington Method has been used with great success on dressage horses working at every level, improving their physicality and mental stability in ways that improve the horse's life not only on the most basic level—alleviating stiffness, eliminating stress, improving appetite, encouraging socialization—but also in more particular, profound areas that ultimately better performance. With merely a *change in the way you think about your horse* and perhaps 5 to 10 minutes of specialized work each day, you can improve your horse's attitude, performance, and way of going in degrees that no amount of repetitive longeing and lateral work, or whip and spur could ever match.

▪▪▪▪▪▪About My Method and How It Works

The three components of the Tellington Method—*TTouch bodywork*, *Ground Exercises*, and *Ridden Work*—were conceived of intuitively and resulted in what I initially thought of as a series of "miraculous" changes in the horses with which I worked. Since those first astounding moments, the Tellington Method has scientifically demonstrated that it engages the left and right brain of the rider and the horse, resulting in an "awakened" state wherein both rider and horse are better prepared to learn and better able to perform in a multitude of scenarios.

3.1 A–C The Tellington Method is made up of *TTouches* (A); *Ground Exercises* and in-hand training with obstacles in my Playground of Higher Learning (B); and *Ridden Work* (C).

In an attempt to find science to support the positive results I experienced early in my work, I studied brain activity in horses undergoing my training techniques during the summer of 1984 and 1985. I did this alongside Anna Wise, a leading authority on electroencephalography (EEG)—the recording of the electrical activity in the brain—and the Awakened Mind™, the most effective state of mental functioning, as coined by psychobiologist and biophysicist C. Maxwell Cade in the 1970s with whom Wise worked closely (see p. 31). But before we get into what Wise and I discovered, let me briefly explain her work.

......About the Left Brain and Right Brain

Most people have some idea of "the two sides of the brain." You hear from many sources on many subjects that the left side of the brain controls logic and language, and is sequential and linear (among other things), and the right side controls intuition and creativity, and is random and holistic (see sidebar, p. 30). What is important to know is that you also learn differently with each side of the brain (as does the horse and any animal). The *left* brain absorbs words, processes them, and integrates them when understanding is present. The *right* brain takes in color, sound, and form.

Ideally, for the optimal learning experience and the most thorough grasp of what you are studying, both sides are involved in the process. Although each hemisphere is unique in the type of information it processes, it complements the other and constantly communicates with it, so *together* they can generate your perception of the world. Your brain hemispheres are *balanced*. When you only use the left brain, you are limited to a Newtonian reality (matter is self-contained and three-dimensional—see my discussion of riding with *intention* on p. 60). When you address the right brain, as well, you have limitless potential.

Do You Ride with Your Left Brain or Your Right Brain?

Although in reality there is much crossover and shared responsibility when it comes to the two brain hemispheres, each of us naturally operates in a manner that can probably be classified as either "left-brained" or "right-brained." For example, does math come easily to you? You are probably "left-brained." More comfortable with a paintbrush than a calculator? You qualify as a "right-brainer." Knowing which way you lean can help you spend some time balancing your overly logical or overly creative tendencies.

Your goal is to *actively* ride with *both* sides of your brain! The learning and thinking process is enhanced when *both* sides participate in a balanced manner. Take this quick "hemispheric dominance" quiz to help you determine your strengths and weaknesses.

Left Brain or Right Brain?

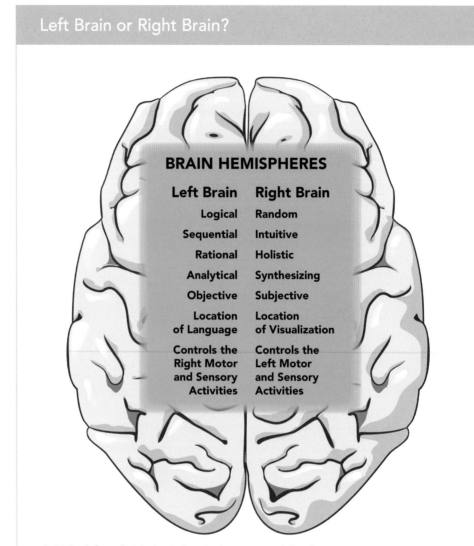

BRAIN HEMISPHERES

Left Brain	Right Brain
Logical	Random
Sequential	Intuitive
Rational	Holistic
Analytical	Synthesizing
Objective	Subjective
Location of Language	Location of Visualization
Controls the Right Motor and Sensory Activities	Controls the Left Motor and Sensory Activities

3.2 The left and right brain hemispheres—a quick reference.

The brain is commonly described as having two hemispheres—the left and the right (fig. 3.2). Popular psychology has long noted that certain functions such as logic and creativity are "lateralized"—that is, located in the left or right hemisphere—hence the common question, "Are you left-brained, or right-brained?"

It is generally thought that the left hemisphere is the home of language and it processes information logically and sequentially, while the right hemisphere is more visual and processes intuitively and randomly. The extent of specialized brain function remains under investigation.

Quiz

1. Is your grooming box/tack trunk:
   a) neat and organized, with everything labeled and in its place, or
   b) overflowing with all the stuff you might need.

2. When you are learning a new movement, is it easier for you to:
   a) memorize the sequence of aids and talk your way through it, or
   b) watch your trainer ride and imitate her actions?

3. When your trainer is speaking to you, do you respond more to:
   a) her words (*what* is said), or
   b) the word's pitch and feeling (*how* it is said)?

4. When you audit a clinic, do you:
   a) take copious and well-organized notes on your laptop, or
   b) never take your eyes off the riders and trainers so you don't miss a single action or movement?

5. Is it easier to remember people's:
   a) names, or
   b) faces?

If you answered with all or mostly "a's," you are likely left-brain dominant and you need to really focus on trying to bring more "heART" to your riding (see p. 14). If you answered with all or mostly "b's," you have a tendency to be emotive, perhaps so much so that the immense amount of feeling you ride with clouds your ability to perform, as well as that of your horse. You need to weave a little more clarity into your riding and training. Remember, hemispheric *balance* is your aim!

.... About the "Awakened Mind"

Now, there's a little more to this idea of attaining optimal performance through hemispheric balance. Using an instrument called a Mind Mirror, which is a portable EEG "computer" attached to a headband outfitted with electrodes, C. Maxwell Cade measured the brainwave patterns in both the left and right brain hemispheres of healers, spiritual teachers, advanced meditators, and his own students. He found a pattern in frequency type—brainwaves are categorized by frequency, or speed of electrical impulse, into beta, alpha, theta, and delta (see sidebar, p. 32)—that by his estimation exhibited the "lucid aware-

The Four Brainwave Frequencies

According to the official website of Anna Wise (www.annawise.com), the four brainwave frequencies are:

Beta   Normal thinking state, active external awareness, and thought process.

Alpha   Detached awareness, visualization, sensory imagery—"a bridge between the conscious and subconscious mind."

Theta   Subconscious mind—present in dreaming sleep, deep meditation, and the "storehouse" of creative inspiration.

Delta   Unconscious mind, sleep state, but when present alongside other waves in a waking state, it provides intuition, empathetic attunement, and instinctual insight.

ness" of meditation "coexistent with thought processes." He called this specialized state the "Awakened Mind."

Anna Wise developed her own work with the Awakened Mind, expanding the research beyond spirituality and healing to incorporate the minds of artists, scientists, inventors, and businessmen. She found that the brainwave patterns during brief moments of high performance and creativity were the same as those found in the experienced meditators' Awakened Mind state. In her bestselling book *The High Performance Mind* (Tarcher, 1997), she explained the Awakened Mind as that feeling of, "Ah-ha! I got it! Everything makes sense now…Exhilarated, you know that you know! You have a sense of understanding on all levels…Your intuitive insight into old problems makes them seem simple and easy to handle, possibly even insignificant."

Wise determined that the "high performance mind" was a "trainable" state, and once there, an individual could become a better problem solver; turn into an effective leader; improve communication skills; gain control of his or her emotions; and be healthier, more relaxed, and less stressed. Her work explains that the two brain hemispheres I've already talked about, left and right, are both needed to perform fully in the world. "Optimally, both hemispheres operate symmetrically," Wise writes, "but an asymmetrical pattern frequently occurs…brainwave training will improve the balance between hemispheres."

Wise is careful to point out that, despite the left/logical and right/creative constructs with which you are familiar, you actually think in *both* hemispheres and create in *both* hemispheres. Therefore the shift that needs to occur to

In a Nutshell: What Is the Tellington TTouch?

Tellington TTouches are a collection of circles, lifts, and slides done with the hands and fingertips over various parts of the horse's body. The contact is applied in such a way to activate the function of cells in order to stimulate the body's potential for healing and learning. Use of *TTouch* on your horse provides a means to:

- Enhance trust

- Release tension

- Increase flexibility

- Overcome habitual holding patterns that lead to resistance

- Aid a horse in recovery from illness or injury

The standard TTouch circle is a one-and-one-quarter circle, easily perfected by visualizing the face of a clock. You start at the bottom of the circle at six o'clock and with your fingers, push the skin once around past six to stop at nine o'clock. You use varying pressures (the firmness with which you apply a TTouch) and tempos (the time it takes to get around the circle). The pressure scale is from 1 to 10 and the tempo from 1 to 3 seconds (see p. 262 for more on the pressures). My use of the clock face and numerically

guided pressures and tempos stimulates the logical (right) side of your brain.

Lifts and slides are used to connect *TTouch* circles, activate circulation, enhance breathing, and give the horse's body time to process incoming information.

I have given my ever-increasing collection of *TTouches* interesting names intended to invoke the way in which you place your hands on your horse's body. This is an intentional use of the creative or intuitive (left) side of your brain.

In the back of this book, you will find my collection of *TTouches* categorized as:

- Circle TTouches

- Lifting and Stroking TTouches

- Other TTouch Bodywork

To further aid you in your search for the best means of connecting with your horse, I have also indexed them as:

- TTouches for Trust

- TTouches for Awareness

- TTouches for Health

- TTouches for Performance

Please refer to the Tellington Method Quick Reference Center, where you can read about each one in more detail (p. 262).

achieve the Awakened Mind is not so much a movement from left brain to right brain as it is "an expansion from up to down—beginning with the *thinking* waves of beta and adding the *creative* aspects of alpha, theta, and delta in both hemispheres simultaneously."

3.3 A & B Practicing *TTouch* on yourself and other humans, helps you ride free from stress, with confidence, and connected to the horse. Here, I perform *TTouches* on Ingrid Klimke: *Rib Lifts* to support breathing (A), and *Octopus TTouch* to differentiate muscles in the leg for enhanced aiding (B).

What All This Has to Do with You and Your Horse

During my first study with Anna Wise, she attached a Mind Mirror headband to me and to a number of my students as we did circular *TTouches* on each other. She found that while performing *TTouch*, not only did I, and my students, consistently operate in a form of the Awakened Mind state, but the people *receiving* the *TTouches* exhibited the same brainwave patterns (figs. 3.3 A & B).

This leads to Conclusion Number 1: *Practicing TTouch on your horse—as I and my students did on each other—allows you to function in an Awakened Mind state, and prepares you to ride free from stress, with confidence, and in connection with your horse.*

Wise next attached a Mind Mirror headband to a horse. As soon as I began doing circular *TTouches* on the horse's body, the screen lit up both hemispheres of his brain, sometimes close to the specific pattern of my own brainwaves (figs. 3.4 A–D).

Conclusion Number 2: *Practicing TTouch activates your horse's "thinking" beta brain waves—initiating what I like to think of as a "state of learning."*

The following summer we took the study a step further and introduced a remote headband that enabled us to measure the horse's brainwave patterns while he was in motion. Sure enough, whenever the horse took the shortened steps around the turns in the *Ground Exercise* I call the *Labyrinth*, for example, the beta brainwaves lit up (fig. 3.5).

3.4 A–D Practicing *TTouch* on your horse activates both the left and right hemispheres of *your* brain, as well as *your horse's* brain! It improves the ability to focus, learn, and perform. Ingrid Klimke does *Mouth TTouches* to improve contact as well as decrease resistance to training (A); *Shoulder Release* to loosen tight muscles in the forehand and neck and lengthen stride (B); *Hind Leg Circles* to improve suppleness and engagement (C); and *Tail Pulls* to build confidence, trust, and a connection through the entire spine (D).

3.5 *Ground Exercises* and *Ridden Work* using the *Labyrinth* help to ready your horse for training sessions by activating his beta brainwaves, bringing him into what I like to call a special "learning state," while simultaneously enhancing balance and focus.

This brings us to Conclusion Number 3: *The Labyrinth, an exercise from my Playground of Higher Learning, helps bring a horse into a state conducive to absorbing new lessons.*

This was science indicating that horses receiving *TTouch* and doing Tellington Method *Ground Exercises* came into a receptive, calm state of mind with both left and right hemispheres engaged, allowing them to readily absorb new information. A horse working in this state learns faster and is safer to ride because his capacity to think overrides his primary instinct of flight. This allows training time to be reduced and helps riders avoid mindless repetition, which can inhibit a horse's brilliance and "sparkle," as well as prevent reliance on force, which can cause pain, fear, and tension.

I have also found that because of this enhanced state of learning, *TTouch* can even improve a particular movement or skill without the horse ever practicing the movement or skill itself. I describe an example of this in the case of the gelding Heartbreaker—a dressage horse who would not load—later in this book (p. 144). Along with my fellow practitioners, I worked with him using *TTouches* and my *Ground Exercises*, and although we did not work on trailer-loading specifically, we improved his overall performance, and ultimately, it helped solve the problem with loading. Now *that* was amazing!

........The Difference between Tellington TTouch and Equine Massage

Every successful human athlete makes sport massage part of his physical care regimen in order to reduce stress, improve performance, and prevent injury. Today, many riders are realizing the importance of this kind of bodywork for horses, as well.

You may think of my *TTouch* techniques as a type of equine massage, but there are three major differences between Tellington *TTouch* bodywork and the accepted standard for massaging horses:

1   *TTouch* is applied in a way to ensure that the horse does not resist or react in pain. Some traditional sport-massage methods are so painful that the horse receiving therapy will actually try to defend himself by kicking or biting. I've worked on world-class dressage horses in three different countries who had been massaged so painfully they were dangerous to work around.

Because my goal, and the goal of Tellington Method practitioners, is to develop trust in the horse, the pressure you apply with *TTouch* is on a variable scale and chosen to enhance confidence, as well as support a sense of well-being (see the sidebar on p. 33 and a description of the specific pressures in the Tellington Method Quick Reference Center,

p. 262). This method attends to the mind and the soul as much as the body. Combining the bodywork with specialized *Ground Exercises* and Tellington Tools (equipment) for work under saddle allows the horse to integrate the new feelings TTouch elicits and helps the horse find a new balance and way of moving with the rider on board (figs. 3.6 A–F).

2 Rather than simply addressing the musculoskeletal system, the intention of *TTouch* is to also address the "intelligence" of the horse's body at the *cellular level*, thereby supporting the *healing potential* of the body. My interest is in activating cellular communication in support of the "whole being." By holding the potential for and *intention* of ideal cellular function, you can promote wellness of body, mind, and spirit (see more about intention on p. 60).

Are Our Cells "Smart"?

Dr. Deepak Chopra, renowned author and founder of Alliance for a New Humanity (www.anhglobal.org), is perhaps one of the most prominent modern figures to successfully meld the spiritual with the scientific. As he explains, in your own body—and I'll add in your horse's body—"In every moment, each cell is communicating with every other cell, carrying out hundreds of thousands of activities all at once. Our cells can simultaneously digest a meal, destroy cancer cells, eliminate waste, and make a baby . . . all without our conscious awareness" (www.chopra.com). To ignore this "cellular intelligence," and to fail to communicate with the cells through physical touch and intention, is to disable the body's own ability to heal itself and function efficiently and optimally.

In addition, experiments suggest that energy exists between living tissues; that cells communicate via this form of energy; and that human emotion and intention can directly influence cellular matter. In *The Divine Matrix* (Hay House, 2007), Gregg Braden summarizes a collection of studies that seem to show that each time you touch another creature, thereby leaving a trace of your DNA (your cellular matter) behind, you are influencing the recipient, not only at the time of the contact, but long after. The quality of this influence is dependent on you being aware of this cellular connection, and ideally, choosing to nurture it, as is possible through the regular use of *TTouch*.

By combining *TTouch* with the Tellington Method's *Ground Exercises* and *Ridden Work*, *TTouch* becomes an integral part of the interspecies experience between horse and rider. Unlike appointment-based sports massage that often takes place on a weekly or monthly basis and operates *outside* the daily dressage training schedule, *TTouch* used wisely is woven into every interaction with the horse, from the daily and mundane to the final moments in an international competition. It facilitates and enhances grooming; saddling; working in hand; warming up; cooling down; training on your own or under the watchful eye of a coach or instructor; and handling your horse in the stable, the arena, and all areas in between.

The "aware" rider can use *TTouch* to read her horse's body and behavior, as well as investigate and address why the horse is physically or mentally reluctant or unable to sustain a posture; perform a movement or transition; or balance, bend, extend, or collect as his development dictates. *TTouch* gives the rider a means to bridge what she observes and feels in every interaction with her horse in a way that is constructive, nonviolent, and effective. It is an opportunity to embed a form of bodywork in the horse's training that will truly optimize the horse-and-rider experience at every turn.

3.6 A–F TTouch is not just another method of equine massage. *TTouches* are chosen specifically to suit the individual horse and his physical, mental, and emotional needs. In addition, they are applied with varying degrees of pressure, depending on the horse, his preference, and the issues at hand.

Here, I am working on Magali Delgado's dressage horse Mandarin: the *Clouded Leopard TTouch* with a 3 pressure to bring awareness and circulation (A); the *Bear TTouch* with a 5 pressure to "aerate" the muscles (B); the *Rhino TTouch* with a 6 pressure (C); *Neck Rocking* with a level neck to invite lengthening of the neck (D); finding a connection between my two hands (E); and connecting Mandarin's abdominal muscles with his hindquarters (F).

THE TRAINING SCALE—
MOVING FROM THEN TO NOW

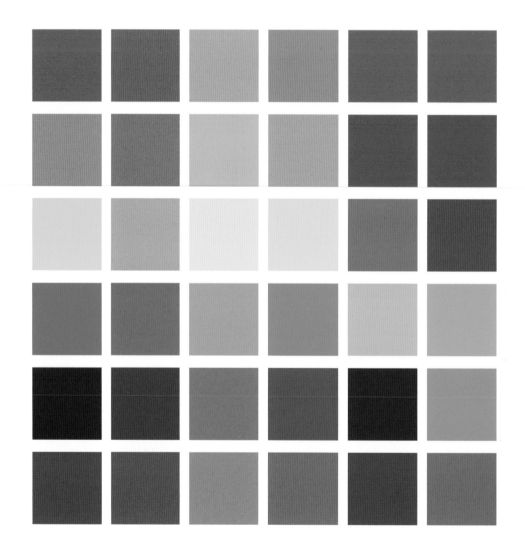

4

FEW EFFORTS IN THIS WORLD COULD BE LIKENED TO THAT OF THE development of the dressage rider and her horse. Theirs is truly a remarkable journey. Like many popular sports and even other riding disciplines, the study of dressage provides the rider a practical procedural focus: perfect required maneuvers; demonstrate them in a series of tests; and over a period of time, improve the horse's condition and way of going while bettering her own riding skill.

But dressage goes one step further. It provides a universal and timeless "ideal"—an end-goal representative not just of the sport of dressage, but of man and horse as partners in work and play. Dressage is the fusion of two beings into one, each voluntarily offering his best to the other while communicating via the most subtle of signals, and the delicate yet powerful dance that is the result.

Throughout the world, millions of dollars, hours, days, years, and lifetimes are devoted to the pursuit of this ideal. To some, it surely seems an effort in futility—the Holy Grail of "throughness" and togetherness never to be found. Others progress, stumble, and try again. And still others are among those few who achieve the elevated status of "Top Dressage Rider," their name, their mount's name, and even their Freestyle music recognized in riding arenas around the globe.

What separates these categories of individuals? Money, certainly. Ability, of course. Time, perhaps. But always, always the horse. Top dressage horses are years in the making. They accumulate knowledge and conditioning in carefully planned stages, gradually growing and developing into the mythical-like steeds we see in the Grand Prix arena or the exhibition hall. To make it through what will likely be nine years of preliminary training, and then an undeterminable number of years confirming, "finishing," and polishing, these horses must be sane, sound, and—as the FEI now dictates in its rule book—"happy" (see p. 256).

In this book I examine a number of ways I feel happiness can be achieved for the dressage horse, and I push some long-established boundaries in that effort. However, I think it is important that we begin on common ground, with

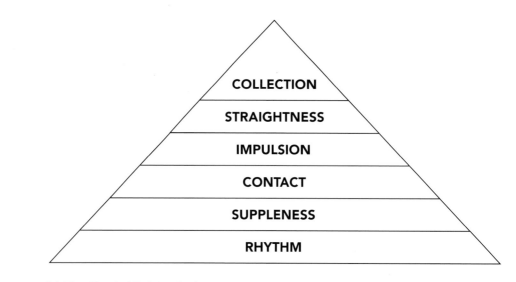

4.1 The Classical Training Scale.

a point of reference every dressage rider is, or should be, familiar with: the Classical Training Scale.

......Common Ground: The Classical Training Scale

It has long been accepted that in order to progress as a horse-and-rider team in the art of dressage, whether for personal pleasure or for sport, the partners must ascend through the six stages of the Classical Training Scale (fig. 4.1). (Although the terms "Classical Training Scale" and "Classical Training Pyramid" are often used interchangeably, in this book I will call it the Classical Training Scale.) My friend Klaus Balkenhol is quoted in his biography *Klaus Balkenhol: The Man and His Training Methods* by Britta Schöffman (Trafalgar Square Books, 2007) as follows:

> *The classical training principles are the foundation of all riding. Through them, a horse acquires the necessary strength to perform the movements demanded in high-level competition without injury…The only thing we must be sure to do is preserve the horse's natural grace through the classical training principles. In my opinion, this includes caring for horses appropriately, providing good training, plenty of love, and knowing and understanding the Training Scale. The Training Scale remains the ultimate measure of quality because only with its help can one manage to develop a horse under saddle carefully and responsibly. This is not something I or some old "cavaliers" have invented—it's a system that has evolved over centuries and has proven itself over time.*

4.2 Klaus Balkenhol, chairman of the Xenophon Society—an organization established to promote and protect the ideals of classical riding, and most importantly to respect the horse in his physical and spiritual form—is a huge proponent of the importance of the Classical Training Scale. My inclusion in the 2011 Xenophon Society Symposium helped underline the ways the Tellington Method dovetails with the culture of classical riding.

As Klaus Balkenhol states, the Classical Training Scale was developed over time through the aggregate expertise of some of history's greatest riders and horsemen (fig. 4.2). Espoused by the German National Equestrian Federation (FN), it has proven through the years to be the most sensible, safe, sane way to train a horse—to take him from gangly and green to the most advanced realms of perfectly syncopated movement and "self-carriage." The stages are intentionally architectural in nature—they build one upon the other, and an "upper," more advanced level cannot be built before the previous level (its foundation) has been properly laid. This ensures sufficient time is taken and the horse's body and mind are allowed to acclimate to new demands before additional ones are made. Some of you may be working at the bottom of the Scale—others at the very top. And some may be struggling on several levels, or even all six.

There are many fine texts available that fully illustrate the six principles of the Training Scale and how to use them in your dressage training. I mention the principles only briefly here, in the sense and sequence that the Training Scale dictates, to give you a common base of reference from which to work. Everything that I discuss on the pages to come—every training technique, method, and theory—can be applied to and used within this single foundation.

Rhythm

A horse has three basic gaits, and each has its own distinct rhythm or pure beat of movement (walk = four beats; trot = two beats; canter = three beats). In all three gaits, the horse should take regular steps, resulting in even, steady, cadenced paces. This is the foundation of dressage and should *never* be compromised.

Suppleness

This stage refers to both *physical* suppleness (involving the muscles and other body parts) and *mental* suppleness (inner tranquility and an easy state of mind). The horse should demonstrate the ability to bend his body both laterally (side to side) and longitudinally (front to back) while exhibiting a contented and engaged "expression" in eyes, ears, and tail, for example.

Contact

This term refers to the rider's connection with the horse's mouth. The horse should accept the bit and the rider's hands, and be willing to go forward "into" them with his jaw relaxed; his poll the highest point; and his nose on or just in front of the vertical.

Impulsion

This stage is about "pushing power" or energy "flowing" forward through the horse from the hindquarters. All horses have a degree of natural impulsion—some more than others—but additional impulsion should develop as the dressage horse's musculature changes and he becomes stronger through his back.

Straightness

All horses, like all humans, are naturally crooked to some degree. When the horse's body is correctly aligned, the hind legs follow the tracks of the front legs, whether on a straight line or a curved path (a circle, for instance); the horse works evenly on both sides of his body; and he accepts weight evenly on both hind legs (as it pertains to the gradual progression of shifting the horse's weight from front to back—a fundamental concept of dressage training, see below).

Collection

The pinnacle of the Training Scale is when the horse carries more weight on his hindquarters than on his forehand (essentially reversing his natural inclination for "front-heaviness" by changing both his physicality and his way of "thinking" how he should move). He lowers his croup, showing more flexion in his hind joints, while simultaneously lifting his forehand. This is called "self-carriage," an essential part of the end goal of dressage training. When done correctly and ridden well, the horse actually moves in a way that is more beautiful and more efficient.

......What's Gone Wrong with the Classical Training Scale?

All that I've said so far isn't new, and indeed as I mentioned earlier, you could find these same points and proclamations in a dozen other books. But why, if the classical system is so worthy and time-proven, do riders and trainers have such a difficult job studying and faithfully applying the Training Scale? Why do they slip up, skip steps, and deviate from that which is spelled out for them time and again? We see the results in our training arenas and on our show grounds today: rushing through levels of the Training Scale only serves to burn horses out, damaging them (and sometimes ruining them) both physically and mentally. In an attempt to speed the process or streamline the training curve, riders require of their dressage horses what the horses have not been sufficiently prepared to give. I feel this is happening for several reasons:

1 Our natural impatience and the desire to achieve the most esteemed levels of dressage as soon as possible encourages us to "cheat" and chalk it up to just being human. After all, as mortal beings, time is not on our side. Add to this modern society's demands on the average horseperson's day-to-day schedule (most riders only have a couple of hours a day, or even a week, to devote to their dressage riding), and you begin to see how easy it is to rush a horse even when you have the very best of intentions.

2 The second reason we see this trend in modern dressage training is the development of finer, more athletic horses, meticulously molded over the years specifically for the sport of dressage. These wonders of selective breeding are often born with a natural ability to perform the most advanced movements, seemingly without the aid of years of traditional training and preparation. This outstanding natural athletic ability, which in some cases has even been labeled "freakish" by commentators and judges, combined with a human desire to achieve the highest levels of dressage training, and to get there *fast*, has created real problems within the industry, and the horses—athletically inclined or not—are paying the price.

3 I also feel there is a far more fundamental reason riders and trainers deviate from the principles of the Training Scale. I think in some cases, maybe even most, individuals have a hard time grasping the concepts as illustrated by the terms and the standard "pyramid" diagram (see fig. 4.1). This has to do with left- and right-brain learning, which I discussed on page 29. The traditional way the Training Scale is taught is entirely left-brain based—it has to do with logic, term memorization, and sensible progression. If you can incorporate right-brain learning techniques—in this case color and visual aids intended to inspire emotion—into the learning of the principles, then your mind and body are more likely to successfully assimilate the concepts, understand them, and use them consistently.

4 Finally, I think we should reconsider the classical principles that were developed by the great horsemen of the past and view each of the six in a slightly different way. Perhaps, the order of when they are addressed within the pyramid structure can be adjusted to better reflect a horse's individual needs as well as the rider's inherent involvement in the training of the principles. In other words, this is not a series of steps to ascend, but a flowing and ever-changing list of prerequisites, all of which are integral to the development of a happy and successful horse-and-rider team. With this in mind, get ready to look at the same six principles *outside* the traditional pyramid structure—in a different way altogether.

Adding a New Foundation

So what does a *modern* Training Scale look like? Let's begin with the elements within it. I believe they remain essentially the same—Rhythm, Suppleness, Contact, Impulsion, Straightness, and Collection—with one major addition at the pyramid's base: *Balance* (fig. 4.3).

What do I mean by Balance? I am talking about something bigger than simply physical stability and equal weight distribution; I am talking about equipoise (a state of equilibrium) between interacting elements within both horse and rider, and I'm talking about mental and emotional steadiness. When I say the word Balance, I mean mental, physical, and emotional well-being. Take a moment to revisit the quote from Klaus Balkenhol on page 42. There he says that "caring for horses appropriately, providing good training, plenty of love, and knowing and understanding the Training Scale…" are of the utmost importance to your success as a dressage rider. It makes sense, then, to actually include care, respect, love, and all those things ("heART") that create well-being in the horse, in the Training Scale itself.

Upon a base of Balance, you will find you are far better prepared to face the challenges in teaching your horse the movements required in the dressage arena. You will be properly grounded in the horse-and-rider relationship. You will be more patient, more understanding, more tolerant, more compassionate,

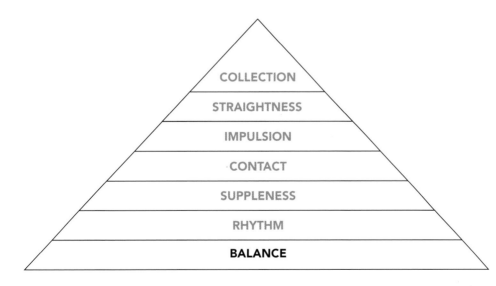

4.3 The Tellington Training Scale.

and more forgiving—of yourself and of your horse. When you can apply these traits to training your horse, you can apply them to your relationships with other people. (And so we see a primary example of how your pursuit of dressage can change the world around you. I'm going to talk more about this as I go on—I feel it is so important!)

When your horse is balanced, he has the care and lifestyle necessary to ensure sanity and happiness. This translates into proper nutrition, turnout, and socialization with other horses, as well as a number of other areas of concern (I discuss specific ways to create an atmosphere of well-being in chapter 10, p. 176. When the horse is happy and healthy, he is free to focus energy and attention to the learning of new skills and the development of his physical self.

Consider the studies that have been done with school children, and how they learn best. It has been found that a child's learning ability is optimal when things are going well at home: he has a supportive family; a nutritious breakfast; a general lack of stress in his life; friends he associates with regularly; and he spends time outdoors. For example, according to the Food Research and Action Center of Washington, DC, studies show that children perform better on tests and show improved cognitive function, attention, and memory after having a good breakfast (Child Nutrition Fact Sheet, www. frac.org). Studies published by the University of California, Irvine, show that stress—even short-term—can impair brain-cell communication in the brain's learning and memory region. And, the Institute for Outdoor Learning (www. outdoor-learning.org) cites "increased physical, mental, and spiritual health" as a benefit of learning outside the classroom.

Your dressage horse is a student in school, with years of education before him, or perhaps he is already on the brink of earning a doctorate. Either way, it only makes sense to provide him a lifestyle and environment that supports this learning. *Balance*, therefore, is where dressage training begins.

Going from "Learning" the Training Scale to "Feeling" It

What Color Means in This Book

Earlier, I broached the ideas of left-brain and right-brain riding, and how dressage has become a primarily left-brain activity. I have, in fact, used the seven colors of the rainbow as a theme in this book to help engage the right brain. It is not by accident that I chose these colors for this purpose. The rainbow is a symbol that transcends time and cultural difference. It is still relevant today and is often used to represent hope and change. In addition, the *seven colors of the rainbow* offer you *seven ways* to add color and "feeling" to the seven principles in the Tellington Training Scale. Let me explain.

The Effect of Color Wavelength and Frequency

Part of what you react to when you experience a color is its wavelength and frequency. Color, because its wavelengths are within the range that humans can perceive, is a form of "visible light," which in turn is a form of electromagnetic radiation. Electromagnetic radiation carries energy that interacts with matter around it.

In the rainbow, red and orange have the longest wavelengths and the lowest frequency, while indigo and violet have the shortest wavelengths and the highest frequency. The other colors on the spectrum fall somewhere in between. Red, with the longest wavelength, is highly energizing, appears nearer than it is, and actually stimulates the physical self, raising the pulse rate. Violet, on the other hand, with the shortest wavelength, can have a meditative effect.

You often see this aspect of color perception employed in interior design. I specifically remember a chain of restaurants from the 1960s and 70s that decorated their interior with shades of red and orange exclusively. They are both strong colors that actually stimulate the body, which I'm sure translates to many as a form of "hunger"! The result is a customer who eats fast, eats more, and spends more.

You can employ this color effect in your training. Perhaps your horse is lethargic one day, and you need a way to put some "spring" in his step. Wear a red shirt and ride in a mirrored indoor where you can see yourself. The color will invigorate you, and your increased intensity will stimulate your horse. I should note here that it's thought that horses perceive color differently than humans, so it is more difficult to affect them directly in this process. (I cover the effect of color on horses in more detail in the section on creating an atmosphere of well-being, beginning on p. 176.)

How Color Affects Us

Very simply, the human eye is able to distinguish color because the cells of the retina vary in their sensitivity and ability to see light of different wavelengths. After being perceived by the eye, color affects us in several ways. Our culture also assigns meaning to color via politics, religion, and contemporary trends. This, whether you like it or not, affects how you react to a color when you see it—both the imagery that comes to mind and how you feel in its presence.

The meaning and symbolism assigned to the colors most familiar to us give colors the power to communicate, heal, and impact the learning process, and they give us the means to manipulate color and use it to our best advantage. There is a whole field of study dedicated to color theory. Graphic and interior designers, artists, and business-to-business consultants spend time and big money on the ideas surrounding color and its affects on humankind. There is no reason we as riders shouldn't take color theory as seriously as those in other industries.

As mentioned, the colors of particular interest to me in this book are the seven colors of the rainbow (fig. 4.4). Why? Well, the rainbow is a symbol that has a place in legend, in contemporary society, and in science, which states that rainbows are the result of water drops in the air and sunlight illuminating them from behind at a low-altitude angle.

Greek mythology says that the rainbow is a path between earth and heaven; in Hindu mythology it is a bow of the gods; in Norse mythology it is a bridge between the homes of gods and humans; and according to Christianity and Judaism, the rainbow was a sign of God's promise never to destroy the earth with flood waters again (following the story of Noah and the Ark in the Old Testament).

The rainbow today is often considered a sign of hope or change. And that is why it is an appropriate color theme for this book. As I explained in the section on left- and right-brain learning, my goal is to engage you in your entirety in this process of learning how to ride and train your dressage horse more effectively and joyfully. In order to do that, you need to inject meaning into every level of this journey. And the colors of the rainbow are simply laden with meaning.

Sir Isaac Newton, who you will meet again in the section about riding with *intention* (see p. 60), is credited for naming the seven colors of the rainbow:

RED
ORANGE
YELLOW
GREEN
BLUE
INDIGO
VIOLET

I first became interested in the meaning of these seven colors when I read the work of Edgar Cayce in the 1970s. Cayce was a psychic who could see people's "auras," which he said were characterized by color. This led him

4.4 The rainbow is a timeless symbol—one that has meaning in all cultures, both spiritually and scientifically.

to examine the seven colors of the rainbow and assign personality traits to them, among other things. In his book *Auras,* Cayce includes the following explanation of the seven colors:

Red: Vigor and energy
Orange: Vitality, thoughtfulness, consideration of others, self-control
Yellow: Health, well-being
Green: Healing, helpful, strong, friendly
Blue: Contemplation, spirituality
Indigo and Violet: Progressive levels of seeking, soulfulness

In Christianity, as another example, color symbolism is primarily used in banners, vestments, and artwork. L. K. Alchin of the online encyclopedia Medieval Life and Times (and other popular sites devoted to early Christianity) attaches the following meanings to the seven colors:

Red: Power, importance, martyrdom, atonement
Orange: Courage, endurance, strength
Yellow: Renewal, hope, light
Green: Fertility, hope, bountifulness
Blue: Heaven, hope, good health
Indigo and Violet: Royalty

In the study of Chakras the seven colors are assigned to positions on the body, and again acquire meaning associated with the corresponding Chakra. Chakras are energy centers along the spine and based at major branchings of the human nervous system (a concept originating in Hindu practices that has now evolved and appropriated a number of interpretations, in both Eastern and Western religion/medicine):

Red: Stability, sensuality, security

Orange: Creativity, joyfulness, enthusiasm

Yellow: Power, expansiveness, growth

Green: Love, passion, devotion

Blue: Communicativeness, independence, thoughtfulness

Indigo: Intuition, visual consciousness, clarity

Violet: Universal consciousness, unity

Distinct themes exist in these different interpretations, and of course, these are only a few sample interpretations amongst the thousands that exist. However, for your purposes of becoming emotionally involved in the dressage training process ("dressage as art"), the meanings I have included here will suffice. They enable you to attach feeling to each color, so when those colors are attached to words and ideas, they can "come alive" within you. This book has been designed with these colors in mind, with the intent that the meaning associated with each color of the rainbow can empower you on your journey to become a better equestrian.

Adding Color to the Tellington Training Scale

When you think about the seven principles of the Tellington Training Scale, you need to visualize a color. And when you see that color, you need to "feel" something deep inside—a movement, an identification, an "aha!" even. In this section I've provided examples of how I assign colors to the Training Scale, but as a learning device, it is important that the colors are relevant in *your* world and in *your* riding experience. In other words, use what I've provided to inspire you to make this exercise your own. Perhaps it suits your learning style to use the colors I've assigned here. Perhaps you have other ideas altogether. The goal is to involve *both* sides of your brain in this process, so please don't feel corralled or cornered by my suggestions. Instead, think of them as an invitation to turn on the creativity faucet and let it flow.

In my example, I'll begin at the base, with Balance, and work up from there:

- To *Balance* I've assigned the color *violet*. To review, Balance, our new addition to the Training Scale, is the idea of mental, physical, and emotional well-being we now know to be integral to a horse's ability to learn the intricate aids and movements involved in dressage and be willing to perform them. Violet to me means spiritual mastery, inspiration, and the responsibility that goes along with the color once reserved for royalty—that is, taking care of others, or *noblesse oblige* (the French saying that means privilege entails responsibility).

- To *Rhythm* goes the color *electric indigo*, representing mastery of physical self and intuition. (Indigo commonly comes in different shades; is the version with "sparkle"—perfect for attaining Rhythm!)

- The principle of *Suppleness* gets the color *blue*, which is calming, relaxing, and yet intense enough to enhance flow and communication rather than put everyone to sleep. Thinking calm, cool, blue while in the saddle results in a horse that is as relaxed, and yet alert, as you are. We had a key phrase that we used for this at the Pacific Coast School of Horsemanship—"relaxed erectness." Being *supple* is not just being *relaxed*. It is being "loose" while maintaining a degree of "positive tension" to enable athletic movement.

- To *Contact* goes *green*, to show the merging of body and spirit and harmony. To me Contact is about more than a connection between rider's hand and horse's mouth—it is also the connection of the seat, legs, heart, and soul. It is a melding of both inner and outer beings.

- To *Impulsion* goes the color *yellow*, which indicates happiness and good health. A happy horse blooming with health will burst forth and forward with energy to spare.

- To *Straightness* I've assigned the color *orange*, which to me represents self-control and equilibrium. Incorporate this "feeling" of equilibrium when you ride and you will help your horse travel straight on both curved and straight lines.

- Finally, *Collection* gets the color *red*, representative of passion and energy. And remember what I said about red on page 49: since it is the color with the longest wavelength, it has the most stimulating effect on your body. If you are energized, your horse will be, too.

These colors and their meanings are of course somewhat subjective, but the point is the result: a vibrant, breathing image that immediately inspires feeling (fig. 4.5). You cannot walk away without an imprint of this figure on

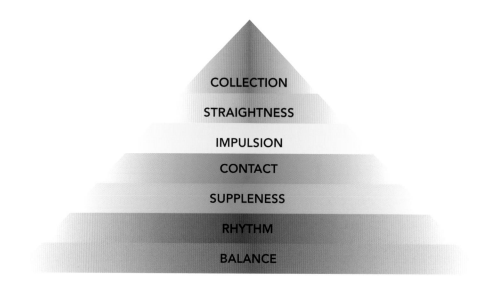

4.5 The Tellington Training Scale *in color.*

your brain. And when you ride, you can picture your cumulative goal as an explosion of color, as fireworks in a clear night sky, rather than simply ticking off a static mental list.

There is more to assigning colors to the Training Scale than constructing a useful learning tool. All along I've said that my hope is to reinspire dressage riders, reinvigorate them, and reinject their riding with what I sense is lacking in so many cases today—feeling and connection. For example, Suppleness is no longer just a word with a long definition—it is now simple. It is the color blue. You immediately feel calm when you think of it, and this calms your horse, clearing the pathways for better communication between you and allowing for a supple horse in body and a relaxed horse in mind.

Contact is no longer about the mechanics of getting the horse on the bit and keeping him there: now it is green, and you can see your body melding with the horse's at every point of contact as you move harmoniously around the arena.

See what I mean?

Take another look at the Tellington Training Scale and assign it these colors laden with meaning to make it your own. This first step in "ownership" adds yet another level of "feel" to the dressage training process: It is no longer simply a directive sent down from equestrians many years gone; now it is an interactive device intended to inspire critical thought and application of technique. Now you're no longer simply receiving marching orders and following them (then giving your horse his own marching orders and expecting him to follow them). Instead you are physically, mentally, and emotionally engrossed in the process of creating a balanced, supple, "brilliant" dressage horse, and you're inviting your horse to participate in what will ultimately be great fun for you both.

Redesigning the Training Scale as a Mind Map®

Popular psychology author Tony Buzan wrote his first books on "Mind Mapping" in the late 1960s and early 1970s. His books, lecture tours, and now software (www.iMindMap.com) have popularized his technique of diagramming words, ideas, tasks, and other items around central key words or ideas, to the extent that it is used throughout the world for a wide variety of purposes. This graphical method of taking notes can help generate, visualize, and classify ideas, and is a way of using both the left and right brains when organizing and studying information.

I am a huge fan of Mind Maps, as I find them a far more effective way of brainstorming than your traditional outline, and in my case, a better study tool because of the way they implement both color and imagery to engage memory.

It occurred to me as I was working on this book (and in fact, while I was creating a Mind Map during the book's early days before it really took form) that perhaps part of the reason many riders find it difficult to use the Training Scale and abide by its principles is that they don't understand it as it is always presented—that is, in a linear and one-dimensional form. Memorization of the principles and the order in which they should be pursued is not enough if you don't have a real idea what each principle means. I've had students who could sit on their horse and tell me that their ultimate goal was "throughness," but when I asked them what that meant, and what it looked and felt like, they hadn't the faintest idea how to explain it.

The act of creating the Mind Map is as important as the end result, so I encourage you to follow along with the example I have provided here, and then try the process on your own, using the words, colors, and imagery that makes sense to you and how you understand the Training Scale and its role in pursuing your dressage dreams with your horse.

Step 1 Choose a central word or idea from which all other words and ideas will radiate. Tony Buzan recommends keeping this to a single word, as that gives you more room to "play," although for our purposes in this example I am going to use "training" and "scale" together as one "idea" (fig. 4.6 A). Another way to start might be with your name, or your horse's.

Step 2 Use color and an image to illustrate this idea. What do you picture when you hear the central word or words spoken? When I hear "Training Scale," I immediately think of a pyramid, such as the ones in Egypt. This image comes

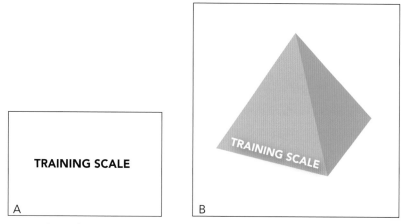

4.6 A–B Transform the Training Scale's usual appearance as a pyramid into a Mind Map to improve its usefulness as a tool in your dressage studies. Step 1: Choose a central word or idea (A). Step 2: Add color and images (B).

to mind for several reasons: the traditional illustration and interchangeable name for the Training Scale is the Training Pyramid, and the pyramids are ancient, strong, and beautiful symbols that have withstood the sands of time. I picture the words and the pyramid in gold—a color often aligned with idealism, values, and success; it is also the color of sand. This completes the imagery of the pyramid at the heart of my Mind Map (fig. 4.6 B).

Step 3 Radiate outward with each of the seven principles in our Tellington Training Scale (see p. 54). In the last section, I assigned each a color within the traditional pyramid diagram to help attach feeling or emotion to each step in the

Creating Your Own Mind Map

Tony Buzan, the author who popularized Mind Mapping as a brainstorming and studying technique, offers the following guidelines for creating a Mind Map on the website www.iMindMap.com.

1 Use one key word per branch of the Mind Map.

2 The length of the word should be the length of the branch.

3 Use color.

4 Use key images.

5 Aim for clarity.

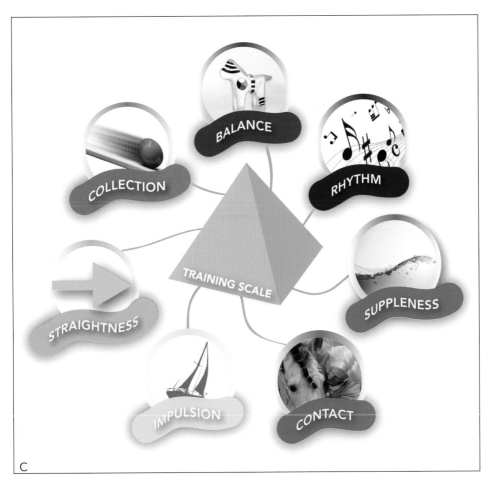

4.6 C Step 3: Radiate outward from your center point (C).

dressage training process. I've used those colors again here in my Mind Map. I've also assigned each principle an image that helps me get in touch with the feel necessary to ride with brilliance, rather than simply mechanics (fig. 4.6 C):

- **Balance** is an image of my "Hopi Horse," held in my own hands. This little figure embodies "heART" to me, which is an integral part of the new base of well-being.

- **Rhythm** is musical notes.

- **Suppleness** is a warm wave in a tropical sea.

- **Contact** is a rider and horse, head to head, and heart to heart. The exchange of energy and love is so important here.

- **Impulsion** is a beautiful boat with full sails.

- **Straightness** is an image of an arrow.

- **Collection** is a rolling ball—its movement is flowing and continuous from back to front, in any direction.

Step 4 From each principle within the Training Scale, you can map out further, with exercises, techniques, bodywork, and sources of inspiration that can help you and your horse along the way. For example, I have added my Tellington Method recommendations (fig. 4.6 D).

.. ....When All Is Said and Done

You may think that this chapter was daring in its attempt to modernize the way we think about what has long been the central pillar of all dressage training. In reality, I'm a stalwart proponent of the Classical Training Scale and all that it stands for. However, as admirable as its principles may be, and as elevated as the thinking may have been at the time of its conception, it does horses little good if a) it is misused; b) it is misunderstood; c) you can't control your horse; or d) you are tense, angry, fearful, or frustrated. My hope is that this chapter served to engage you with what has already been deemed as good, in order to help make it better.

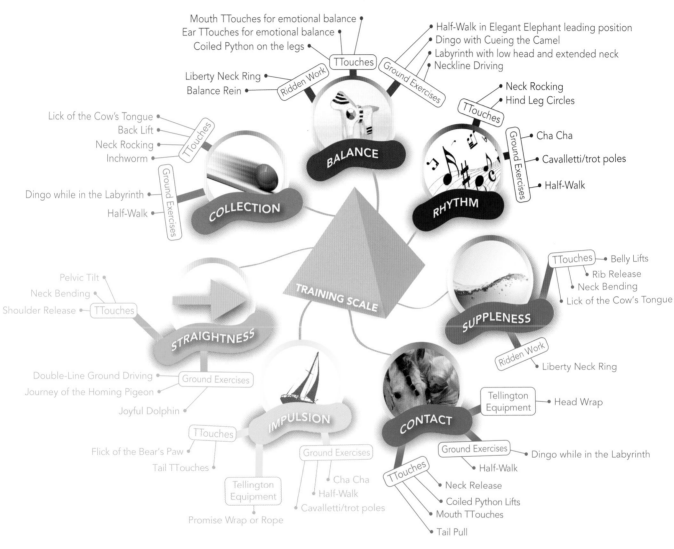

Mouth TTouches for emotional balance •
Ear TTouches for emotional balance •
Coiled Python on the legs •
TTouches

• Half-Walk in Elegant Elephant leading position
• Dingo with Cueing the Camel
• Labyrinth with low head and extended neck
• Neckline Driving
Ground Exercises

Ridden Work
Liberty Neck Ring •
Balance Rein •

• Neck Rocking
• Hind Leg Circles
TTouches

Lick of the Cow's Tongue •
Back Lift •
Neck Rocking •
Inchworm •
TTouches

• Cha Cha
Ground Exercises
• Cavalletti/trot poles
• Half-Walk

Dingo while in the Labyrinth •
Half-Walk •
Ground Exercises

COLLECTION

BALANCE

RHYTHM

TRAINING SCALE

TTouches
• Belly Lifts
• Rib Release
• Neck Bending
• Lick of the Cow's Tongue

Pelvic Tilt •
Neck Bending •
Shoulder Release •
TTouches

STRAIGHTNESS

SUPPLENESS

Ridden Work
• Liberty Neck Ring

Double-Line Ground Driving •
Journey of the Homing Pigeon •
Ground Exercises

Joyful Dolphin •

Tellington Equipment
• Head Wrap

IMPULSION

CONTACT

Flick of the Bear's Paw •
Tail TTouches •
TTouches

Ground Exercises
• Dingo while in the Labyrinth
• Half-Walk

Ground Exercises
Cha Cha
Half-Walk
Cavalletti/trot poles

TTouches
• Neck Release
• Coiled Python Lifts
• Mouth TTouches

Tellington Equipment

Promise Wrap or Rope

• Tail Pull

D

4.6 D Step 4: Illustrate further sources of inspiration (D).

RIDING WITH INTENTION

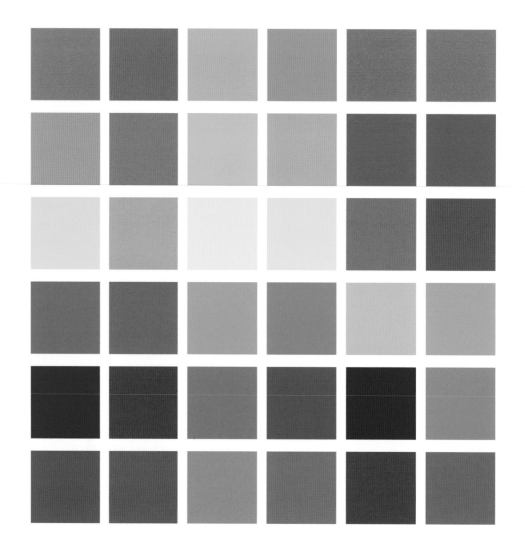

5

NOW WANT TO RETURN TO TWO CONCEPTS I TOUCHED UPON AT THE beginning of this book: *feel* and *"heART"* (see pp. 13 and 14). I hope to truly help you construct such a strong foundation of well-being for your horse that, regardless of your ultimate competitive success (if that is indeed your goal), you will be able to maintain a healthy, happy partner over many years—one who is not only strong and vibrant physically, but present and willing in everything you do together, in and out of the saddle, in and out of the ring.

This means you very well may have to change how you ride. When I say "how you ride," I don't mean the timing of your aids or the way you hold the reins (although I will touch on these later in the book—see p. 223). I mean what you bring to the saddle as an emotional partner, as well as an athletic one. Each one of you has a number of (usually) untapped resources within your own body that, when identified and explored as a source of improved communication with your horse, can open gates to whole new arenas.

Tapping the Power of Intent

The determination to act in a certain way—that is, your *intent*—can empower you. This is no secret, and certainly isn't a novel idea on my part. In fact, *intention* has become a buzzword of sorts. Not only does it have a spiritual connotation, as it can mean the object for which a prayer or pious act is offered, but for years scientists have used the term "intention" or "intentionality" when referring to the act of "targeting your thoughts" in an attempt to change physical reality.

It is my feeling that "riding with intention" is integral to success in the ring, whether training or competing. The degree to which you accept the power inherent in this idea is up to you, but I hope you can agree that holding an ideal in your heart and mind creates a distinct pathway "from here to there." This is not unrelated to the practice of visualization popular with sport psychologists and used for many years by riders at all levels and in all disciplines (I speak more to the matter of visualization on p. 245).

Author Lynne McTaggert (*The Field*; *The Intention Experiment*; and most recently *The Bond*) has spent years researching studies done by scientists around the globe in an effort to prove the *actual* power of intention—that is, that every thought you have is "a tangible energy with the power to transform." And, it's not just in a metaphysical sense, but in very much a physical one.

The classical laws of motion and gravity with which we are all most familiar are those professed by Isaac Newton, and they teach you that "matter" is three-dimensional and self-contained, and influence (of one "thing" upon another) requires physical force or impact. So, for example, you apply your (three-dimensional) leg on your horse's (three-dimensional) side in an effort to "push" him over. However, the introduction of quantum theory to the international body of scientific thought offers a more complex—and in my opinion, far more interesting and inspiring—view of reality, in that "things" are not in fact isolated, but involved in a "web of dynamic interrelationships."

According to McTaggert's research, a diverse group of scientists has shown that because of interconnectivity at a subatomic level (everywhere atoms and molecules are constantly exchanging information), human intention can not only affect inanimate objects (pencils, chairs), but living systems, too (chicks, mice, cats, and dogs, for example). Experiments on human subjects have demonstrated that, using intention, one person can change the fight-or-flight responses of another. "Directed intention appears to manifest itself as both electrical and magnetic energy, visible and measurable by sensitive equipment," McTaggert writes in *The Intention Experiment*. "When we enter a crowded room, when we engage with our partners and our children, when we gaze up at the sky, we may be creating and even influencing at every moment."

What's exciting about all of this is that intention is not some special gift born only to an elite few. It is a learned skill, and one that you can teach yourself. I highly recommend you read Lynne McTaggert's books and refer to her "Intention Exercises" in *The Intention Experiment* in order to fully develop what I like to call your "intention potential." In the meantime, I'd like to get you started with a few steps you can take to begin to "ride with intention" and open up a whole new world for you and your horse to joyfully explore.

Seven Steps to Riding with Intention

Step 1 Set skepticism aside. As riders and trainers, we are willing to try all manner of tack, techniques, and methods, often at any price, in an effort to move up a level, win a medal, or simply "dance" with our horse for a few magical minutes in the quiet light of a summer evening. The idea that "thought" can affect physical reality may be difficult for you to accept at first, but it comes without cost and with infinite promise. Why not open your mind and give it a try?

Step 2   *Intention*, as you can use it to change your riding and your life, must be a "purposeful plan." It must be an understanding of a *course of action* necessary to achieving a desired result, so simply focusing on "a picture-perfect pirouette" is not going to get you results. Instead, you must meld the steps necessary to achieving that end into your daily barn rituals and riding practice.

Step 3   Regularly clear your mind and slow your brain waves. You can do this through breathing exercises, which I discuss in more detail later in the book, but which primarily focus on slow, rhythmical breathing, in through the nose and out through pursed lips, using your diaphragm (your belly should slightly protrude on the "ins" and pull in toward your spine on the "outs"—see p. 241).

Step 4   Learn to be "in the moment" and "attend to it" fully and completely, allowing thoughts to enter and exit without judgment or emotion. One meditation teacher my coauthor Rebecca Didier once worked with described this as "acknowledging, touching, then letting go." In order to use intention in your riding, you need to be fully present with each step your horse takes, free of distractions and stressors from other parts of your life, or even posed by your horse himself. You need to be aware of sensations caused by your surroundings (the soft leather reins in your hands, the dog barking by the barn, the wind in the trees, the heat of the sun or its glare on the white fence, the muffled thump of your horse's feet in the arena footing, the lesson going on in the neighboring ring), but they should be accepted without judgment. Acknowledge them, "touch" them, and then "let them go." Catch yourself forming an opinion ("That annoying dog is barking, so the farrier must be here early,") and move away from it. Don't interpret the situation; just be part of it.

Step 5   Seek and find empathy and *heart coherence*. (I explore heart coherence in greater detail, beginning on p. 67.) You need to empathetically connect with your horse: You must *ride with compassion* before you can *ride with intention*.

Step 6   State your intention specifically. McTaggert recommends using the "news report checklist" of *who*, *what*, *when*, *where*, *why*, and *how* to ensure you include detailed information and a "purposeful plan." For example, perhaps it would sound something like this: "On the next diagonal line coming up after this short side, Midnight will perform a flawless, smooth extension with marvelous impulsion and suspension as I imperceptibly become more supple with my seat while 'giving' with my hands to allow his energy to flow forward from his hindquarters, over his topline, and into the soft contact."

One sunny morning in Pebble Beach, California, now over 40 years ago, I rode a lovely six-year-old Hungarian stallion named Brado onto the cross-country course for practice before an eventing competition. Brado had been shipped from Virginia to my Pacific Coast Research Farm and School of Horsemanship a few weeks earlier. He had recently failed to make the Olympic eventing team because he was very spooky and resistant when it came to jumping ditches.

Pebble Beach had one of the premier cross-country courses at that time, including many natural water ditches. Since I had competed for many years successfully at events held there, I chose to see if I could use that course to change Brado's mind about ditches.

I casually approached the first ditch out on the course, just to see what he would do. The horse stopped dead in his tracks, about 40 feet in front of the ditch, and assumed the stiff-legged, hard-necked posture I've often seen in stallions when they become resistant. Rather than fighting with Brado, which is what, from reports, everyone else had already tried without success, I immediately "emptied my head like a gourd."

Robert van Gulik wrote a series of Chinese detective stories, often based on Chinese legend, that starred a protagonist named "Judge Dee." I learned the phrase "empty my head like a gourd"

5.1 This old and rather dark photo shows Brado and me clearing a big ditch on the Pebble Beach course just three days after I held the intention he would lose his fear and be safe and confident. This was our first event together, and we won many.

in a Judge Dee story about a fourteenth-century blind samurai who could never be defeated because he knew to "empty his head like a hollowed gourd," which according to the story, made him see far more clearly than eyesight could make possible. I think imagining your head as a hollowed out gourd is a great visual way to rid yourself of unwanted left-brain "chatter," doubts, and negative self-talk, thus leaving room for a positive outcome and an actual space open to "infinite possibilities."

As Brado and I confronted that first ditch in Pebble Beach, I sat quietly. I didn't allow him to go left, right, or back, but I didn't urge him to go forward. I simply rid my mind of any preconceived ideas of what he would do or what he could accomplish, and then I held the intention that he would lose his fear and go forward when he felt safe and confident.

Only a few minutes passed before Brado walked forward on his own, without any urging or insistence from me. He jumped the ditch easily, and I *never* had a single stop at a ditch in all the years I competed with this wonderful horse after that day (fig. 5.1).

Step 7 Let go of an outcome. As when learning to be "in the moment," acknowledge the result, touch it, and let it go (see Step 4). Your goal is for riding to become a series of "small intentions" that lead to a greater one—that of dressage as *art*. You cannot become consumed by failure, by mistakes, by missteps. They are but single brush strokes on your canvas, each of which adds depth, color, and meaning to your final portrait.

"From the peace in our world to the healing in our bodies, from all our relationships and romances to the careers we pursue, our conversation with the world is constant and never ending...if we're conscious, by definition, we're creating."

—Gregg Braden, *The Divine Matrix*

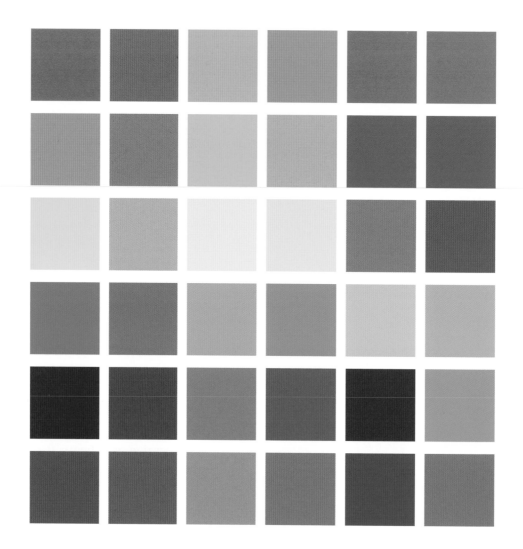

6

.. ....More than a Muscle

We now have scientific evidence that the heart does more than simply service the human circulatory system as a "blood pump." It is in constant communication with the brain in order to direct various other bodily systems so they all work in harmony. As you perceive and react to the world, your brain sends messages to your heart. And, amazingly, the heart talks right back, with its rhythmic activity sending us emotional signals that, in effect, govern our life.

Heart Rate, Heart Rhythm, and How They are Meaningful

Heart rate is the number of times your heart beats per minute, and *heart rhythm* (heart rate pattern) is the repetitive action of your heart—its cadence (or tempo). The health of your heart is determined by both rate and rhythm.

Heart rate is measured with a *heart rate monitor* (such as the wristwatch-type used by many athletes in training), or by taking your pulse. Heart rhythm is recorded by an electrocardiogram (ECG), which captures the heart's electrical activity. Today there are portable ECG devices, or *heart rhythm monitors*, that enable you to evaluate your heart's electrical impulses throughout your daily activities.

According to an article "Heart rate variability and the prediction of ventricular arrhythmias," appearing in the Oxford University Press' *QJM: An International Journal of Medicine*, heart rate variability (HRV) is the temporal (time) variation between sequences of consecutive heartbeats. It is a measure of the balance between sympathetic mediators of heart rate (that is, epinephrine and norepinephrine—see more about them on p. 192), which *increase* the rate of cardiac contraction, and parasympathetic mediators of heart rate (acetylcholine, for example) that lead to a *decrease* in heart rate (Reed, Robertson, and Addison, Volume 98, Issue 2, pp. 87–95). "Although counterintuitive," write the authors, "it is possible that HRV confers a survival advantage. Any system exhibiting intrinsic variability is primed to respond rapidly and appropriately to demands placed upon it."

Heart Rate Feedback Trainers—
The Future of Top Performance?

A new development in biofeedback technology, the heart rate feedback trainer, monitors heart rate patterns and helps people develop skills to increase physiological harmony and ability. This promises to greatly impact performance in clinical, academic, workplace, and sports settings.

For example, the emWave® PC system is a software and hardware program that collects pulse data through a finger or ear-clip sensor that plugs into your computer. It then translates your heart rate patterns into graphics so you can watch in real time how your thoughts and emotions affect them. This enables you to learn how to regulate your emotions and develop methods of managing stress, anxiety, fear, and sadness, to name just a few. You can find out more at www.emwavepc.org.

I like to have students at my clinics and seminars use a portable version of the device, which slips neatly into a shirt or jacket pocket and emits a musical "pinging" sound indicating heart coherence. The pocket-size device is effective in helping the rider focus, breathe calmly, and slow down—often a necessary transition from the daily stresses of job, family, and commute to your time in the saddle.

Today we understand that HRV is in fact a normal and a dynamic demonstration of our inner emotional state and the neurotransmitters that send signals from brain to heart and vice versa. Studies using heart rhythm monitors show that negative emotional states—such as stress, anger, and frustration—impact HRV, causing a random and jagged rhythm pattern. In contrast, positive emotional states such as appreciation, love, and compassion cause coherent and ordered rhythm patterns.

"HRV dynamics are particularly sensitive to changes in emotional states," says Dr. Ellen Kaye Gehrke, who uses working with horses as a way to improve the organizational and leadership skills of international business clients on her ranch in California. She and a team of researchers from the Institute of HeartMath®—a recognized global leader in researching emotional physiology, stress management, the physiology of heart-brain research, and how students learn (www.heartmath.org)—studied the effects of the human heart on the horse, and vice versa. "Positive and negative emotions can readily be distinguished by changes in heart rhythm patterns...During the experience of

Heart Rhythm Awareness

A heart that beats too fast or too slow, or irregularly, creates an irregular heart rhythm called an *arrhythmia*. While some arrhythmias are life-threatening, others occur in normal, healthy hearts. It should be noted that while not always, arrhythmias can be cause for medical concern, and irregular heart rhythms paired with symptoms such as dizzyness, fainting, or shortness of breath should be reported to your physician.

negative emotions such as anger, frustration, anxiety, sadness or depression, heart rhythms become more erratic or disordered (or incoherent). Conversely, sustained positive emotions such as appreciation, love, or compassion are associated with a highly ordered, or coherent, pattern" (Mistral, Kip, "Heart to Heart," *Horse Connection Magazine*, August 2007).

In *The Heartmath Solution*, Doc Childre and Howard Martin provide a good example of how the slightest emotional change can show up immediately in an individual's HRV pattern. "A fairly calm business manager at one of our seminars was hooked up to the heart rhythm monitor," they write. "As he began to do the stressful exercise of counting backward from two hundred by seventeens, his HRV pattern revealed his heart was changing erratically. (This same erratic pattern occurs when we feel stress from any frustration or anxiety.) But when he focused on his heart by appreciating someone he loved, his HRV quickly shifted to a smoothly ordered, coherent pattern."

But how does your horse "feel" your heart? After all, the distance from the usual points of contact via the saddle (seat and legs) and bridle (hands) to the torso (the physical "home" of your heart muscle) is significant enough to most likely prevent subtleties of heart rate and rhythm to make a huge impact—or is it?

......Exchanging Energy

The study of energy fields is central to many different therapies and disciplines, including traditional Indian medicine, Reiki, acupuncture, Tai Chi, shiatsu, and aromatherapy, to name just a few. According to these disciplines, and to some aspects of the study of quantum theory, your body receives, stores, and transmits information via electromagnetic energy fields that run through you and surround you (see my discussion of riding with intention on

Two Hearts As One

According to a study published in *The Veterinary Journal* (July 2009), it has now been proven what many horse people have long intuitively known: an increase in a human's heart rate affects the heart rate of the horse she is handling or riding. Researchers at the Swedish University of Agricultural Sciences measured the heart rate in horses and humans as they walked or rode past a point where the human was told to expect an umbrella to open (fig. 6.1). Though the umbrella never opened, the heart rate of both horses and humans increased as they passed the point in question.

6.1 When you are riding or handling your horse and your heart rate increases due to anxiety or anticipation (whether due to excitement or trepidation), your horse's heart rate will increase, as well. When my heart rate remains steady in the face of possible or definite obstacles—such as the open umbrella here—my horse "feels" it, and maintains a steadiness of his own, which is reflected in his physical and mental state.

p. 60, and the effects of wavelength and frequency of color on p. 49). When you touch another creature, you exchange energy.

It has been found that the heart radiates the strongest electromagnetic field in the body. According to data from the Institute of HeartMath, the heart has enough power that an electrocardiogram can read it in every cell of your body, and a magnetometer can actually measure it radiating into the space around you, up to 8 to 10 feet in all directions.

It has been consistently shown in my work with the Tellington Method that horses are sensitive to human heart energy fields, and vice versa. This suggests that those who incorporate the Tellington Method into their daily interactions with their horse are, in fact, engaging their four-legged friends at "heart level" (figs. 6.2 A & B). Now, the real question is how can this be of benefit?

.......Heart Rhythm Coherence

Coherence is defined as a logical, orderly, and aesthetically consistent relationship of parts. Understanding how the mental and emotional energy, emanated and controlled by your heart, can become coherent, and learning to manage this energy can be a powerful force in your work with horses. It's called "heart rhythm coherence" (fig. 6.3). As I'm sure you can guess by now, positive emotional states produce coherence within human systems, and this in turn can drastically improve your effectiveness when addressing tasks, large and small.

Most of us have experienced this on more than one occasion: perhaps your child gives you a hug and a kiss before he or she goes off to school, or your significant other reminds you how much he or she loves you before you hop in the car to go to the barn. Your positive emotional state, in this case the result of an exposure to *love* and *caring*, makes the mundane magical and the difficult a little easier. You may find yourself humming while you warm up your horse, perhaps with more patience than usual, and the movements you've struggled to grasp until now suddenly seem to come more easily.

According to the Institute of HeartMath, research has shown that "sustained positive emotions lead to a highly efficient and regenerative functional mode associated with increased coherence in heart rhythm patterns and greater harmony among physiological systems." In other words, when you handle your horse or ride him with positive emotions weighting the scale, your body will react to his movement and the demands of your schooling figure or test more smoothly, cohesively, and in a more skilled manner than it will when you are anxious or angry, for example.

And, even better, research has also shown that human beings can regulate their own *heart rhythm coherence* by actively generating positive feelings and intentions. You can achieve a higher performance state by "thinking good

6.2 A & B Whenever you make contact with another creature, you affect each other via an exchange of energy. The strongest source of electromagnetic current in the body is the heart. Incorporating *TTouches* into your work with your horse therefore engages him at "heart level." Belli Balkenhol's dressage horse Dablino is extremely tall, and he carries his head very high, both a symptom and a cause of his sensitivity and reactivity. I encourage his trust here by placing one hand on the noseband of his halter and the other on his crest near his poll (A).

Note that he is so tall that I am standing on a mounting block to perform this exercise. With clear intent and a calm heart, I put light pressure on the noseband and use small, circular *Clouded Leopard TTouches* on his crest to ask him to lower his head, which he does as you can see by my altered stance (B).

With spooky or overreactive horses, finding another means of communicating with them is of significant value—transmitting assuredness and peace of mind heart to heart can be your key to breaking through the haze of panic or the clutter of worry that can interfere with your horse's ability to learn and to perform.

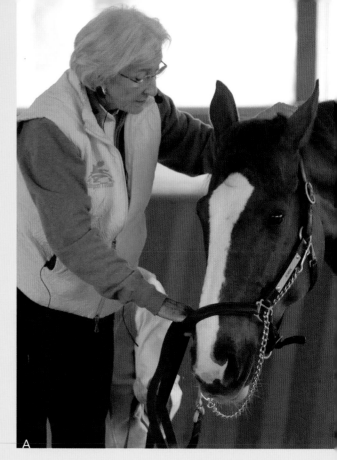

A

B

6.3 A positive emotional state, both in you and in your horse, contributes to heart rhythm coherence, which has been proven to increase effectiveness when addressing tasks—or in other words, it improves performance. The presence of love and caring in one's life are important factors in the generation of a positive emotional state, and human beings are also blessed with the ability to control (to a great degree) the amount of positivity or negativity in their thoughts and intentions.

Being thankful and showing thanks are basic steps in promoting a positive emotional state in you and in your horse. Here, French dressage rider Magali Delgado and I share our immense gratitude with one of her wonderful Lusitano stallions, Nacarado, during a *TTouch* session. We are doing light *Raccoon TTouches* on his head to soothe and relax him. Our moment of interspecies connection and coherence in body, mind, and spirit is a special gift.

thoughts." As studies continue to show how the heart can be the control center of all that you do, technology is providing tools to help us (see sidebar, p. 68).

Practical Steps to Becoming Coherent in Your Riding and Your Life

If you've come this far, you may have begun to understand the true power the heart possesses—it goes above and beyond that which we have traditionally allotted it. "Thinking positively," is the crux of the matter, and because this is not a new concept, I am willing to bet that whether or not you are finding it easy to believe that you can impact your horse at "heart level," you can be convinced to inject positivity in your life that may currently be lacking. It

Everything You Feel, Your Horse Feels, Too

Heart rate increases at times of excitement, stress, and perceived pain (see also the sidebar on p. 70). Studies show that pain experienced by healthy volunteers increased heart rate by up to 11 percent (Tousignant-Laflamme, Y., Rainville, P., Marchand, S., 2005). Because of the exchange of energy I've already discussed, it therefore stands to reason that when your heart rate spikes because something "hurts," your horse senses your pain, both mentally and physically.

I've seen this exhibited time and time again: an individual riding through pain, whether due to acute injury or chronic illness, on a tense, worried, and often overly compressed horse who has difficulty stepping under himself, stretching forward, and rounding his back.

Neither horse nor rider enjoys their time together in such a scenario. The rider may think he or she is doing the right thing by staying in the saddle and "riding through it," but I feel that this often leads to physical problems in the horse that are further detrimental to the partnership and can even be permanently damaging to the pair's ability to communicate. If the act of riding increases or accentuates pain in your body in any way, it behooves you to find ways to alleviate the physical stress you are experiencing before pursuing an active dressage training program in earnest.

will only serve to make you feel better, and the residual effects (heart coherence, for one) are, as they say, "gravy."

Best-selling author Gregg Braden writes in *The Divine Matrix*, "I've rarely seen people trapped in the positive patterns of joy in their lives. Almost universally, the situations that cause people to feel stuck have roots in what are considered negative feelings."

This statement is so, *so* true when I apply it to working with horses. I cannot think of a single example of a happy, confident, pain-free rider who professed a lack of improvement on her own part and on the part of her horse. Most often, the rider with such a "positive" sense of reality sees progress as inherent and constant. This kind of rider takes "backward" steps that are a natural part of the educational process in stride. On the other hand, the unhappy, fearful, frustrated, or pain-ridden rider is usually unable to gauge minute changes for the better and be thankful or buoyed by them. Her "negative" perspective colors everything and suspends progress in relationships, both with horses and people.

How do you replace negative emotional patterns with positive ones? I have a few easy exercises that I regularly use to remind myself to think positively and find heart coherence, whether at home or in the barn.

Exercises for Finding Heart Coherence

1   Reserve a time each day to recall three things for which you are thankful—big or small. Make them specific: rain in a hot dry climate, a loved one's health, your dog's eager greeting at the end of a long day. I like to say, "Hold your thanks in your heart and mind" for a few moments (dwell on what it is you are thankful for, think about it, and appreciate it), and note how you feel physically as you do so. Later, if you sense that negativity is gaining ground—perhaps you are angered by a barnmate's lack of cleanliness—you can remember this feeling and summon it. For years I have included the message, "Think of three things for which you are thankful" at the end of my voicemail greeting. That's how integral I feel it is to a healthy self and a healthy society.

2   Choose a new, positive response to an old and hurtful pattern. Instead of feeling impatient in traffic during your commute to the barn, consider it "slack time," and use the extra moments of quiet to run through your test in your mind. Instead of feeling frustrated by your horse's inattention in the ring, think of it as evidence of his interest in his surroundings and his spark for life, which can translate to animation and impulsion in another riding situation.

3   Smile. That's right. As trite as it sounds and as hokey as you may feel, riding with a smile on your lips translates into general positivity and suppleness in your body while dissipating stress and/or worry. I learned this trick from my mother, the late Marion Hood. When I was young and catch-riding in Edmonton, Alberta, Canada, my mother used to stand along the fence line of the show ring, and every time I passed her she'd say, "Smile, Dear!" This simple reminder helped keep me relaxed in competition, and reminded me that I was there because I loved horses and riding was (and is) *fun*!

In addition, there are physiological reasons for smiling when you are riding. Eckart Meyners, a specialist in riding and kinetics for more than 30 years who often presents on behalf of the German National Equestrian Federation (FN), says that when you smile you "activate

6.4 A & B As can be seen, Ingrid Klimke and I are happy with our horses! It has been shown that smiling releases serotonin, the "feel-good hormone," and if you feel good, your attitude has a positive impact on your horse. In addition, smiling affects chains of muscles from your face all the way to your feet, so smiling enables you to better follow the horse's movement with your body. Plus, it makes riding *fun*! I enjoyed sharing this idea with Ingrid.

muscle chains running from your face through your neck area, and your pelvis all the way to your feet (figs. 6.4 A & B). A rider who is smiling will naturally follow the horse's movement with her body" (*Rider Fitness: Body & Brain*, Trafalgar Square Books, 2011).

4 Be sincere. A random and fleeting moment of appreciation or affection is of course a good thing. But your heart and mind know the difference between an automated feeling and a sincere desire. For example, if you go around the ring smiling on the outside but gritting your teeth on the inside, thinking the whole time how ridiculous you look, then the benefits of smiling in the first place are cancelled out. If you tell your partner you love him or her, but do so half-heartedly while checking email and thinking about the half-gallon of chocolate ice cream in the freezer, you haven't made the best use of such important words! *Sincerity* is the source of *power*. The results you experience in the saddle will directly correlate with the amount of sincerity you can muster during these simple lessons in positive emotion.

5 Summon your "intention potential." Heart coherence is simply one corner of the canvas upon which your dressage art will appear. Remember what you learned about riding with intention in the last chapter (see p. 60). You must learn to apply positive emotion with focused intention and consistency in order to connect with your horse at heart level and transform your dressage explorations into an experience your horse enjoys as much as you do.

Riding Whisper with Intention and Heart Coherence

I met the mare Whisper at one of my clinics in 2010. Her rider was frustrated with herself and with her horse because she wasn't able to get the degree of engagement she needed from the mare to prepare her for the upper dressage levels—and this was a rider who had successfully brought along seven horses to Grand Prix. This issue was in spite of several years of careful training and what I saw to be skillful riding. Whisper's lack of collection was certainly not due to an ineffective rider, nor was it an absence of "try" on the mare's part.

I watched the two struggling together, observing the rider's discouragement and frustration, and what I felt to be the mare's depression and resignation. After hearing their story, it was my opinion that Whisper's difficulties were influenced by two past colic surgeries, which I felt made it more difficult for her to physically connect her front and hind end. She carried a rather "heavy"

6.5 A & B Opening my heart and visualizing Whisper's perfection (riding with *intention*) helped transform her attitude and way of going—shown in both before and after photos with the *Promise Wrap* to promote a sense of connection from her hindquarters. In the before picture, Whisper's rider is having difficulty engaging her (A). Later, Whisper is connected, forward, and coming through her back (B).

belly that I thought inhibited her freedom to achieve collected movement to some degree. I added the *Promise Wrap* around her hindquarters to encourage Whisper to bring her back up and come into better balance, but I still didn't see the kind of willingness and engagement of which I just knew she was capable. I asked if I could ride her.

When I mounted, I immediately opened my heart and held a feeling of love and appreciation for Whisper and how hard I knew she was working. I thought about how beautiful she was and formed a picture in my mind of her perfection and her potential. Whisper became light in my hands and very responsive to my leg aids. Her center of gravity shifted back, her forehand became lighter, and I felt a change in her heart, as though she was "smiling." The feeling of "oneness" I had with Whisper was remarkable (figs. 6.5 A & B).

This is a wonderful example of the importance of riding with intention and heart coherence, and illustrates how your attitude affects performance. Practicing with a smile on your lips, an open heart, and a desire to flow together with your horse, can have a huge effect on performance and take the horse-human relationship to new and inspiring levels.

"Throw your heart over the fence and the rest will follow."

—Norman Vincent Peale,
author of *The Power of Positive Thinking*, 1898–1993

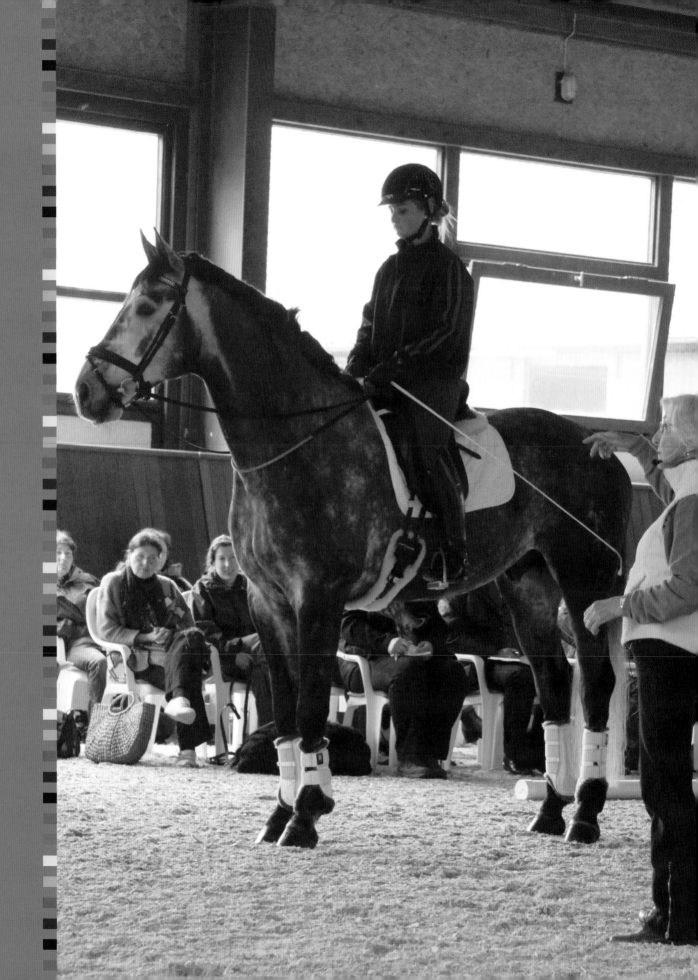

PART TWO

DRESSAGE AND THE
TELLINGTON METHOD

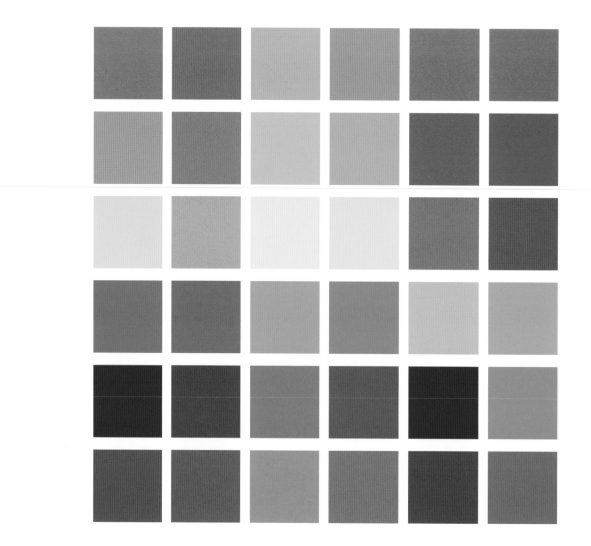

7

SO HOW CAN YOU TAKE THE DIFFERENT IDEAS AND COMPONENTS that make up the Tellington Method, which I discussed at length in Part One, and translate them into a language that makes sense for the sport of dressage? When it comes to applying all you have learned so far, you may wonder just where to begin. Honestly, *where* the change starts isn't as important as, quite simply, it *starting*.

Perhaps you have strategically adhered to the principles outlined in the Training Scale, but there is one area, or several, where you and your horse struggle or get stuck. This "stumbling block" can serve as your starting point. In chapter 8 (p. 94), I provide specific *TTouches, Ground Exercises,* and *Ridden Work* according to the Training Scale, as well as guidance for creating a daily *TTouch* plan for your horse.

It may be that your horse displays one of many common training, behavioral, or health problems, in which case, let me assure you, you are by no means alone. This, too, can provide your intial reason for using the Tellington Method in your daily horse care and riding routine. Perhaps your horse suffers from stress related to travel or recurring health issues. Maybe he takes a long time to warm up, or even after a lengthy time spent easing him into a workout, he remains stiff and reticent in his work. I provide real-life examples that demonstrate how the Tellington Method can go a long way to solving these kinds of problems in chapter 9 (p. 120).

But before I approach issues with the Training Scale, and before I troubleshoot common problems with behavior and performance, I would like to illustrate the specific areas of physical and psychological development my *Method* addresses so you can better understand its potential in aiding in your horse's existence as a happy and healthy athlete. I have designed a "pie" that shows what I like to call the "Seven Cs": *Comfort; Confidence; Capacity for Learning; Coordination; Cooperation; Connection with Rider;* and *Change* (fig. 7.1). It is my opinion that the Seven Cs are *equal* in weight and importance— none must precede the other—and, in fact, it is best if the horse has all seven in place from the very beginning of his development as a dressage mount.

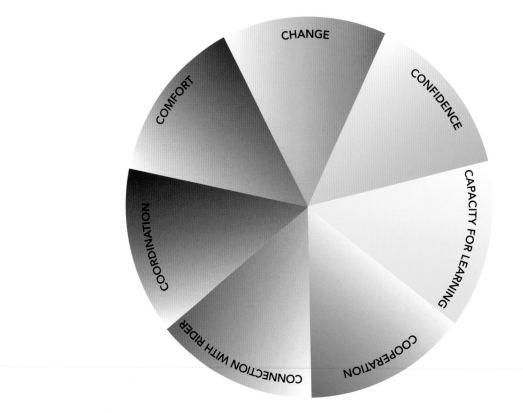

7.1 The Seven Cs.

Therefore, you should aim to apply them in equal measure when you picture them as the symmetrical pieces of a very colorful pie.

The Tellington Method not only enables horse and rider to confirm the classical training principles—plus *Balance*—via engagement of both hemispheres of the brain, it also verifies every step along the way via these Seven Cs. Each of them is fundamentally necessary for any horse, no matter how naturally talented, to learn and eventually excel at dressage; therefore, it should be your goal to address each of them with the same focus you apply to the principles of the Training Scale.

I briefly describe the Seven Cs on the pages that follow, and each of them is a necessary ingredient to improving your horse's dressage ability while solving common problems. In addition, I remind you that each of the Seven Cs is assigned a *color*, the same as its parallel element in the Tellington Training Scale (see p. 54). I also provide guidance in *targeting your intention* in the process of establishing the Seven Cs as integral facets of your horse's training.

Comfort

Dressage horses are athletes. Their body works hard to bend, flex, collect, and extend thus leading to physical soreness in particular areas; fatigue; and often unsoundness. My unique form of bodywork—*TTouch*—enables you to treat existing soreness or injury, and prevent development of chronic problems. First and foremost a dressage horse needs to be *comfortable* to perform (fig. 7.2).

The Color: *Comfort* is the color *violet*, the color of *Balance*—mental, physical, and emotional well-being (see p. 52).

The Intention: Target your thoughts so they encompass your horse's mental, physical, and emotional well-being. Think of his muscles, joints, and ligaments working together in concert, of his body being free of discomfort, of his movement being uninhibited.

7.2 A dressage horses performs best when he is comfortable and free from pain. *TTouch* has been proven to both prevent and treat the physical wear and tear that comes with the years of serious training and conditioning necessary in order to compete the sport horse. For example, *Belly Lifts* with a towel can help relax tight back muscles and avoid soreness in this area, and they can significantly improve a horse's ability to consistently work over the back and come "through."

Confidence

Highly bred for spirit and animation in the competitive arena, many dressage horses may be of particular sensitivity, often making them excitable, skittish, and spooky (figs. 7.3 A & B). In addition, overtraining or heavy-handed discipline can create timidity or fearfulness that leads to trouble in new or tense situations. My series of *Ground Exercises*, combined with *TTouches*, can increase confidence in the most timid of animals. Specifically, *TTouches* override the instinctual flight reflex and teach the horse to "think" rather than "react." A dressage horse needs to be *confident* to learn new lessons and give his best in competitive environments.

The Color: *Confidence* is the color *orange*, the color of *Straightness* (see p. 53). A confident horse moves assuredly ahead, every cell directed as one from Point A to Point B.

The Intention: Target your thoughts so you hand your horse the ability to be sure of himself in his surroundings. He is king of his castle, he balks at nothing, shies at no one. And don't forget, *your own confidence* provides him all the impetus he needs to stride assuredly forward.

Capacity for Learning

Dressage horses are expected to learn and remember countless aids and cues for various movements—knowledge accumulated over a number of years. In addition, dressage tests differ from level to level, and in order to increase collection or animation, new exercises are introduced throughout a horse's lifetime. When a horse learns to trust his rider, this trust will override the fear and flight instinct, and the horse's *Capacity for Learning* is enhanced, assuring progress from one level of performance to the next (fig. 7.4).

The Color: *Capacity for Learning* is *yellow* for *Impulsion* (see p. 53). When your horse is open and ready to absorb new lessons, when he is eager to participate, he is propelled forward in both his ability to perform and his ability to associate with humans and other animals.

The Intention: Target your thoughts so you imagine your horse gobbling up lessons the way he gobbles up grass, moving steadily, hungrily, without hesitation, bite after bite, seemingly insatiable.

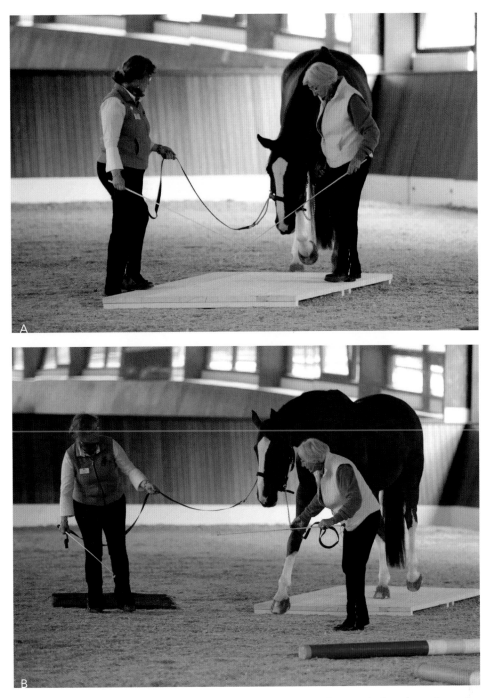

7.3 A & B Some dressage horses today have a tendency to be timid, skittish, and spooky, lacking the ability to deal with new or unusual obstacles or surroundings. *Ground Exercises* combined with *TTouches* can increase confidence and help reactive, anxiety-ridden horses deal with day-to-day challenges in a calm, safe manner. This confidence will translate quickly into improved performance in the dressage arena.

A simple exercise like learning to step on a flat wood surface or even a black stall mat in the arena can help to ground and focus a reactive horse. After our work together, Dablino becomes less suspicious and more willing to approach, pass, and traverse unusual footing or strange sights; he learns to *think* rather than simply *react*.

7.4 Dressage horses are expected to learn and remember aids, movements, aural cues. They spend a lifetime in the classroom, with numerous "quizzes" and tests. Their capacity for learning, for absorbing new information and retaining old, can be improved with the Tellington Method, in particular work in the *Labyrinth* to gain focus and mental, physical, and emotional balance, as we are doing with Dablino here.

Coordination

The intricate, delicate movements of dressage are indeed an art form—a dance. Muscles are flexed, legs are crossed, and motion suspended. This demands an incredible amount of athleticism—namely *Coordination*. While not all horses are born with excellent coordination, you can markedly improve this characteristic (figs. 7.5 A & B). A *coordinated* dressage horse will be able to score better at his current level and progress more easily up the ladder to higher levels of training.

The Color: *Coordination* is the color *electric indigo* for *Rhythm* (see p. 53). Coordination is one of the keys to rhythm, and further evidence of mastery of the physical self.

7.5 A & B Not all horses are born with the coordination they need to perform movements in the competitive dressage arena. *TTouches*, *Ground Exercises* and *Ridden Work*, however, have been shown to improve the horse's proprioception (his ability to understand where his body is in space) and handle it, and namely his feet and legs, appropriately.

Cavalletti and gridwork such as Ingrid Klimke demonstrates here will improve coordination significantly with the addition of *Front Leg Circles*, *Hind Leg Circles*, *Lick of the Cow's Tongue*, and *Tail Pulls*, which give the horse a sense of connection throughout his body. Work in the *Labyrinth* with careful attention to navigation and balance around corners can also bring many rewards.

The Intention: Target your thoughts so you see your horse's basic gaits as if they are steps of a dance. Visualize each step perfected, each foot clearly and perfectly placed, each sideways movement fluid as if the horse were more liquid than solid.

Cooperation

Horse and rider can only be truly connected through *Cooperation*. Dressage lessons are hard and the aids for different movements can be similar, or they consist of a combination of multiple cues. An argumentative horse who puts up a fight whenever he is challenged or whose first inclination is to refuse to try something new will have a hard time progressing upward through the Tellington Training Scale. Use of my *Method* has shown to improve a horse's inclination to work *with* rather than *against* his rider. A dressage horse who *cooperates* every step along the way can make day-to-day training a true pleasure rather than an uncomfortable—and dangerous—struggle for supremacy (fig. 7.6).

The Color: *Cooperation* is the color *green* for *Contact* (see p. 53). There is no connection without cooperation. A horse accepting of the hand, responsive to the seat and leg, and who is "one with you" in mind and matter, is in tune with the basic premise of dressage.

The Intention: Target your thoughts so your relationship with your horse is clear. This should be a partnership based on interdependence and balance, neither one of you more needy than the other. Your horse should willingly and joyfully give and receive just as freely as you do.

Connection with Rider

Many of the horse-and-rider teams at the top of dressage sport represent true partnerships, usually many years in the making. It is beyond a doubt that the most successful of them are intuitively communicating via a carefully established and nurtured connection. Through *TTouches*, *Ground Exercises*, and *Ridden Work*, the Tellington Method offers myriad ways to be with your horse and form or further your relationship. When a dressage horse is *connected with his rider* he will be more in tune to her aids and try harder to perform when asked (fig. 7.7).

The Color: *Connection with Rider* is the color *blue* for *Suppleness* (see p. 53). Blue and suppleness together enhance the flow of communication, integral for true connection. Think of the clear blue waters of the ocean as they wave and roll, ebb and flow, connecting distant lands and creatures above and below.

7.6 Dressage can be an exercise in frustration when your horse pits his will against yours every step of the way. The premise of the Tellington Method is to help horses discover ways to work *with* their rider and handler, and to improve their attitude and work ethic because lessons are interesting and pain-free. My techniques can instill a general desire to cooperate, as exhibited here by Heartbreaker (see more about him on p. 144). When we began work with Heartbreaker the platform and pool noodles inspired massive anxiety and a fight to escape. After a day's work using my *Method*, he cooperated with our requests in a quiet, interested, and pleasant manner.

7.7 Dressage with "heART" requires a true connection be established between you and the horse. This enables communication to flow both ways, uninterrupted, and completely clear to both "sender" and "receiver." I take a moment on one of Ingrid Klimke's horses to target my thoughts and connect with my mount. Note the horse's soft expression—open and ready to listen to what I have to say. The *Balance Rein* around his neck gives him a sense of freedom that encourages connection with me—his rider.

The Intention: Target your thoughts so you have in your mind a vision of one being, a centaur-like creature, horse and rider connected in such a manner as to make it difficult to determine where one begins and the other ends.

Change

I include this principle because this book is about *transformation*. It is about *changing your mind* so you can *change your horse*—that is, the way your horse thinks, the way he feels, the way he behaves, and the way he performs (figs. 7.8 A–C). And *you* need to remember that change is indeed possible, and it may be easier than you think! Training your horse with a predetermined idea, such as "He always breaks gait in this corner," or "He hates tempi changes and will never like them," or "He's just not very talented," assumes that change is too difficult or unlikely to achieve. This is detrimental to your horse ever improving in areas of difficulty, and it certainly prevents the two of you from reaching your potential.

In addition, your horse is your teacher. Challenges you face alongside him are your opportunities to develop a new understanding or skill. Believe in the possibility for change for the better, on your horse's part and on your own, and you may find you are pleasantly surprised by the relationship and the rapport that awaits you. Through the years, my organization, Tellington TTouch Training, has logged countless case studies of people giving their horse a fresh start and, in a relatively short time, having that horse completely change his attitude and way of going. Trust me! You can be one of these success stories.

The Color: *Change* is the color *red* for *Collection* (see p. 53). Collection has always been the pinnacle of the Training Scale, the end goal of dressage. It is also representative of change: a change in the way the horse carries himself; a change in the way you communicate with him; and ideally, a change in how you will forever go about attaining future riding goals.

The Intention: Target your thoughts so you envision your horse in a state of metamorphosis. His learning curve and your learning curve are both necessary in order for him to ultimately grow wings and "fly."

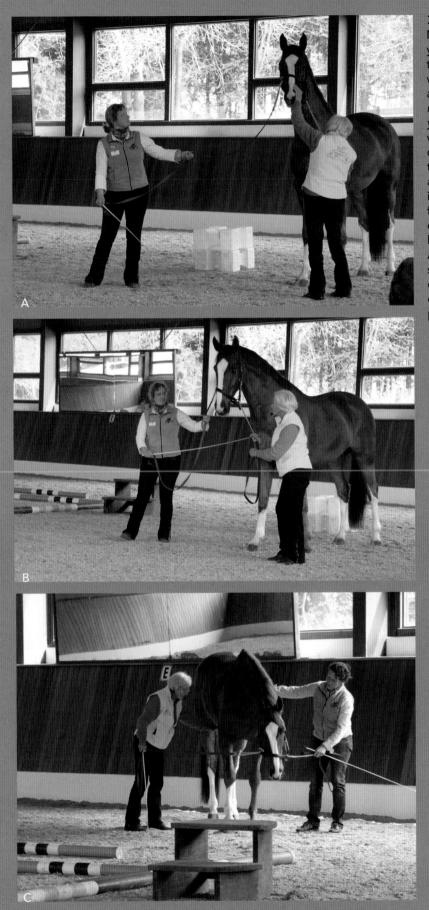

7.8 A–C With the Tellington Method you can break free of your old patterns, clear long-time hurdles, and ignore what might once have borne an impasse. *Change your mind and you can change your horse.* Every horse, whatever the problem or challenge, has the potential to change for the better and become all you can imagine for him. Dablino, for instance, responds to our work by progressively lowering his very high head. And this fairly small, perhaps seemingly insignificant change can be a gateway to bigger changes in his confidence and performance under saddle.

GETTING SPECIFIC: CHOOSING *TTOUCHES*, *GROUND EXERCISES*, AND *RIDDEN WORK*

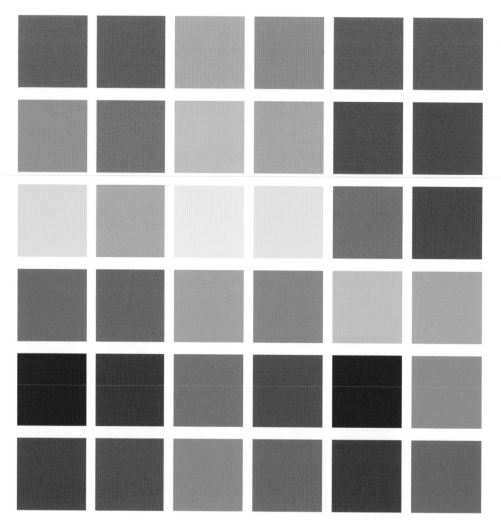

8

THE TELLINGTON METHOD PHILOSOPHY IS TO TEACH YOUR HORSE to think rather than *react;* to build trust; and to connect with your *heart,* your *head,* and your *hands.* We've already discussed how to connect with your heart and your head—now it is time to use your hands. In order to incorporate my *Method's* components in your dressage training you must understand ways to apply them to the Training Scale itself. This enables you to begin to customize a Tellington Method program for *your* dressage horse, with all his strengths, weaknesses, charms, and idiosyncracies in mind.

8.1 Another look at the Tellington Training Scale (see p. 47).

......Applying My Method to the Tellington Training Scale

Balance

Balance, the first element and the base of the Tellington Training Scale, represents physical, mental, and emotional well-being (fig. 8.1 and see p. 47). Here are nine Tellington Method exercises to improve your horse's balance:

High-Tech Tools for Improving Rhythm

Dressage riders have long used a metronome to determine the beats per minute (bpm) of their horse's gaits. This helps the rider develop a consistent and rhythmic tempo, and is also invaluable when planning a Freestyle program.

Equiapps.com offers a fabulous metronome app called EquiTempo that emits a regular tick sound at a predetermined rate, helping you mark time as you ride, and offering adjustability in order to customize the appropriate bpm for your horse. I regularly use the EquiTempo app with my students. It's brilliant! You can set it for any tempo at the walk, trot, and canter to accommodate a slow or speedy horse. Both horse and rider respond to the rhythmic beat, and I find horses appear to enjoy the audible tempo, proactively adjusting their stride to the steady "tick, tick, tick."

TTouches
- *Coiled Python* on the legs
- *Mouth TTouches* for emotional balance (fig. 8.2)
- *Ear TTouches* for emotional balance

Ground Exercises
- *Labyrinth* with low head and extended neck
- *Neckline Driving*
- *Dingo* with *Cueing the Camel*
- *Half-Walk* in *Elegant Elephant* leading position

Ridden Work
- *Balance Rein*
- *Liberty Neck Ring*

The Color: *Balance* is the color *violet*, the color of *Comfort* (see p. 85).

The Intention: Target your thoughts so they encompass your horse's physical, mental, and emotional well-being.

8.2 Mouth TTouches as I am performing on Dablino contribute to the horse's emotional balance. The muzzle has a direct connection to the limbic system, the parts of the brain that control emotions, behavior, and learning retention (long-term memory). Your horse may be resistant in the beginning, but he will soon learn to accept and will appear to enjoy *TTouches* on the mouth and nostrils.

Rhythm

Rhythm, the second element in the Tellington Training Scale, can be a challenge—riders often struggle throughout progressive work with their horse to keep the rhythm of his gaits true and unspoiled. Here are five exercises to help maintain your horse's rhythm:

TTouches
- *Hind Leg Circles*
- *Neck Rocking*

Ground Exercises
- *Cha Cha*
- *Cavalletti*/trot poles
- *Half-Walk* (fig. 8.3)

The Color: *Rhythm* is the color *electric indigo* for *Coordination* (see p. 88).

The Intention: Target your thoughts so you see your horse dancing.

8.3 The *Half-Walk* on the ground (or in the saddle) improves the horse's rhythm. I bend slightly forward and give subtle signals on the chain between my thumb and forefinger to encourage Dablino to take careful, measured, slow steps.

Suppleness

Suppleness aims for both relaxation of mind and elasticity in body, and *TTouches* are a fantastic way to achieve it. Here are five exercises for a suppler mount:

TTouches
- *Lick of the Cows Tongue* (fig. 8.4)
- *Rib Release*
- *Neck Bending*
- *Belly Lifts*

Ridden Work
- *Liberty Neck Ring*

The Color: *Suppleness* is the color *blue* for *Connection with Rider* (see p. 90).

The Intention: Target your thoughts so have in your mind a vision of one being, a centaur.

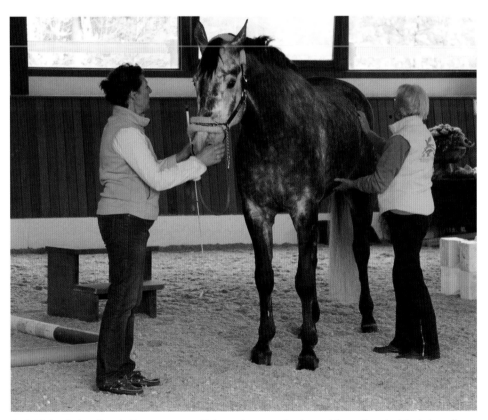

8.4 Lick of the Cow's Tongue—parallel strokes on the barrel from just behind the elbow all the way back to the flank—helps ensure a horse that is supple in mind and body. This *TTouch* raises the back and softens the back muscles.

8.5 Noting the high head and (negative) tension in Heartbreaker prior to a ridden session, I stand slightly to one side of his hindquarters and perform *Tail Pulls*, which relax the back and neck, activate cranial-sacral fluid through the spine, and create a sense of connection in his body. All these will help him overcome spooking and reacting to clapping and other sounds or movement from spectators.

Contact

Contact is one of the easiest elements to mishandle. When "gone wrong" (inconsistent, behind the vertical, tilted head), contact is also one of the most common problems dealt with by riders at every level. Here are six ways to improve contact:

Tellington Equipment
- *Head Wrap*

TTouches
- *Neck Release*
- *Coiled Python Lifts* on the jaw
- *Mouth TTouches*
- *Neck Rocking*
- *Tail Pull* (fig. 8.5)

The Color: *Contact* is the color *green* for *Cooperation* (see p. 90).

The Intention: Target your thoughts so your horse gives and receives just as freely as you do.

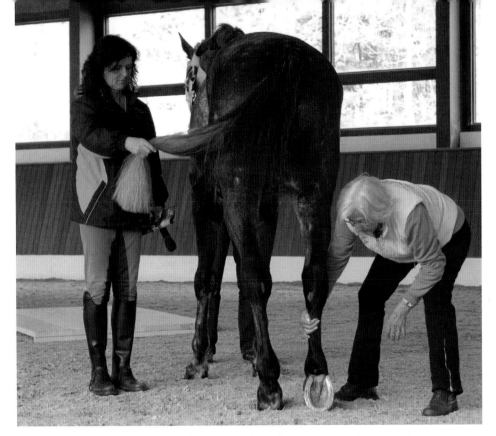

8.6 *Hind Leg Circles* lengthen the horse's stride and improve suppleness and engagement. Resting the toe of the hoof 6 to 8 inches behind the other hind foot encourages the horse to relax the muscles in his hindquarters.

Impulsion

Impulsion is an element that's all about energy flowing forward through the horse. Here are four ways to improve your horse's impulsion:

Tellington Equipment
- *Promise Wrap or Rope*

TTouches
- *Flick of the Bear's Paw*
- *Hind Leg Circles* (fig. 8.6)
- *Tail TTouches*

The Color: *Impulsion* is *yellow* for Capacity for *Learning* (see p. 86).

The Intention: Target your thoughts so your horse eagerly moves forward through life just as he eagerly moves forward through his lessons.

Straightness

I explain *Straightness* as it applies to the definition from the Classical Training Scale (p. 42)—the horse's hind legs should follow the tracks of the front, on both straight and curved lines. Here are six ways to improve your horse's straightness:

TTouches
- *Pelvic Tilt*
- *Neck Bending*
- *Shoulder Release*

Ground Exercises
- *Double-Line Ground Driving*
- *Journey of the Homing Pigeon* (fig. 8.7)
- *Joyful Dolphin*

The Color: *Straightness* is the color *orange*, the color of *Confidence* (see p. 86).

The Intention: Target your thoughts so your horse is sure of himself in his surroundings.

Collection

Collection, of course, is the end goal, and it depends a great deal on the work done before it is attempted. Most horses require progressive conditioning to enable them to shift their weight off their forehand and onto their hindquarters, as collection necessitates. Here are six ways to improve your horse's ability to attain and maintain collection:

TTouches
- *Lick of the Cow's Tongue*
- *Back Lift*
- *Neck Rocking*
- *Inchworm*

Ground Exercises
- *Dingo* while in the *Labyrinth* (fig. 8.8)
- *Half-Walk*

The Color: *Collection* is the color *red* for *Change* (see p. 92).

The Intention: Target your thoughts so you envision your horse in a state of metamorphosis, with a beautiful, enthralling end result.

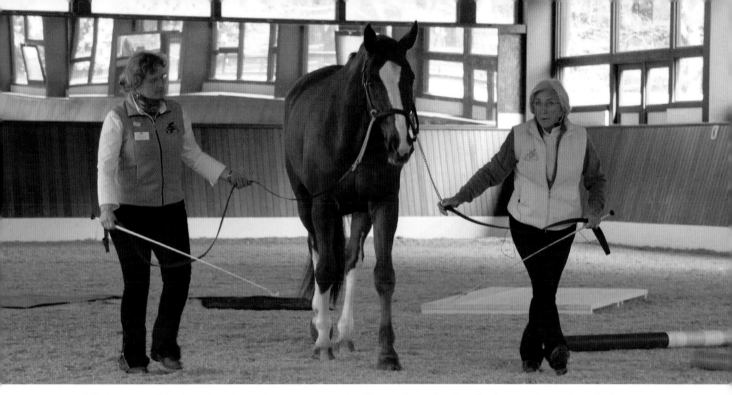

8.7 *Journey of the Homing Pigeon* is a two-person leading position that instills a sense of security, rebalances the horse who has difficulty bending or traveling in one direction, and improves straightness. This exercise engages both sides of the horse's brain, and calms those who are nervous or anxious.

8.8 *Dingo* teaches the horse to respond to clear, precise signals for "go" and "whoa" on the ground, which carry over into your ridden work. It involves a series of *strokes* (on the back) and *scoops* (on the croup) with the *Tellington Wand* while simultaneously signaling on the lead line.

While in the *Labyrinth*, working your horse "between two hands" in this way improves your horse's focus and progressively lightens his forehand while redistributing weight to his hindquarters—collection. *Dingo* is usually done without a second handler, but here it gives Dablino a feeling of security.

.......Upkeep: Creating a TTouch Program

It is easy to incorporate a regular *TTouch* routine into your horse's day. The number of *TTouches* you include, and the length of time you spend on each can vary with your own schedule, your horse's needs according to the Training Scale, and with specific training, behavioral, or health issues in mind. This *TTouch* addition to your care and management plan can be a fun, relaxing way to bond with your horse out of the saddle.

Begin by assessing your horse's body. I recommend using my easy method of *Flat-Hand Body Exploration* (figs. 8.9 A & B). Although the *Flat-Hand Body Exploration* is commonly thought to be for physical assessment, how your horse accepts the contact over every area of his body will also give you a sense of how confident and trusting he is. You may also find "hot" or "cold" areas possibly indicating stiffness or soreness, but your primary interest in your initial body assessment is the level of trust between you and the horse.

Flat-Hand Body Exploration

Step 1 Beginning on the near side of your horse, place your left hand softly at the junction of the horse's head and neck, just behind the ear.

Step 2 Slide the hand smoothly over your horse's entire body and legs. You can also alternate in a smooth rhythmical fashion between both your left and right hands.

Step 3 Feel for hot or cold areas, swellings, lumps, indentations, changes in muscle tone, and differences in hair quality. Particularly note sensitive areas where the horse appears to avoid contact, raises his head, switches his tail, steps back or to the side, pins his ears, or threatens to kick. Record areas of concern for your attention later, once your "physical inspection" is complete.

I consider this form of *Flat-Hand Exploration* a means to monitor a horse's sense of trust, as well as stress, soreness, and sensitivity. Remember: The second "T" in *TTouch* stands for *Trust*. When your horse is reactive to this basic *Flat-Hand Exploration*, his trust in you is limited and his stress level is high.

The Daily TTouch Plan

In 1996, Judith Balkenhol asked me to compose a "Daily TTouch Plan" for each of the horses in her barn. Here is the basic plan I created for Goldstern, her husband's Olympic-gold-medal-winning horse. It's been updated so it can be adapted to fit today's dressage horse and the modern-day dressage rider's schedule, and I

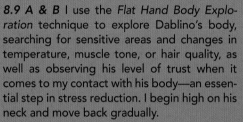

8.9 A & B I use the *Flat Hand Body Exploration* technique to explore Dablino's body, searching for sensitive areas and changes in temperature, muscle tone, or hair quality, as well as observing his level of trust when it comes to my contact with his body—an essential step in stress reduction. I begin high on his neck and move back gradually.

show you some of the steps of the customized plan I devised for Judith's daughter, Anabel (figs. 8.10 A–F). Your goal should be to use TTouch for at least 5 to 10 minutes a day, choosing from the suggested list that follows. Note: an upper-level horse will benefit from double to triple this time allotment.

Once your horse adapts to *TTouch*, I find it most beneficial to work on the horse free in the stall. But when it is necessary to perform your daily upkeep in the cross-ties, make certain they are long enough that his nose can lower to chest level (see more about cross-tying on p. 191). I generally begin on the neck, move to the tail, and end up back with the head, but you can also begin with the head and vary the areas you work on, depending upon your horse's level and training schedule. As you'll see in the steps that follow there is a modified program for more advanced horses.

Neck

Step 1   *Lower the Head* to the point that your horse's poll is level or just below the withers.

Step 2   Perform two-second, *Clouded Leopard TTouches* using a 2 or 3 pressure with two-second connecting slides, covering the neck in three rows running parallel to the top of the neck on both sides of your horse (see p. 262 for a description of the TTouch Pressure Scale).

Step 3   When your horse appears to be sensitive to the *Clouded Leopard TTouch*, apply *Abalone TTouches* or *Lying Leopard TTouches* in the same three rows.

Step 4   Apply gentle, rhythmic *Neck Rocking* with the crest of the neck parallel to the ground. Keeping the horse's neck level, hold the cheekpiece of the halter with one hand and bend the neck slightly to the side you are standing on while making slow *Bear TTouches* that press gently into the neck muscle

8.10 A–F Here, I work with Anabel ("Belli") Balkenhol to develop a routine of *TTouches* that could be helpful to relieve stress in her horse Dablino. We work outside of the stable in the sunshine, and Dablino is held with a person on each side, because he is often reactive to grooming in the cross-ties. Here he is able to stand quietly. Belli does connected *Clouded Leopard TTouches* on his back with a light pressure (A). I calm him with a hand on his shoulder and ask him to *Lower the Head* while Belli moves lightly along his back (B). Dablino stands quietly while she does *Abalone TTouches* along the flank area where he has been known to be sensitive (C). Belli then asks him to *Lower the Head* by stroking his upper lip lightly and inviting him down with her own lowered hand—a move that can work like magic to lower a high head (D). Next she does a *Heart Hug*, forming a circle with *Abalone TTouches* on Dablino's chest balanced with her left hand on his withers (E). Belli begins *Neck Rocking* with one hand on the crest and the other on the underside of Dablino's neck. Rocking back and forth loosens the tight underside of the neck, releases tension in the neck and back, and improves breathing (F).

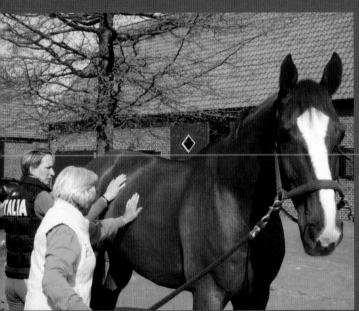

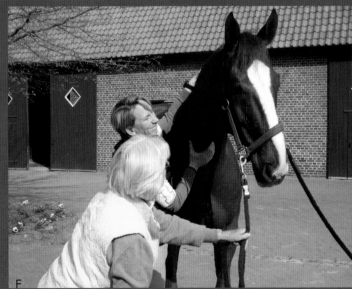

with the other hand. Work from the top of the neck under the first cervical vertebra to the shoulder. Breathe in as you make a circle (2 pressure) and breathe out slowly through pursed lips as you press slowly into the muscle while bending the horse's head a little in your direction.

An alternative is to actually move the horse's crest toward you with one hand while you "bear slowly and gently into the muscle" with the *Bear TTouches* with the other hand. This has the effect of releasing tight muscles and increasing circulation. When your horse throws his head or resists this step, his neck may be sore, in which case, apply *Abalone TTouch* followed by a *Python Lift.*

Step 4 (Variation) *Inchworm, Mane Slides,* and *Shoulder Release* can be done on alternating days.

Back

Step 1 Raise the horse's back with a *Back Lift.*

Step 2 Perform *Lying Leopard TTouches* along the back with a 2 or 3 pressure and two-second circles connected with slow slides. Hold the intention in the slide so that the horse feels this connection between circles. Cover each side of the back, from withers to croup, with two, precise, long lines of connected circles. One line should run approximately 4 inches down from the spine, and the second line 4 inches below that. Two minutes of this *TTouch* on each side increases circulation, enhances suppleness, and releases tight muscles.

Step 3 When the horse is relaxed, proceed with slow *Lick of the Cow's Tongue* from the abdomen over the back—again, two minutes on each side. I pay particular attention to keeping my slides precisely perpendicular (90 degrees) to the ground, beginning a little on the opposite side of the belly midline and ending by closing over the back.

Step 4 Follow with *Tarantulas Pulling the Plow* in long lines running parallel to the spine.

Step 5 (For Intermediate and Grand Prix Competitors) Once a week include a session covering the entire barrel with two-second *Coiled Python Lifts* in a conscious pattern to release lactic acid and support circulation, and finish with *Belly Lifts* to encourage deep breathing. *Springbok TTouch* over the over the 4th and 5th lumbar vertebrae—the horse's "power pack"—can restore impulsion. I also like to combine *Rib Release, Neck Bending,* and *Tail TTouches* for this level horse.

Belly

Step 1 As noted in Step 5 on p. 108, *Belly Lifts* are deeply relaxing before or after *TTouches* are performed on the back and barrel. For *Belly Lifts* use a long bath towel, folded so it is 6 inches wide, and wrapped around the horse's barrel. Hold one end on your side of the spine and initiate the *Belly Lifts* with the other end. You can stablize your elbow against your hip in order to lift and release slowly, as if you are doing a *Python Lift* on the belly.

Step 2 Perform *Abalone TTouches* or *Lying Leopard TTouches* on the entire abdominal area from elbow to flank—two-second circles with a 2 pressure, followed by slow releases. If your horse is sensitive in the flank area use a sheepskin mitt to perform the *TTouches*. (Note: When your horse remains reactive in the flank even after several sessions, I recommend having him checked for ulcers—see more on this on p. 178.)

Front Legs and Shoulders

Step 1 Do slow *Coiled Python Lifts* from elbow to hoof.

Step 1 (Variation) Perform *Rainbow TTouch* and *Octopus TTouch*, including the whole shoulder and down to the hooves, on alternating days.

Step 2 Perform *Front Leg Circles* in both directions to release the horse's shoulders and back.

Hind Legs and Hindquarters

Step 1 Begin with rhythmic, connected *Clouded Leopard TTouches* in 3-inch circles at a 3 to 4 pressure on the hind end.

Step 2 Perform *Hind Leg Circles* on one leg at a time, both low and high, then do them with each leg brought forward and under the belly to activate the hind legs for piaffe and passage.

Step 3 Do three or four two-second *Abalone TTouches* with pause over and around the stifle joint, as a way to provide strength and stability to the piaffe and passage.

Step 4 Follow with *Pelvic Tilt*.

Step 5 Then add a few *Zigzag TTouches* and *Octopus TTouches* from the horse's croup down to each hoof.

Step 6 Return to the legs and circle each hoof in both directions, spiraling down to the ground. Make two small *Hind Leg Circles* in each direction, followed by two or three large ones.

Step 7 Do *Coiled Python Lifts* that last two seconds each, with a three-second pause at the top of the lift on the back and front of each leg, from stifle to hoof. Perform this twice on each leg.

Tail

Step 1 *Tail Work* helps the horse overcome fear of noise behind him, and it connects him through his whole body. Circle the tail in both directions with one hand near the base of the dock and one 10 inches lower. Pull on the tail slowly with both hands and hold for four seconds, then slowly release.

Step 2 Do *Hair Slides* on small clumps of hair, from the top of the tail to the end. This relaxes the horse through the croup, back, and neck, without detracting from impulsion and a forward tendency.

Head

Step 1 Perform slow *Lying Leopard TTouches* or *Baby Chimp TTouches* in connected lines from your horse's nose to his ears. This helps to increase circulation (particularly after use of a tight noseband—see more on this on p. 206). Do the *TTouches* over his eyes and his forehead to help him relax and focus, followed by *Hair Slides* on his forelock. Continue this segment for five minutes.

Mouth

Step 1 Begin with *Clouded Leopard TTouches* or *Baby Chimp TTouches* with the backs of your fingers, whichever is easier for you and most acceptable to your horse around the mouth and chin. Slide your hand under his upper lip onto the gums above the teeth and inside the lower lip. Tap the horse's tongue with your fingers if you can stabilize your hand safely. This work around the mouth and nostrils affects the limbic system, which controls the fight-or-flight reflex. Note: These *TTouches* can be very beneficial when applied just prior to saddling at a show.

Ears

Step 1 Standing in front of the horse and giving him enough space so he does not feel crowded, ask him to *Lower the Head* with your left hand on the left side of the noseband of the halter. If your horse is resistant to this in the beginning, stand on a safe stool so you can easily reach his ears.

Step 2 Make a few smooth *Hair Slides* on your horse's forelock. Starting at the center of the poll with the palm of your right hand, make a circle around the base of one of your horse's ears, and stroke the ear smoothly from base to tip. This develops trust and releases tension and stress. Fold the ear between your thumb and fingers when you reach its middle. Note: Tempo makes a difference. To calm your horse, use slow slides; to activate him, make the slides a little quicker.

The Perfect Warm-Up: Getting Supple without Losing that "Sparkle"

The Tellington Method gives you a valuable alternative to longeing or scheduling lengthy riding sessions to "work the horse down" in preparation for a lesson or test. Using 10 minutes of *TTouches* before you mount—particularly *Ear TTouches* to create focused calmness and *Lick of the Cow's Tongue* to supple your horse—you can prepare your horse as much as 30 minutes of longeing or riding ever can, while conserving the horse's energy (aka "sparkle") at the same time. TTouch prior to mounting also develops trust between horse and rider and an attitude of cooperation in the horse—one of the important Seven Cs (see p. 90).

The *TTouch* session effective for warm-up can be such that *all* riders can easily build it into their routine before mounting. When time does not allow, it can become part of a groom's preparations prior to tacking up your horse, allowing her to check the state of your horse's body from nose to tail, encompassing the horse's withers, back, ribs, abdomen, and croup.

Therein lies one of the many gifts of *TTouch*. Time spent with *TTouch* on the body can shorten necessary warm-up time while effectively bringing the mind of the horse into a relaxed and cooperative state. It allows a rider to spend a quiet moment with her horse, which often results in the horse's increased willingness and ability to perform.

Over the years I've enjoyed working with several of Klaus Balkenhol's horses, including Gracioso and Garçon, before major competitions. Often I would do a 30-minute *TTouch* routine each morning they were to compete, followed by a few specific *TTouches* to calm or invigorate about seven minutes before the horse was saddled.

Everyday Warm-Ups: A Five-Minute Routine

Step 1   A few minutes of *Ear TTouches* can calm a horse when done with a medium tempo. It is important not to do them too slowly, because they can relax the horse too much. To energize, stroke more quickly with a pressure your horse accepts readily.

Step 2   *Tail TTouches,* especially the one where you hold with a slow release similar to a back stretch for a person, are helpful for horses who are high-strung or nervous, as they make a connection through the whole body (fig. 8.11 A).

Step 3   *Lick of the Cow's Tongue* from girth to flank and repeated two times on each side helps to supple your horse before you're in the saddle.

Step 4   *Lowering the Head* (figs. 8.11 B & C) followed by *Neck Rocking* gets your horse listening to you and ready to go.

Step 4   (Variation) *Front and Hind Leg Circles* can be performed on alternating days.

Competition Plan-of-Action

Dressage horses, like any other performance horses, can suffer from a great deal of stress due to their competitive schedule. The stress can stem from a variety of sources: travel to and from (see p. 128 for more about trailering), strange accommodations, intense and chaotic environments, and the nerves of handlers and riders. I have found *TTouch* to be hugely helpful in calming a horse prior to and during competition.

When applying a complete *TTouch* routine during competition, you should have performed *TTouch* on your horse before—you need to know how much he needs to relax in a competitive situation, and conversely, in some scenarios, how much stimulation is needed to prepare him to perform. Achieving this balance takes a little practice, as there is a fine line between relaxing, activating, and fine-tuning. Different horses may respond in different ways to specific *TTouches.* Furthermore, one horse may react to one particular *TTouch* differently, depending on the day.

The first time I worked at home with Klaus Balkenhol's gold-medal-winning dressage horse Goldstern, he became so relaxed he would not respond normally to the aids. So the following day, I used a faster tempo and more activating *TTouches;* the result was he was optimally responsive. (See more about my work with Goldstern on p. 153.)

A

8.11 A–C *Tail TTouches* (A) and *Lowering the Head* (B & C) are two good exercises to use in your regular warm-up routine, as they encourage a calm attitude, trust, and cooperation prior to beginning your work (or "play"!) session. Heartbreaker obviously enjoys the attention he is getting here. Note: These *TTouches* can also be done before you mount. ➞

B

C

Note: Whenever possible, perform these *TTouch* routines in the stall with your horse free (loose, without a halter). Assuming an attitude of trust and cooperation in the hours before you enter the arena will ultimately pay off in competition.

TTouch on the Road

One of the easiest *TTouches* to incorporate in your regular horse care routine, *Ear TTouch*, has many uses during competition (fig. 8.12). Keep in mind that a simple, five-minute Ear TTouch session can be used to:

- Help your horse relax after travel.

- Accustom your horse to new surroundings so he eats and sleeps better.

- Shorten warm-up time, allowing your horse to reserve the energy he needs for a top performance.

- Calm and focus the nervous horse, and stabilize pulse and respiration prior to entering the arena.

- Bring heart rate and respiration into normal ranges and shorten recovery time following a performance.

- Increase appetite and desire to hydrate (lengthen session to 10 minutes of medium pressure and tempo for this effect).

Recommended Routine: Before Warm-Up

When you will work your horse under saddle a few hours before you compete, I recommend spending 20 minutes on *TTouches* before he is saddled. This can save you a long warm-up that can potentially take away the edge he needs for top performance. I recommend the following routine, which should be adjusted according to your horse's needs and preferences:

Step 1 *Back Lifts* and *Lick of the Cow's Tongue* on the horse's barrel and from hip to hip over his croup, using a pressure and tempo the horse enjoys. Note that you may have to stand on a stool to reach the croup adequately.

Step 2 *Lowering the Head.*

Step 3 Two minutes of stimulating *Ear TTouches* to activate the horse.

8.12 Ingrid Klimke performs *Ear TTouches*. These have myriad functions during competition, including calming and focusing an excited horse, shortening recovery time, and increasing appetite and the desire to hydrate.

Step 4   Thirty seconds of *Neck Rocking*.

Step 5   Activating *Troika TTouch* over the back and hindquarters.

Step 6   Arched *Tail Circles* and *Tail Pulls* with a slow release.

Step 7   Four minutes of *Rib Releases* and *Neck Bends*.

Step 8   *Front and Hind Leg Circles.*

Step 9   *Coiled Python Lifts, Rainbow TTouch,* or *Octopus TTouch*—whichever is most comfortable for you to apply and best for the temperament and mood of the horse.

Step 10   (Variation One)—To stimulate: end the session with *Noah's March,* alternating both hands to cover your horse's whole body.

Step 10   (Variation Two)—To enhance Collection and Suppleness: end the session by outlining the horse's entire body with strokes of the *Tellington Wand.* (See more about the Tellington Tools on p. 263.) Stroke along the underside of the neck, over the chest, down the front legs to the ground, and then under the belly and down the front of the hind legs. Finish by outlining the horse's topline, over the croup and down the back of the hind legs. Use the same pressure you would if you were painting the horse's body with a paintbrush in order to give the horse a sense of connection in his whole body.

Step 10   (Variation Three)—To activate a tired horse: when your horse has competed in several classes and does not have the energy and impulsion you would like, make the *TTouches* named in the prior steps more invigorating (apply with a faster tempo) and end with *Flick of the Bear's Paw* over the entire body.

Recommended Routine: Before Test

I recommend that 6 to 10 minutes before saddling your horse prior to competition, you perform the following routine as a "Wake up!" for your horse:

Step 1   *Ear Slides* with the horse's neck level, activating from the base of the ear to its tip with even pressure all over and the ear at 90 degrees to the topline of the horse.

Step 2   *Mouth TTouches* under your horse's upper lip and *Lying Leopard TTouches* on his chin for an emotional and mental flexibility that influences his overall Balance.

Step 3   *Neck Rocking* with the top of the neck level.

Step 4   One minute of *Troika TTouches* using a medium tempo and pressure, applied on both sides of the back from the midline to approximately 8 inches below the spine.

Step 5   *Activating Lick of the Cow's Tongue* (but again, be sure to respect the ideal tempo and pressure for the horse on that day).

Step 6   End with activating *Coiled Python Lifts* or *Octopus TTouches* applied with exuberance!

Recommended Routine: Immediately Following Test

• Remove your saddle, but leave the saddle pad in place, or place a thick towel over the back, and do quiet *Zigzag TTouches* from withers to loin.

• After the horse is washed and cooled off, allow him to relax in his stall while you go over the whole body with *Coiled Python Lifts* to prevent lactic-acid buildup in the muscles. Combine *Lying Leopard TTouch*, *Abalone TTouch*, or *Chimp TTouch* with the *Coiled Python Lifts*, depending what is most comfortable for your hands and for your horse.

Recommended Routine: The Day After

How much *TTouch* your horse needs the day after a show depends on the level at which you are competing. The higher the level, the more time it takes to keep the horse's body in ideal condition.

• For the higher-level horse, repeat the *TTouch* session I recommended for use before the morning warm-up ride at a show (see p. 115).

• When you are riding at the lower levels, you may choose to spend a little less time on the post-competition routine; however, don't forget that once you are acquainted with *TTouch*, you will derive as much benefit from applying it as you horse gets from receiving it! Consider every moment spent incorporating it into your regular horse care regimen a step forward in your journey together (fig. 8.13).

Note: At the show grounds, when *you* are riding in the competition, it behooves you to have another person, or your groom, prepared to perform your Tellington Method routine so you can rest and prepare for your test. I do, however, recommend that you reserve just a few minutes before mounting to do some *TTouches* on your horse's face and ears yourself. This simple act deepens the connection and communication between you and your horse prior to asking him to give you his all.

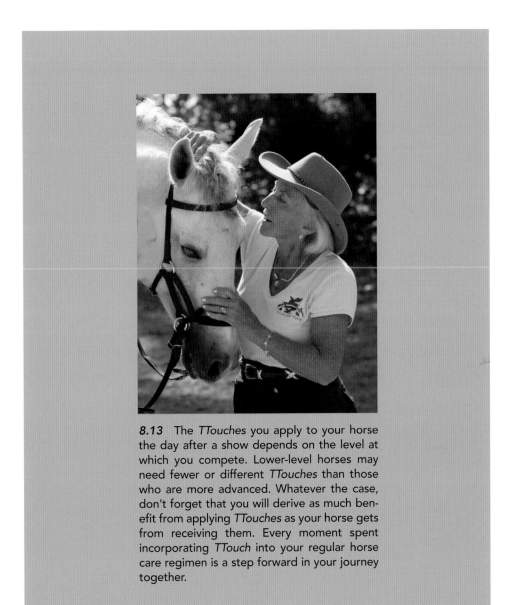

8.13 The *TTouches* you apply to your horse the day after a show depends on the level at which you compete. Lower-level horses may need fewer or different *TTouches* than those who are more advanced. Whatever the case, don't forget that you will derive as much benefit from applying *TTouches* as your horse gets from receiving them. Every moment spent incorporating *TTouch* into your regular horse care regimen is a step forward in your journey together.

CHANGING PERSPECTIVE:
STORIES OF SOLVING BEHAVIORAL,
TRAINING, AND HEALTH PROBLEMS

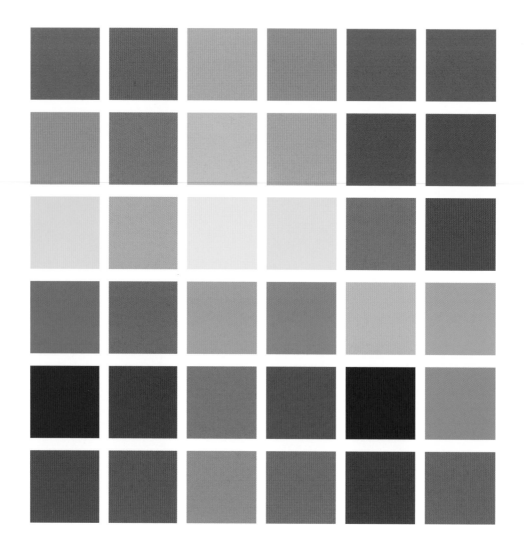

9

I MUST MENTION BEFORE I BEGIN THIS CHAPTER THAT MANY OF THE causes of behavioral, training, and health problems I have seen in dressage arenas and barns around the world can be alleviated by working to create an "atmosphere of well-being" in the life of your dressage horse. I closely examine the elements of this atmosphere of well-being in chapter 10, beginning on p. 176. First, however, I'll recount tales of a few common problems that I have, time and again, found solvable with conscientious application of the Tellington Method.

.......Problem-Solving Tales: Common Issues and Tellington Method Solutions

Slowing "Rushiness" and Calming Anxiety

In May of 2008, I spent two days working with Ingrid Klimke—German eventer, dressage rider, and daughter of the late Dr. Reiner Klimke (see p. 21 for a story about my time spent working with him). I first met Ingrid many years ago while visiting her father's stable and demonstrating *TTouch* for the reduction of the stress caused by travel and competition. In a way, I was coming full circle, as Ingrid had invited me to show her *TTouches* that she and her groom could use on her horse Abraxxas in preparation for the upcoming Olympics in Beijing (where she and Abraxxas would win team gold, a feat they repeated in London in 2012).

Ingrid hoped the Tellington Method could help reduce the stress of distant travel and competing overseas. Stress relief is one of the main aims of my work for performance horses, and it can be beneficial in many different anxiety-causing scenarios (see more on stress on p. 188).

Over the two days I was at Ingrid's stable, we worked with several of her horses, in addition to Abraxxas. She had a four-year-old mare she described as "dominant," with a tendency to run ahead of Ingrid's leg—the mare was too forward under saddle and difficult to rate (figs. 9.1 A–F). After observing the

9.1 A–F I worked with Ingrid Klimke and her young mare in 2008—the horse was "rushy" and too forward, which I attributed to a lack of Balance. I did *TTouches* on the mare, including light *Raccoon TTouches* on her face to soothe and relax her (A). Ingrid had wonderful luck improving the mare's confidence and also shifting her weight from forward to back with a *Balance Rein, Lindell Sidepull,* and *Promise Wrap* (B & C), which she used in the *Labyrinth* and over *Cavalletti* (D & E). The result was a happy trot, that was forward without being "rushy" (F).

mare being ridden at the walk, trot, and canter, I felt these issues were due to a lack of mental and physical *Balance*—the first element in the Tellington Training Scale (p. 47)—resulting in what amounted to "rushiness."

I asked Ingrid to dismount so I could check the mare's neck, back, and haunches for areas that showed sensitivity. Just like humans, it is common for horses to have muscles that are a little sore or tight, and a few minutes of *Lying Leopard TTouch* using a light pressure can provide relief. I showed Ingrid how her groom could achieve this, then spent about 20 minutes performing *Lick of the Cow's Tongue* on the mare's body to give her an increased sense of her back and rump, as well as connect her from forehand to hindquarters.

Then, Ingrid discovered a new side to the lovely mare when she rode with a combination of the *Balance Rein*, *Lindell Sidepull*, and *Promise Wrap*. With the *Balance Rein* around her neck and the *Promise Wrap* around her hindquarters, the mare had encouragement to bring her back up and come into better balance, quite naturally. The *Promise Wrap* gave the mare a sense of being "contained," and thus more confidence. Ingrid said she felt a good shift in the mare's balance and in her attitude, and that she was no longer running ahead of the leg.

It was during this visit that I introduced Ingrid to the *Liberty Neck Ring*, a stiff, adjustable ring made of lariat rope used around the horse's neck. I have found that riding with the *Liberty Neck Ring* can help calm the typically nervous or anxious horse, slow the rushing one, and improve your overall balance, as well as your horse's.

A year after my visit, Ingrid sent me an email stating: "I have to tell you how much I love to ride in the *Liberty Neck Ring*. It is fantastic! I am riding

Changing Perspective: Stories of Solving Behavioral, Training, and Health Problems

9.2 A & B Riding with the *Balance Rein* clearly raises the horse's back, as well as increasing suppleness and lengthening of the neck—here at the trot and the canter.

Abraxxas without a saddle and only with the *Ring,* and we feel so close and he is listening so very well."

Riding your horse with the *Liberty Neck Ring* seems to create a field of trust and a special partnership that eludes words. Just try it!

Raising the Back and Lengthening the Body

Many years ago Belli Balkenhol (Klaus and Judith Balkenhol's daughter and a lovely rider—you see her working with Dablino in many examples in this book) used the *Balance Rein* to improve her horse's tempi changes. The addition of the *Balance Rein* during training sessions helped her horse come through and work over the back in ways that had previously been difficult to achieve (figs. 9.2 A & B).

This benefit of the *Balance Rein* was evident at the Xenophon Society Symposium in 2011, as well, where one prominent Austrian dressage trainer stated his plan to integrate the *Balance Rein* into his training and instruction upon returning home. He saw how, with the help of the *Balance Rein*, the horses raised their back, allowing for lengthening of the neck, as well as increasing in suppleness, flexibility, and looseness of the topline (and, in fact, the horse's whole body) with very little effort on the part of the rider.

Interestingly, at the symposium I gave with Reiner Klimke in Los Angeles, California, in February of 1999 (see sidebar on p. 21), many of the riders found that warming up their horses with the *Balance Rein* and *Promise Wrap* made the horses more supple, confident, and willing from the get-go (find more about warming up on p. 111). At the event, there was a flapping sheet of plastic at the end of the indoor arena at the Los Angeles Equestrian Center that was causing some trouble with a number of horses. But, with the help of the *Promise Wrap*, even nervous horses could be ridden into the arena and past the flapping plastic on a long rein—as per Dr. Klimke's instructions—without panicking.

Rediscovering Rhythm and Elasticity

In 1992, I was presenting at an equestrian trade show in Hamburg, Germany, and one of the demo horses was a massive black Hanoverian gelding—he was 18 hands, and too tall to fit on the stage provided. With each step this gelding jerked his right hind leg up, almost as high as his left hock. Although it may sound like stringhalt, the movement was much higher and more exaggerated than commonly seen in such cases.

The gelding's owner had been told that perhaps stifle surgery could help the horse, but because the stifle never locked or caught and the horse did not hesitate when asked to back up, I thought there was likely another reason for his irregular stride. He had incredibly tight muscles in his neck and back—even his gaskin muscles were hard to the touch.

I performed 45 minutes of *TTouch* bodywork, including *Python Lifts* on his legs, back, and neck; *Inchworm* on his neck; *Lowering the Head*; *Ear TTouches*; and *Front and Hind Leg Circles*. When we walked him out, he was able to move with about a 70-percent reduction in leg jerking.

I encouraged the gelding's owner not to give up on him, but to ride him more often in a long, relaxed frame. The horse had been ridden in a short, compressed frame so often his muscles had lost their elasticity, with a detrimental effect on his whole body, and ultimately, on his gaits.

It is remarkable to me that all the great classic books on dressage indicate the importance of riding the horse in a lengthened frame to allow the neck to stretch and relax, but rarely is it done as often as it should be during a schooling session. Prolonged contraction of the muscles of the neck and back, necessary for advanced collected movements, restricts the horse's breathing, and over time can cause stress and a great deal of resistance.

Connecting the High-Headed, Strung-Out Horse

I remember one young, sensitive, hot Hanoverian working at First Level who had a tendency to be slightly high-headed and strung out. I worked with him and his rider at the symposium with Dr. Klimke. The horse had never been under a covered grandstand, such as the one we were in, and was extremely tense and overflexed when warmed up the first morning. It was also noteworthy that he was very nervous in hand and had difficulty standing still.

I worked with the young horse on *Lowering the Head*, and did *Back Lifts*, and lots of *Lick of the Cow's Tongue* circular *TTouches* over his entire barrel, increasing his body awareness through connecting circular *TTouch*. We worked in a halter and lead in the *Labyrinth* and did *Journey of the Homing Pigeon* with the intention to teach him to *stop and think* rather than simply *react* when he was nervous. My goal was to get him to stand, walk forward, and halt again, with his neck level and straight, thus changing his tendency to start and stop with his head up and back tight, which was causing him to fall on his forehand and out of balance when he was asked to lower his head.

The circular *TTouches* visibly improved the horse's posture, and in-hand *Ground Exercises* helped him to lengthen his neck and relax. After one hour he came trotting into the cavernous Los Angeles arena on a long, loose rein, moving freely and with confidence. This extraordinary transformation was made partly possible by the rider's addition of the *Balance Rein* and *Promise Wrap*, which gave him a feeling of "containment" without his rider having to shorten her reins.

By the second day of the symposium, the young horse was really tuned in to his rider and her aids, and she was amazed by the difference. This story clearly shows how *TTouch* is effective in relaxing horses, allowing them to release fear and stress. And, in combination with my *Ground Exercises* and Tellington Tools such as the *Balance Rein* and *Promise Wrap*, the effects of *TTouch* deepen, allowing for significant changes in behavior.

Reversing the Effects of Too Much, Too Soon

In 1994, I did a three-week intensive clinic in Mexico that featured a young Andalusian mare named Insignia. She was a highly sensitive mare capable of explosive responses whenever she perceived a form of restraint. While she was admittedly of the type and whose facial and other features as well as conformation predisposed her to overreaction (I wrote a book detailing what your horse's features and posture can tell you about his personality called *Getting in TTouch with Your Horse*), this characteristic had been amplified by asking her for too much too early in her life.

She had been taught the passage and piaffe in hand at the age of two (movements she now resorted to when she was nervous or asked to stand quietly by a handler), and was habitually ridden in a contracted head-and-neck frame with little regard for the position of her back, which tended to be dropped. In my opinion the resulting discomfort from being asked to perform high-level movements for which her body was not yet prepared, and being ridden in such a disunited and incorrect frame, combined to overwhelm her general good sense and good nature and make her prone to hysteria.

Insignia was a wonderful teacher because she reminded me, and my team, of the importance of lowering a nervous horse's head to interrupt instinctive fight-or-flight patterns. We did *Mouth TTouches* to stimulate her limbic system, *Ear TTouches* to relax her, and *Tail TTouches* to release her pelvis and raise her back.

By the end of the three-week course and with daily *TTouches* and *Ground Exercises* from the Playground of Higher Learning, Insignia was no longer reactive. She became trusting, her posture changed, and she so improved she could be ridden in the *Lindell Sidepull* and even bridleless. The manager of her stable felt the changes in the mare profound enough to use her for beginner riding lessons.

Transcending Trailering Trouble

When you train and compete in dressage, traveling with your horse is quite simply a matter of course. Even if you do the majority of your training from "home base," there will still be clinics and shows to attend some distance away, at some point "down the road." And of course, if you compete at the upper levels or on an international scale, then both you and your horse face an entirely different set of travel challenges, including flying on planes, crossing time zones, and waiting in quarantine.

Trailering problems can run the gamut, from the horse not wanting to enter it in the first place, to working himself into a state once he's in and secured. I've frequently worked with horses at both ends of the spectrum and all the places in between, and I find that trailering problems can be symptomatic of tension and fear in general. I have specialized in safe ways to load and haul horses since I first competed across the United States in 100-mile endurance rides and three-day events in the 1960s and '70s.

In 2001, while a student at the Ontario Veterinary College at the University of Guelph, Ontario, Canada, Stephanie Shanahan conducted a study of what she termed "loading stress in the horse" and measured the effectiveness of the Tellington Method in dealing with horses termed "problem loaders." Her team timed problem loaders and measured their heart rate during an attempted loading prior to a two-week-long, every-other-day Tellington Method training schedule, and then again at the end of the two weeks. Four of the ten problem loaders loaded within seven minutes, and three in less than 30 seconds. All of them demonstrated significantly lower heart rates as compared to the initial attempt.

In spring of 2011, I heard from a woman who had attended one of my weeklong trainings. "Sally" had a seven-year-old, 17-hand Warmblood, who she said had a "bad start." She felt the horse had been pushed hard as a four-year-old and had torn some muscles down the back of his hind leg, which hadn't been rehabilitated properly. He was hot and reactive, and she'd been badly injured in an accident with the horse.

Sally had regularly performed *TTouch* on the horse and felt he was improving in mind and body, but she was having trouble with trailering—he loaded fine, but once in, he threw himself around, rocked the trailer, and pawed constantly, leaving him in a sweat by the time they arrived at their destination.

This scenario is the perfect example of how a horse's level of stress and behavior under saddle will be communicated in very specific circumstances. The horse's story pointed to a lack of mental and emotional balance—not necessarily a fear of horse trailers. I recommended that Sally work on improving her horse's *Balance* all around (remember that *Balance* is the base of the Tellington Training Scale—see p. 47). Stroking him with the *Wand*, using *Coiled Python TTouches* from the elbows to the hooves, *Lowering the Head*, *Ear TTouches*, and then working over the *Platform* and under pieces of plastic or pool noodles helped him overcome his claustrophobia in the trailer, and at the same time, his performance under saddle improved dramatically.

Many years ago Tellington Method practitioner Ella Bittel, freshly graduated from the University of Veterinary Medicine, Hannover, spent several months working with me in Europe. At the end of the summer I left her with a very special assignment: to work with a horse in Klaus Balkenhol's stable—an 18-hand gelding going at Grand Prix level. The horse had so much to offer in the dressage arena, but no one had been able to load him. Several experts had attempted to work with him without success. I left Ella with the suggestion that she take as long as necessary to retrain the extremely talented gelding to load. It has been my experience that while most horse people understand and accept the time required to train a horse under saddle, few spend the hours necessary to properly prepare a horse to travel safely and stress-free in a trailer.

For one month Ella took the gelding through the Playground of Higher Learning (specifically using the trailer-loading steps in my book *The Ultimate Horse Behavior and Training Book*) and used *TTouch* on his body. At the end of the month, not only did the horse load quietly, his dressage had improved greatly—he had a better sense of his body in space, and a greater capacity for and willingness to learn.

Providing Relief in Times of Illness and Injury

There are three primary *TTouches* that I've used for over 35 years to help alleviate acute health problems, such as colic, shock, or trauma. They are *Ear TTouches* and *Belly Lifts* for colic in particular, and *Raccoon TTouches* to alleviate swelling in fresh wounds and bruises.

In the 1980s, I was a founding member of the California Dressage Society (CDS)—now one of the largest dressage organizations in the United States—so whenever I have the opportunity to work with California dressage riders, it is a little like "coming home."

In February of 2008, I was presenting at Equine Affaire when Carol Tice, the CDS Southern Regional Director stopped by my booth to tell me that my *TTouch* demonstration the day before had helped save her horse's life. Carol's students have used *TTouch* to help keep their horses tuned into them during the off season or when they can't ride for years, and she had encouraged four of them to attend my demo for further instruction from the source. During this particular presentation, I had focused on the benefits of *TTouch* in high-stress situations and how it has been proven to help during acute colic episodes while waiting for the veterinarian to arrive.

Carol's horse was recovering from a recent colic surgery, and when her students returned to the barn right after my demo, they found him exhibiting signs of stress. One of the students performed *Ear TTouches*, the horse relaxed, and all seemed well.

However, the next day Carol's horse's condition suddenly took a dramatic turn for the worse—he was spasming, sweating, and thrashing around to such an extent that they couldn't even take his pulse and respiration. Obviously, the situation was serious and the horse needed immediate medical attention, but the horse was in such a state, Carol's students were afraid to try to move him. Three of the four who had attended my demo began to *TTouch* him all over his body, and the calming results were significant enough that they could load him onto the horse trailer and get him to the veterinary hospital, where he recovered.

Carol was convinced that had her students not been at my demonstration, they most likely would not have had a plan of action ready when her horse's condition worsened. And without the help of the *TTouches*, she dared not think of what the consequences might have been.

.......Real-Life Challenges Solved

On the pages that follow you'll read 17 profiles of some of the inspiring dressage partnerships I have been privileged to work with over the course of my career. These stories have kindled a renewed energy and enthusiasm within me for publicizing the fact that we have the tools we need to change the behavior, performance, and health of a sport horse, often in only a few sessions. As you will see, countless competitors have experienced remarkable changes in their horses after using the Tellington Method.

Instilling Confidence and Quelling Volatility

The Partnership: *Klaus Balkenhol and Gracioso*

The Problem: I have worked with German Olympian Klaus Balkenhol and a number of his horses over the years. During the spring of 1995, I spent several days at his facility while we recorded footage for my video *TTouch for Dressage*. During that period I worked with the then 10-year-old Westfalian gelding Gracioso.

Gracioso was extremely nervous around people and when he was first acquired, Klaus would spend day after day, up to half an hour at a time, just standing in the horse's stall, talking to him. Gracioso was volatile both in hand and under saddle; he'd shy and bolt at the slightest movement (tree leaves rustled by the wind, for example) and was very inconsistent because of his inability to concentrate.

Tellington Method Solutions: During my basic Body Exploration (p. 104), I found Gracioso to be highly sensitive to the slightest pressure, especially in his poll area, shoulders, back, and rump. After working with Gracioso for two days at the Balkenhol stable, I accompanied the Balkenhols to Gracioso's first competition of the season. At the show grounds on the first day I attempted to work him in hand outside the stabling area, but the horse was so explosive and high-headed I had to work him in the stable aisle.

On the second day, after 15 minutes of *TTouch* and the *Half-Walk* in the aisle, I was able to take him outside. With the help of an assistant, I led him in *Journey of the Homing Pigeon*, and we did a few more minutes of *Half-Walk*, stroking him all over with the *Wand* while allowing him to watch another horse working in the warm-up arena. When it was apparent he was beginning to accept us and trust us, we returned him to his stall.

That afternoon before his test and working in the stable aisle, we vigorously did *Ear TTouches* and *Flick of the Bear's Paw* on Gracioso's hindquarters. Suddenly, the look in his eye changed and he relaxed, lowered his head, and seemed to focus on me as I switched to *Hair Slides* on his tail. Gracioso then stood quietly and contentedly while he was groomed and saddled.

Other work I did with Gracioso included: *Coiled Python Lifts*; *Rainbow TTouch*; *Front Leg Circles*; *Jellyfish Jiggle*; *Lying Leopard TTouch*; *Abalone TTouch*; and *Mouth TTouches* (figs. 9.3 A–H).

The Happy Ending: As Klaus warmed up Gracioso prior to his class, he couldn't believe how much calmer and more focused his horse was. He'd ride by with a smile on his face and say, "He's totally different!" It usually took Klaus 45 minutes to achieve what this time had taken only five. Gracioso won his first class that day and within the year qualified as an alternate on the German dressage team in the Atlanta Olympics.

Dealing with Distractions

The Partnership: *Adrienne Bessey and Winston Churchill*

The Problem: I met Adrienne and Winston at Equine Affaire in Pomona, California, in 2008. Winston was a 12-year-old Hanoverian gelding who Adrienne had bought in Germany a few years before. She had competed him at Prix St. Georges and Intermediate I with some success, and was hoping to move up to Grand Prix.

Adrienne described Winston as her "dream horse"—the one she'd waited for the 30 years she'd been riding. He was extremely gifted and a fabulous mover, but they had a lot of trouble because he was extremely sensitive to noise and movement around him. At a qualifying class for the Pan American Games, Winston became so upset by the background music playing over the loudspeakers that he spooked and bolted repeatedly during their test until finally Adrienne had to excuse herself. Even at smaller shows, strange sounds would frighten the gelding so much, Adrienne was unable to regain his focus for hours.

Winston was so nervous on the first afternoon we worked together that his movement consisted of a series of leaps, spins, and running backward. Although he was saddled, Adrienne agreed it was best to work him from the ground because of his tendency to bolt under saddle when startled.

Tellington Method Solutions: We worked with Winston in the *Labyrinth* and asked him to *Lower the Head*. It is important to note that he, as I've seen in other horses, could not lower his head until his girth had been loosened (see p. 219 for more about girthing issues). By the end of the session, the change was noticeable, and he walked out of the arena slowly, with his head lowered, breathing normally. The second day he was already much improved, and I could stroke him with the *Wand*, do *Dingo*, and ask him to step onto a wooden platform without him tensing up or overreacting. Those in the audience could see he was beginning to think rather than just react, and he was making some good decisions. In fact, many who had seen him enter the ring the day before couldn't believe he was the same horse!

The Happy Ending: On the third day I offered to work on Winston during my *TTouch* demonstration in a small arena surrounded by rattling, clanking metal bleachers filled with chattering bystanders. Adrienne thought he would be terrified! But in just two days of work we had already gained enough ground for Winston to stand in this enclosed space without startling or bolting.

Adrienne was so impressed by the change in her horse that she continued to do *TTouches* on him at home, and she relayed to me later that the "scary things" Winston had always shied at didn't seem to bother him in the least anymore. She couldn't wait for show season to begin.

Focusing the Overly Playful, High-Energy Horse

The Partnership: *Nicole Uphoff and Rembrandt*

The Problem: I worked with Nicole and her then 18-year-old, two-time Olympic gold-medal-winning dressage horse Rembrandt or "Remmy" in my 1995 video *TTouch for Dressage*. Nicole told me that Rembrandt had always been resistant to having his ears handled and she did not believe it would be possible for me to demonstrate *Ear TTouch* for the cameras.

Remmy's resistance to having his ears groomed or touched in any way was interesting to me because of his reputation and tendency to be very "playful" when first mounted. To be successful at the Grand Prix level, a winning performance depends upon power and brilliance and high energy—that "sparkle" I've talked about. So, there is a downside to working off excess energy in the warm-up arena, but at the same time, one "bobble" or playful jump to the side can lose a championship.

It is just these kinds of antics that can be avoided with a few minutes of quiet *Ear TTouch* in the stall prior to mounting; they focus the horse before he has to perform. And so it was worth working with Remmy and getting him to accept *TTouch* on his ears.

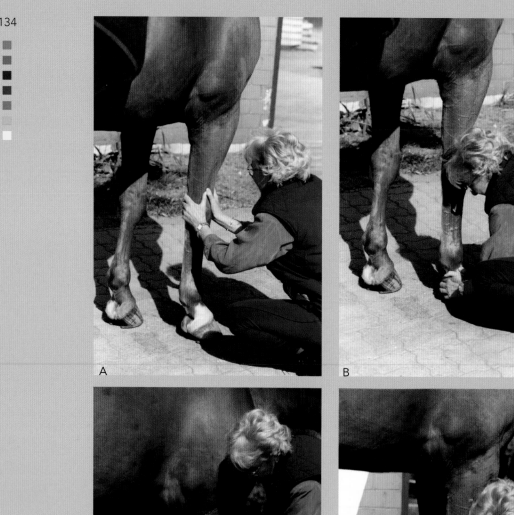

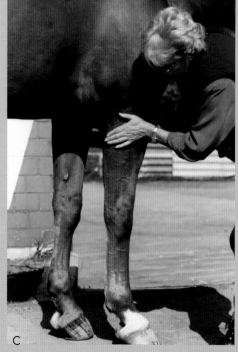

F

H

9.3 A–H In 1995, I worked with Klaus Balkenhol's Westfalian gelding Gracioso, who was an inconsistent performer due to spookiness, nervousness, and an inability to concentrate. I used a number of body and ground exercise techniques with Gracioso, including: *Coiled Python Lifts* from elbow to ankle to "ground" him, increase confidence, and improve proprioception (A & B); *Rainbow TTouch* to energize in preparation for performance and make the horse more aware of his lower limbs (C & D); *Front Leg Circles*, including resting the toe on the ground, to release tension in tight shoulder, neck, and back muscles, and lengthen stride (E); *Jellyfish Jiggle* to free tight muscles and increase circulation in a way the horse enjoys (F); and crossing my hands in a combination of *Lying Leopard TTouch* (to get the finger movement) and *Abalone TTouch* (for the warmth of the hand) (G). Working his nostrils—stretching the edges in every direction and gently reaching inside and doing little circular *TTouches* as far as my fingers would reach—helped calm and stabilize his mental and emotional state, easing his intense fear of his surroundings (H).

Tellington Method Solutions: For the first 40 minutes of work on his body, I did not attempt to handle Rembrandt's head. Instead I focused on basic *TTouches* all over his body, followed by *Leg Circles*. Only at the end of the session did I ask Rembrandt to *Lower the Head*, which he did with ease and complete trust. Much to Nicole's amazement, I was able to do *TTouch* on both of Remmy's ears, and she could do the same.

The Happy Ending: After only about an hour of using *TTouch* on Rembrandt, Nicole was able to ride him without any of his usual antics—none of the jumping around, shying, and playing. She was surprised and very pleased. Nicole said that from the very first moments in the saddle, Rembrandt felt as though he'd already had 30 minutes of warm-up. He was supple and cooperative. The week after we worked together, Rembrandt had one of the highest scores in history for the Grand Prix Special.

Regaining Confidence in the Arena

The Partnership: *Carl Hester, Jennifer Oldham, and Gershwin*

The Problem: In 1995, Gershwin, a German-bred Warmblood gelding, was one of British dressage star Carl Hester's top horses. (Carl won a team gold medal on Uthopia at the London Olympics in 2012.) I was doing a series of evening demonstrations in the United Kingdom to promote my book on horse personality *Getting in TTouch with Your Horse*, and one demo included Gershwin along with his owner, Jennifer Oldham. Carl was scheduled to ride Gershwin in the National Dressage Championships later that week.

When Jennifer first bought Gershwin several years before he was uptight, easily stressed, and extremely difficult. He would react violently to noises or movements—bolting or rearing—and often refused to approach groups of spectators. If frightened while tied he pulled back until he sat on his haunches, shaking all over. His neck was rigid and his back was hollow. He couldn't be touched under the tail or around the hindquarters. Jennifer discovered he had a reputation for being dangerous and had been written off in dressage training circles as unrideable.

Tellington Method Solutions: Jennifer pulled Gershwin out of training and through an equine physiotherapist found a Tellington Method practitioner in the United Kingdom who was offering hands-on clinics. Jennifer took Gershwin to a weekend Tellington Training and said the changes she saw in two days were amazing. She followed up with *TTouch* and my *Ground Exercises* to help Gershwin overcome his fear of whips and contact on his body. She rode him bareback for months with only a *Balance Rein* to help his body recover from its state of stiffness and soreness.

Although her work had improved Gershwin's attitude toward being ridden and had given her a glimpse of how good he could be, Jennifer still felt he lacked confidence and didn't feel he was ready to cope with the pressures of international-level competition. He still often shied dramatically at the judges' stand, flower boxes, and crowds of spectators, and his rider could not accept a ribbon in competition because Gershwin would spin and bolt. In the stable, he would bolt in panic when a plastic feed sac was opened in the stall aisle.

During my first demonstration with him in front of approximately 200 spectators, I focused on *Lowering the Head*, grounding him with *Leg Circles*, and working him around plastic tarps—of which he was terrified. I performed additional *TTouches* and *Ground Exercises* (figs. 9.4 A–N). I rode him without a bit in a *Lindell Sidepull* and then with only the *Neck Ring*, proceeding carefully, step by step. Everyone who knew the horse could not believe I could ride him at the walk, trot, and canter, with only a *Neck Ring*, in an arena full of people.

Three nights later at another evening demonstration, Gershwin returned to the arena, recognized me, lowered his head immediately when asked, and was able to walk under plastic tarps (unimaginable during the first demonstration). I introduced him to the *Labyrinth* for the first time. When he saw it, he stopped dead in his tracks with his head up, "stuck" in a "freeze." I spread the poles twice as wide, lowered his head, and he came quietly throught the *Labyrinth*. This was a turning point in his ability to trust, and as it so often does, the *Labyrinth* brought him into a new state of mental, physical, and emotional balance.

When I rode Gershwin at the end of the evening with only the *Neck Ring,* he felt great at the trot, but at the canter, I sensed he bunched his back muscles and it felt as though he was "jamming" his back up into the saddle. I worked on Gershwin's tight back the next day at Carl Hester's barn, beginning with *TTouch* over his back and loins, and riding him outside using the *Lindell* and again only the *Neck Ring*. While riding with the *Lindell*, I did some special "lifting" exercises with his head and neck, which helped release his back: at the canter, I lifted and opened my hands, inviting and allowing Gershwin to open his throatlatch with his head high and his nose well ahead of the vertical. This shortened and tightened his back even more, and after five or six strides in this elevated position, I released his head. This exercise helped him lengthen his body and experience a more comfortable position for his neck and back, ultimately resulting in a smoother gait at the canter.

That day I also worked to overcome Gershwin's spookiness by incorporating food in our work under saddle. Each time he tensed in a corner of the arena

A

B

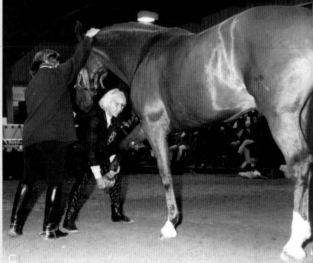

C

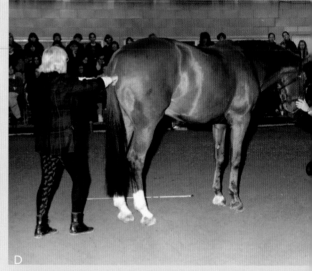

D

9.4 A–N I worked with the Warmblood Gershwin in 1995 while in England. He lacked confidence and was easily stressed. When I first took him into the large arena during my demonstration, his high head carriage indicated his anxiety and reactivity (A). After four sessions of TTouch over a week's time, his head carriage lowered significantly as his confidence grew. I did *Ear TTouches* (B); *Leg Circles* with his front and hind legs to improve suppleness and relax tight back muscles (C); *Pelvic Tilt* and *Tail Pull* to release tension and help connect the horse back to front (D & E); *Neckline Ground Driving* helped deal with confidence issues related to movement behind him and resolved his tendency to spook (F), and we worked in hand through and around a number of obstacles that Gershwin wouldn't have gone near on the first day, including bales of hay and a "tunnel" of criss-crossed *Wands* (G). Riding him bridleless with only a *Balance Rein* and *Neck Ring* improved his emotional balance and revived his willingness to work as a partner with his rider (H–J).

E

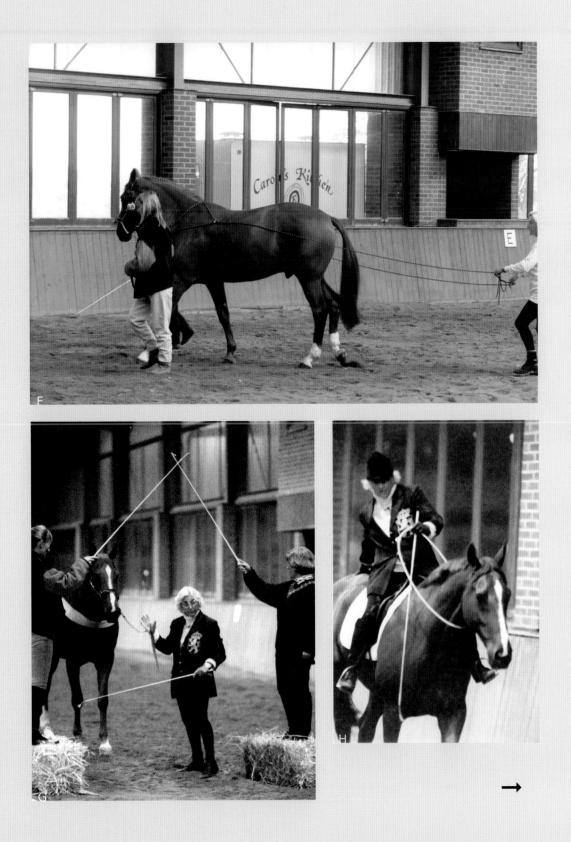

or while passing the van parked outside the fence, I stopped him and fed him a little grain, sometimes from the saddle and sometimes via a ground person. One of the principles of the Tellington Method is to understand the effects that eating has on overcoming the fight-or-flight reflex (see sidebar, p. 201).

The Happy Ending: That weekend Gershwin was back at the showgrounds with Carl and Jennifer, in preparation for the British National Dressage Championships. All the work paid off as he displayed more confidence in each test, each day. This culminated on the last day of the Championships, when he won the Intermediate II Freestyle: he worked in unity with Carl, who finished the test with an extended trot down the centerline with the reins in one hand and his hat in the other—something he had never before had enough confidence to do while riding Gershwin.

Finding the "Forward"

The Partnership: *Merrylyn R. and Holly*

The Problem: "My mare moves like a cart horse!" was the frustrated comment of Merrylyn R. at my weekend training in Santa Fe, New Mexico, in June of 2011. Merrylyn had bought her Irish Sport Horse, Holly, four years before, and was taking dressage lessons regularly, but the performance she dreamed of had eluded her so far. Holly had to be urged with every single stride, and the spurs Merrylyn wore had little effect.

It's often easier to slow down a horse that has too much forward impulsion than to convince a sluggish horse to be more energetic. That was certainly true for Holly. I watched Merrylyn at the walk, trot, and canter, and then asked if I could ride the mare to evaluate the problem from the saddle. Holly had a long stride, so she was actually covering more ground than it felt like from the saddle, but she was not fun to ride, and it certainly didn't look or feel like the mare was having fun, either.

I don't ride with spurs. I'd rather teach a horse to respond to a flutter or press-and-release signal from my lower leg. Holly responded readily to my leg aids by lengthening her stride, but the second I stopped asking for forward motion, she slowed down. I could understand why Merrylyn called the mare a "cart horse"—riding her was frustrating and hard work for the rider!

Tellington Method Solutions: I decided to put a *Promise Wrap* on Holly. As I've mentioned, this is a tool I have used for many years and found useful for horses who are strung out or spooky. Holly responded with a little more forward momentum, but not enough to make much difference. So I switched to the *Promise Rope*, which encourages "forward" by brushing the horse's gaskins with every stride. This can have a miraculous effect, increasing length of stride and tempo without the rider having to work at it. And, wow! There was definitely more "forward"—but not the increase in suppleness through the back and the sense of impulsion that I had hoped for.

So I dismounted, pulled the saddle, and did about 10 minutes of connecting and activating *TTouches*, including *Lick of the Cow's Tongue, Neck Rocking, Tail Pulls*, and *Front and Hind Leg Circles*. I followed this by introducing the *Tellington Training Bit* to the mare. I let her get acquainted with the new feeling in her mouth by leading her from the ground for a few minutes. Then I mounted and asked her to trot on a long loose rein—and she responded with lightness and a willingness to move that was an absolute pleasure.

The Happy Ending: Merrylyn said she had never seen her mare move with such rhythm and balance. The mare now gave the impression that she was enjoying the feeling of "forward" as much as I was. I didn't need to use my legs to maintain the impulsion. When Merrylyn climbed back into the saddle, picked up the reins, and trotted off, she said the feeling was all that she had hoped and dreamed of since the day she had bought the mare. (You can read more about the benefits of the Tellington Training Bit on p. 217.)

Finding a Peaceful Place to Quiet the Mind

The Partnership: *Dodo and Dieter Laugks and Weltall*

The Problem: At my spring 2011 seminar at Klaus Balkenhol's stable near Münster, Germany, Klaus introduced me to Dodo Laugks and suggested I find a time to visit with Dodo and her husband, Dieter, at their dressage stable, a 30-minute drive east of Munich. Dodo manages this spectacular facility and a stable full of lovely Warmbloods owned by Toni and Marina Meggle. Dieter splits his time between his law practice in Dusseldorf and training and showing the Meggle Grand Prix horses.

A few weeks after the Xenophon Seminar, my husband Roland and I stopped at the Laugks' for a one-day visit, and we wound up staying almost a week! I thoroughly enjoyed working with Dodo and her staff, teaching them the Tellington Method and working with many of the horses there.

One of my favorite horses was Meggle's Weltall VA ("Weltall"), a very talented 16-year-old Hanoverian, ridden at Grand Prix by Dieter. Weltall was very hot as a youngster, but big-moving, so he was easily sold at auction and competed at Grand Prix by the time he was eight years old. His piaffe, passage, and trot extensions were world-class, and, ridden by Martin Schaudt, he was a member of the German dressage team for the Athens Olympics in 2004. The team won the gold medal. Following his successes, Weltall experienced on-and-off-again soundness issues, and he was eventually sold to the Meggles.

When I met him, Weltall was extremely tense in the stable, and so defensive on cross-ties I was warned he often attempted to bite or kick when groomed or saddled.

Tellington Method Solutions: I believe that training and trust begins with the basics—namely grooming and saddling. Because of the stress Weltall experienced and his extreme reaction to being in the stable's saddling area, I began by working him free in his stall with no halter and very light *TTouches* over every inch of his body. The goal was to gain his trust, relax him, get him to really feel his body and come into mental and emotional Balance. So, I started with careful *Lying Leopard TTouches* so he felt and grew accustomed to the warmth of my hand. He stood very still as though listening, but if my *TTouch* was too fast or I used too much pressure, he would flash his ears back.

By the second session the following day, two of us could work on Weltall at the same time, still with no restraint. And by the third day, Dodo and Dieter and I could all *TTouch* Weltall at the same time. He enjoyed *Ear TTouch*, but I had to be slow and respectful with *Lick of the Cow's Tongue*. He learned very quickly that when he pinned his ears, I would stop the *TTouch* I was using and find one that he liked. He was very expressive, but at the same time, he never attempted to bite or kick while free in his stall.

We did *Back Lifts* and lots of *Tail TTouch*—and on his legs, *Coiled Python TTouch* and *Octopus TTouch*. Weltall loved light pressure, drifting *TTouches* with the fingernails, especially on his face. A highlight of my work with Weltall came one night after feeding: I sat with Dodo and Weltall's groom Kathy Rath, on the straw, each of us doing *TTouch* on his legs as he stood very still, without a halter, thoroughly enjoying this "bedtime" body session with us. We found that this change of attitude when handled was soon reflected in a newfound willingness and sensational impulsion under saddle. And, following my recommendation, Dodo and Dieter began to only groom and saddle him in the stall, and they and their excellent grooms applied *TTouches* every day.

TTouch bodywork was accompanied by work in hand, which played an important role in stress reduction and building trust. The first day I attempted to lead Weltall into the indoor arena, even with a lead chain over the noseband of his halter, it was impossible. When he saw himself in the mirror, he panicked, and I had to take him out into barn aisle and stroke him all over with the *Wand*. For the first few minutes he was agitated as I stroked his front legs, but soon he settled and accepted the contact. I then stroked his back with the *Wand* and tapped him lightly on the croup to go forward (*Dingo*).

After several steps forward, I tapped him on the chest three times lightly to stop while giving him a clear, "And, Whoa," along with a light "ask-and-release" signal on the lead shank.

The second day of groundwork I was able to lead Weltall into the arena with an assistant in *Journey of the Homing Pigeon*. We then took him through the *Labyrinth* to get him bending, thinking, and listening.

The Happy Ending: In his first competition after my visit, Weltall placed second in two Grand Prix classes, and in the following two shows, he won four Grand Prix classes with really excellent scores. "Weltall is enjoying his *TTouches* a lot," said Dieter in a note following the competition, "and I really want to say thank you from the bottom of my heart. Last weekend we did our first competition after an 11-month break. Weltall was fantastic—very relaxed and not nervous at all. He placed second in the Grand Prix and second in the Grand Prix Freestyle with almost 75 percent. But much more important than this is that you have completely changed his life. His whole body is much softer and for the first time since I've known this horse, I feel he has started to relax in his stall."

These performances qualified him for the 2011 CDI Milan, an international dressage competition and a qualifying event for the 2012 Olympics in London, England. Weltall was brilliant in in the Grand Prix Freestyle in Milan, placing fifth. One of the judges who has known Weltall since before he competed in the 2004 Olympics said he had never seen the horse move so well over his back—Weltall gave the impression of being totally engaged and really enjoying performing. In addition, I was overjoyed to watch him with his head hanging over the door, gently nuzzling the hair of one of the grooms sitting on the ground outside his stall. Since he has been receiving daily *TTouch* sessions, he has truly blossomed. In the fall of 2011, he won 10 Grand Prix classes with marks in the high 70s, and he has gained a new trust in people that is a delight to see (figs. 9.5 A–C).

Making Negative Tension and Nervousness in the Arena a Thing of the Past

The Partnership: *Mandy Zimmerman and Heartbreaker*

The Problem: I met the talented six-year-old gray gelding Heartbreaker at the Xenophon Seminar at Klaus Balkenhol's stable in April of 2011. His rider, Mandy, was a full-time student of Klaus Balkenhol, and the horse had received only the very best in classical dressage training. However, he had an extreme fear of spectators clapping—it took only three of us clapping, during Mandy's

9.5 A–C Weltall enjoys the company of other horses and the *TTouch* of his groom as he grazes (A & B). He now enjoys daily grazing in a paddock. Since Weltall has been receiving daily *TTouch* sessions, he has blossomed. Last year he won 10 Grand Prix, including a remarkable weekend in Ising, Germany, when he won three (C)!

ride the day before the seminar, to make Heartbreaker clamp his tail and bolt forward in a panic. He also was very resistant to trailer-loading—he'd been easy to load the first few times he went to a show, but had become progressively more reluctant.

Tellington Method Solutions: After observing Heartbreaker's fear issues under saddle, I focused on his objection to being loaded—a serious problem in the career of a dressage competitor. It is my experience and opinion that emotional and physical stress can cause resistance to travel (to a show) such as Heartbreaker demonstrated (previously loading fine, but now fighting his handler). A horse can lose his courage, his trust in his rider, and thus his desire to do his best. Mandy needed to see her horse with new eyes, and, in my opinion, her horse wasn't stubborn and combative, he was stressed and afraid.

Rather than "making the outside of the trailer more uncomfortable than the inside"—a common training technique today, which is basically a form of forcing the horse to "submit"—my approach is to use exercises that not only teach the horse to load safely and without injury, but in the process, to develop trust, cooperation, and physical and mental Balance. Heartbreaker showed concern when asked to step onto the trailer ramp. So I moved him away from the trailer. He was also hesitant to step on rubber mats in the arena, as well as a wooden platform. Thirty years ago I would have got after him a little and forced him onto the platform. However, I've learned over time that a minute or so of holding a clear *intention* (a "picture in my mind"—see p. 60) of what I'm asking the horse to do; staying in *heart coherence* (see p. 71); stroking the horse's legs with a *Wand*; lowering his head; and "chunking down" the exercise, paves the way to making him successful without confrontation.

Simple steps, including running the lead up the side of Heartbreaker's halter (see p. 171 for a photo) and laying poles alongside the wooden platform—using our brains instead of our muscles—set us up for success. In addition, my team and I performed *Tail TTouches*, *Ear TTouches*, *Neck Rocking*, and *Dingo* in the *Labyrinth*.

The Happy Ending: The following day, Mandy was able to ride Heartbreaker at the trot and canter with rhythm and cadence, without bolting, while 170 people in the seminar audience applauded enthusiastically. This was a dramatic turnaround after only a short time working with the Tellington Method. Our work on the trailering had, in turn, resolved his nervousness in the arena (figs. 9.6 A–K).

Solving Problems with Stage Fright

The Partnership: *Nadine Capellmann and Gazpacho*

The Problem: When I first worked with Gazpacho in 1995, he had almost torn his stall apart at a recent show due to the fear and stress he felt in unfamiliar situations. Although very talented, this horse was terrified of crowds. His groom described him as easy to handle one day, and extremely touchy the next (the day I first met him, his groom had given up on her attempt to clip him, he was so resistant). He habitually spooked in the aisle of the barn he lived in, and always walked in and out tense, high-headed, shying at whatever might be lying about—lead ropes, dressage whips, buckets, chairs.

Under saddle Gazpacho was again high-headed and tended to come behind the bit when nervous. If pushed onto the bit, he would sometimes stop dead in his tracks, planting his feet and refusing to go forward.

Tellington Method Solutions: Gazpacho didn't want me to touch him at first—even with the lightest of contact—anywhere on his body. He threw his head in the air, backed away, and swung his shoulders into me. So I began with slow, firm *Python Lifts* from the top of his neck, along one side of his body, while steadying him with one hand firmly on the chain lead and his head turned toward me. This flexed position quieted him, relaxed his muscles, and eased his fear of the contact. By the time I began on the opposite side, I could work using both hands as I no longer had to turn his head toward me.

After 20 minutes of *TTouch* I could walk him quietly up and down the barn aisle, his head lowered and his eyes soft, past all the usually "scary" things that he had spooked at only half-an-hour before when he was led out to me.

The next morning Gazpacho reacted very differently to my first *TTouches*—he immediately dropped his head and really began to enjoy them. His nervous behavior returned under saddle, however, and he shied many times—at shadows from the trees hanging over the arena and dark areas in the sand. The usual method for dealing with this behavior was to put him on the bit and make him face the object in a collected frame, but as I mentioned, this often resulted in him bracing his legs and body and refusing to go forward.

I had recently read in a book about African elephant behavior that if you faced an elephant in the wild head on, and the elephant was in a nervous state, there was a fifty-fifty chance that an adrenaline rush in the elephant would result in him charging. However, if you faced the elephant from the side, he would never charge. I theorized that this "fight" tendency was directly related to preparing for "flight": When facing the source of danger, the elephant had to be tense and enough "on edge" to be able to turn and run. But when the danger was to one side or the other, the elephant could just bolt and escape forward.

This all came to mind as I watched Gazpacho in the ring so I suggested he be ridden with a *Balance Rein*. And, instead of forcing him to face the source of his fear and/or move past it, he should be allowed to stand parallel to the source of perceived danger. This change helped him stand quietly and turn his head toward it, as I reassured him with *TTouches* on his crest until he stretched his neck out and went by the object without shying. Since that experience,

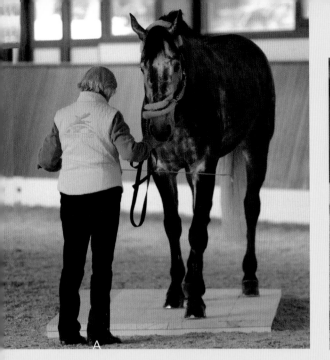

9.6 A–K Heartbreaker reacted strongly to sounds behind him, and was also very resistant to trailer loading. I felt these issues were related, so began work on the trailer-loading. It's generally thought that a horse who does not load is being dominant, but I see the behavior as based in fear. By addressing these specific confidence and trust issues, then the general difficulties under saddle could be more easily handled. I had Heartbreaker stand on different surfaces, including a wooden platform (A); then, two assistants stacked mounting blocks beside the platform. They remained standing at the ready with pool noodles, though they did not lift them yet. I helped Heartbreaker grow accustomed to this slightly more claustrophobic situation (B–D). Once Heartbreaker could pass between the assistants and over the platform without reacting, I took him through the *Labyrinth* to help him absorb the first steps of the lesson and refocus for the next (E). We then crossed the platform with the assistants on the mounting blocks but with the noodles still down (F). Finally, we raised the pool noodles in order to create an "arch" for the horse to practice going under in preparation for loading and being comfortable with movement overhead (G–J). The next day Heartbreaker could be ridden at the trot and canter in the crowded arena, in front of a live, clapping crowd without bolting (K).

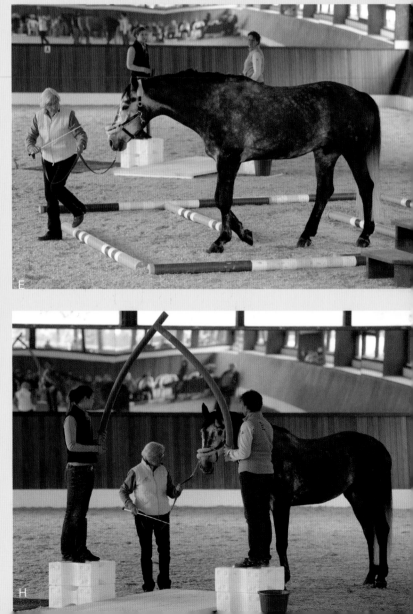

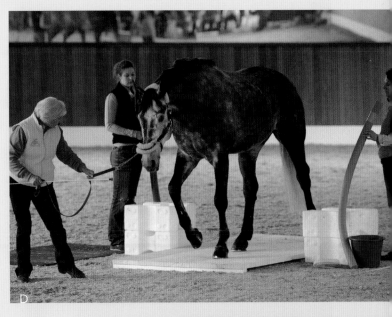

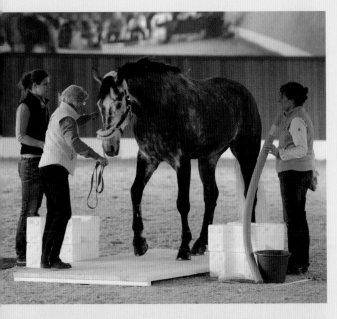

D

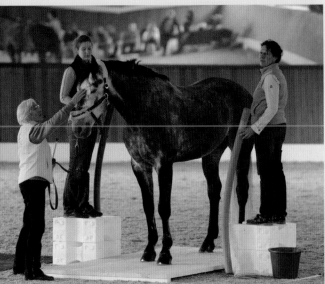

G

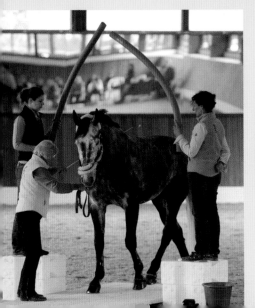
J

A
→

K

instead of facing a spooky horse toward a threatening object, which usually results in a spread-legged, low-headed posture and a startled reaction, I ride him by with his head tipped slightly away with an indirect rein. I have found that this plan of action helps a horse overcome his fear of "scary" things far more quickly than when he must face a threat head-on.

The Happy Ending: I accompanied Nadine and Klaus and Judith Balkenhol to a show at the end of the week. During the early warm-up, Gazpacho spooked at every little thing. He was very tight in the neck and holding his breath. After the warm-up, I did deep *Bear TTouches* on his neck, with rows of connected *Clouded Leopard TTouches* down his back, over his croup, and down to his hocks. As she warmed up prior to their first test, I suggested to Nadine that she slow down, talk to Gazpacho, and use firm strokes along both sides of his neck just behind his ears when it felt like he was going to spook. It paid off—by the time the bell rang, he was much more relaxed than usual, and they placed fourth in the Prix St. Georges.

Improving Balance and Transitions

The Partnership: *Kyra Kyrklund and Matador*

The Problem: I worked with five-time Olympian Kyra Kyrklund and Matador in Northern Germany in July of 1988. Kyra was interested in how the Tellington Method could give Matador an edge in competition. Like so many Grand Prix dressage horses, Matador had powerfully developed neck muscles—overly developed, in my opinion. Overly developed muscles lose their elasticity and restrict blood circulation to the head and neck, and can cause muscle fatigue, resulting in resistance and explosive behavior in some horses.

In addition, Matador's transition from piaffe to passage needed improvement, and because the stallion had lost his ability to draw up his testicles, his lateral transitions were affected by them slapping against the inside of his legs.

Tellington Method Solutions: After my initial exploration I worked Matador's neck with *Lowering the Head* until his poll was slightly below his withers in order to "soften" his muscles. It took at least 20 minutes to gain Matador's trust enough so I could perform *Clouded Leopard TTouch* over the first and second cervical vertebrae. Matador did not want his ears handled, which made sense to me because the triple heater meridian—which, according to Chinese medicine, regulates the flow of energy to the digestive and reproductive systems, among others—encircles the ears and runs down the neck, zigzags over the shoulder and down to the top of the front hooves. Based on previous work I

9.7 I worked with Kyra Kyrklund and the charismatic Matador in 1988. Kyra noted in a March 2011 Eurodressage.com retrospective of Matador's life that the *TTouches* I showed her were very helpful in settling his "hot" tendencies.

had done on stallions with similar issues, I did *TTouches* on the testicles themselves, and worked the base of Matador's ears. During the three-hour session of bodywork, the testicles drew up noticeably for the first time in months.

After performing *TTouch* on Matador's body, I rode him to show Kyra how to use the *Half-Walk*, lifting Matador's head a little higher and ahead of the vertical. I also encouraged her to work on more extensions and spend time on a long rein, with less emphasis on the collected movements, to continue to stretch and lengthen his neck.

The Happy Ending: After our work Kyra felt the difference in Matador was considerable—he had much better balance and smoother transitions. Three days after I worked with Matador, he won the Grand Prix Special at the Hamburg Derby for the very first time. Kyra and Matador went on to compete in the Olympics later that year, in Seoul, South Korea, as members of the Finnish dressage team (fig. 9.7).

Heightening Performance by Lowering Reactivity

The Partnership: *Emile Faurie, Alice Wilson, and Confidential Wendelicht*

The Problem: Confidential Wendelicht ("Ernie") was a 12-year-old gelding that British Olympian and national coach Emile Faurie's student, Alice, was competing at Grand Prix. Ernie had shown great potential, but was inconsistent, tight, and suffered chronic back problems. He did not gain weight no matter how much or how often he was fed.

I was warned that Ernie didn't tolerate strangers and was known to bite and kick. I found him to be excessively reactive to contact anywhere on his body, and especially on his shoulders and back. I also had to have one front leg held up while I worked on his flank area so he couldn't kick me. I've found a significant correlation between flank sensitivity and ulcers and/or a tendency to colic (stress-related), which might have explained his body condition issues.

However, this was many years before ulcers were recognized as a widespread problem in performance horses (see more on this on p. 186).

Tellington Method Solutions: When I tried to do *Leg Circles* with each leg, Ernie could not lift the left hind normally; he jerked his hoof up as high as his hock on the opposite leg, and I could see an extreme spasm all the way through his back and ribs to his shoulders. I was told he had been difficult to shoe on that side for years (no wonder he had back problems and flank sensitivity!) I used *TTouch* on both sides of his body for another hour to encourage relaxation of the left hind leg.

I wanted to improve his movement through the back so I rode him in the *Lindell*, encouraging him to lift his head by exaggerating the lifting of one hand much higher than the other—a technique that is now taught by renowned master of the French school Philippe Karl. I also rode him in the *Liberty Neck Ring* to open his throat—the opposite of what normal collection asked of him.

The Happy Ending: Ernie's movement under saddle improved markedly. His piaffe was better than it had been in years. The head-lifting exercise I introduced to Emile and Alice worked so well to lighten and soften him, they placed sixth in the Intermediate II test and seventh in the Grand Prix Special at the dressage championships for which Ernie had qualified earlier in the year. Emile and Alice hadn't planned on competing him because of his discomfort until they saw the results of our work together.

Relaxing the Tense, Hyper-Attentive Horse

The Partnership: *Klaus Balkenhol and Goldstern*

The Problem: During the spring of 1995, I spent time with Klaus Balkenhol and his horses while we recorded footage for my video *TTouch for Dressage.* Klaus asked me to work with Goldstern, the (then) 14-year-old Westphalian gelding with whom he had won team gold and individual bronze at the 1992 Olympic Games in Barcelona; team gold and individual silver at the 1994 World Equestrian Games; and team gold at the 1993 European Championships (fig. 9.8). Goldstern was a very sensitive horse, curious and sweet by nature, but also hyper-attentive to his surroundings, and very nervous and uncomfortable while being groomed.

Goldstern exhibited these characteristics through a tendency to be high-headed and nervous when at showgrounds and being handled prior to competition, and with incessant head tossing and pawing while on the

9.8 Almost 20 years ago I had my first opportunity to demonstrate to Klaus Balkenhol and his medal-winning horse Goldstern how the Tellington Method can work to improve performance and reduce stress in top performance horses.

cross-ties. This kind of tension while handled on the ground and while being groomed could potentially translate to tension under saddle.

Tellington Method Solutions: I have found that horses that resist grooming are often tight and tense in the back and abdominal muscles. I began by putting Goldstern in *Taming the Tiger* in order help him learn to stand quietly and lower his head while being groomed. Asking him to *Lower the Head* immediately encouraged him to relax his tense neck and back. I continued attention to these areas with *Back Lifts*, and *Taming the Tiger* allowed him to reach back with his head so he could see me, communicate with me, and gain trust in having my hands on his body.

I used *Lying Leopard TTouches* on his neck, shoulders, back, loin, and down the hindquarters, followed by *Raccoon TTouches* under his tail. *Tail TTouches* and *Pearling* further released Goldstern's tense back muscles and helped him to begin to visually relax during the bodywork. His learning to trust my *TTouches* was a significant step toward being able to trust his rider to decide whether or not his surroundings were worth worrying about.

The Happy Ending: By the end of my first session with him, Goldstern was standing quietly in the aisle while I performed *Ear TTouches* on him. The display of tension so obvious before was no longer present. Klaus said that usually Goldstern was tense at the beginning of a workout, but during their next session, the horse felt quite different!

"It was astonishing to see how much the horse changed," Klaus says in the book *Klaus Balkenhol: The Man and His Training Methods*. "He was suddenly transformed, standing there with his ears and neck drooping, totally relaxed. The next day he was still very relaxed and because he was lacking the necessary body tension, he didn't perform well at all. I said to Linda, 'Do you think you could change the dose so he's relaxed but doesn't fall asleep?' The result was incredible. During the next session she worked with 'Goldi' in a slightly different way, and the following day he was just sensational."

I worked with Goldstern prior to his first test at the next competition, and he won both the Grand Prix and Grand Prix Special by a wide margin over the second-place horse. Klaus and Goldstern would go on to win team gold at the 1995 European Championships that year and the Olympic Games in 1996, as well as becoming German National Champion a total of five times before Goldstern was retired in 1997.

Rekindling Enthusiasm in the Experienced Campaigner

The Partnership: *Charlotte Bredahl-Baker and Lugano*

The Problem: Charlotte Bredahl-Baker is a USEF "S" judge and FEI "C" judge. In 1992 Charlotte and her horse, Monsieur, were part of the bronze-medal-winning US Olympic Team in Barcelona, and in 1997, she and her horse Lugano were part of the silver-medal-winning team at the North American Championships.

I worked with Charlotte and Lugano at the symposium I did with Dr. Reiner Klimke in 1999 (see sidebar on p. 21). Lugano had been laid up due to an injury, and Charlotte was concerned that he seemed moody as she brought him back into work. She hoped that the Tellington Method would rekindle some of his enthusiasm.

I found Lugano to be extremely touchy on the hindquarters and flank area, and Charlotte warned that he might kick. She mentioned that his sheath needed cleaning (both his sheath and penis were crusted, upon visual inspection), but that it was near impossible without sedation.

I was certain that this could be a cause for Lugano's lack of enthusiasm. I don't know about you, but if I have so much as a jagged nail I am aware of it and any discomfort until it is fixed. I thought that an extremely crusty sheath could be very inhibiting for a horse who needed exceptional freedom of movement in the hindquarters for piaffe and passage.

Tellington Method Solutions: My sister Robyn worked with Lugano each day of the symposium, using very light *TTouches*, *Lowering the Head*, and concentrating on having him stand still while he was quietly groomed and touched all over his body. Eventually, he stood quietly enough for her to clean his sheath: he stood so still, those observing thought he was tranquilized!

The Happy Ending: Each day, Lugano's piaffe and passage improved and his attitude brightened, and by the end of the symposium, he worked with gusto and his ears up, seeming to enjoy the entire lesson with Dr. Klimke.

Righting the Upside-Down Neck and Improving Suppleness

The Partnership: *Ingred Pollak and Ferry*

The Problem: I was visiting White Fences Equestrian Center near Palm Beach, Florida, in November of 2004 when I met dressage rider Ingred Pollak as she prepared to mount an attractive Warmblood mare named Ferry. Much to my surprise, Ingred recognized me and said she had been interested in the Tellington Method for years and wondered how it might benefit her dressage horses, but she had never observed the work firsthand. I offered to work on Ferry, and she instantly agreed. As it turned out, the eight-year-old mare had a tendency to have a tight back and ewe neck—standing next to the mounting block as we discussed her, Ferry was high-headed with the muscles on the underside of her neck bulging and her back slightly dropped. Despite months of schooling, Ingred said she remained stiff and lacked suppleness, and required 30 minutes or more of warm-up before she began to relax and move freely.

Tellington Method Solutions: The posture Ferry exhibited—a high head and dropped back—was of the kind that can be influenced and often changed in a surprisingly short time using the Tellington Method. Her posture restricted her ability to contract her belly muscles, and contraction of the abdominals is what would allow her to stretch her back and engage her hindquarters. So I began with a *Back Lift*, making contact with my nails just behind the girth and asking the mare to contract her abdominal muscles, lower her head, and breathe deeply. At least 95 percent of horses respond to the *Back Lift* with a sudden upward arching of the back and lowering of the head, but Ferry showed very little response.

I loosened the girth and repeated the *Back Lift*, and this time she raised her back dramatically—but she still did not lower her head. I again considered her tack and realized she had to "release" her jaw in order to extend her neck, so I loosened her cavesson three holes. This was the magic ingredient, and down her head came.

I next taught Ferry to *Lower the Head* when asked with very little pressure on the nose and crest. The signal on the crest was a slight inward and upward move between my thumb and fingers (as opposed to a "push" down), and serves as a cue the rider can use to ask the horse to lower his head from the saddle. Ferry's eyes "softened," and she licked her lips and chewed (signs that she trusted me and what I was doing).

I followed with a few minutes of Inchworm along her topline, then asked Ingred to mount and practice asking Ferry to lower her head from the saddle. They began to warm up at the walk and trot and Ferry's issues were evident—she was stiff-necked, strung-out, and switching her tail. I asked them to stop and did *Shoulder Release*, which can be particularly useful with high-headed horses as it not only releases the neck but frees up the loin area, allowing for engagement of the hind end.

The Happy Ending: Ingred and Ferry moved out once again and Ingred—riding in a half-seat at my request—walked and trotted on a loose rein while encouraging the mare to lower and lengthen her neck by placing her thumb on one side of the mare's crest and her fingers on the other and applying short, light slides toward the ears. Within 10 minutes, Ferry began to engage her hindquarters and lengthen her stride, raising her withers and back and looking like a very different horse: supple, round, and willing, with a light springy trot and moving forward comfortably. The entire exercise had taken about half an hour, and was such an interesting demonstration of what just a few minutes of *TTouches* can do for a horse's overall performance (figs. 9.9 A–H).

Improving Saddle Fit, Elasticity in the Back, and Attitude

The Partnership: *Keri Chapman and Ahot*

The Problem: In 1988 I was a keynote speaker at the Horses International Trade Show in Ontario and gave a one-day demonstration at a nearby farm with my sister, Robyn Hood. One of the horses in the demo was a 10-year-old Hanoverian mare named Ahot who was competed in the junior dressage division by a talented young rider, Keri Chapman.

Ahot was sour and resistant. Judges' comments in previous competitions had said things like, "not supple through the back"; "stiff"; "not enough impulsion"; and "lack of elasticity." When we saw her go at the demo, she was slightly off behind, did not track up consistently, swished her tail when asked

A

B

C

D

E

F

9.9 A–H I met Ingred Pollak and Ferry in Florida in 2004 (A). Ingred had heard of my *Method* but never had the chance to experience it. When I offered to show Ingred how my techniques could work on Ferry—a young mare with tendency to travel with a high head, tight neck, and dropped back—she instantly agreed. Even without a rider, the mare stood with a high head, so I began with a *Back Lift*, applying my curved fingers several inches behind the girth and about 4 inches away from the midline (B). She did not respond at all, and I realized I had to first loosen the girth. Only then did she contract the abdominal muscles and raise her back, slightly lowering her head (C). Before inviting Ferry to *Lower the Head*, it was necessary to loosen the noseband completely (D & E). Next, I lowered her head with Ingred in the saddle. When Ingred trotted off again, Ferry's neck was a little better but she was still stiff (F), so I asked Ingred to stop and I performed *Shoulder Release* (G). Opening the mare's shoulders and releasing her neck enabled Ferry to lift her back, which, in turn, finally allowed for engagement. When Ingred and Ferry moved out again, with Ingred in a half-seat, the change in the mare's way of going was remarkable (H)! ➡

G

H

to move forward, and had a tendency to get behind the vertical and on the forehand, which limited the elevation of her front feet.

Tellington Method Solutions: Robyn and I checked Ahot's saddle and found it very tight in the front area of the panels: an all-too-common situation that and puts pressure on the acupressure point for the diaphragm, causing the horse to drop his back. The saddle was tighter on the left side because Ahot's left shoulder was slightly lower than the right.

We did about 15 minutes of *TTouch* bodywork, including *Lowering the Head* and *Neck Releases* to open the throatlatch area and lengthen the neck muscles. I worked down Ahot's back, using *Raccoon TTouch* about 4 inches away from the spine, over the hindquarters to the buttocks. I did some *Hind Leg Circles* to connect Ahot's back end to her front. When we resaddled Ahot, we used a pad insert to help the saddle sit evenly on her back and put on the *Tellington Training Bit*. I showed Keri how to use the *Wand* from the saddle to help Ahot become aware of her hindquarters.

The Happy Ending: Keri immediately noticed that her seat bones were even on the saddle and she could feel her left leg against Ahot's side for the first time—this was because the saddle was now sitting evenly. The change in Ahot's attitude and movement was remarkable. Her tail stopped swishing and she moved forward freely, tracking up with her hind legs and swinging her back. Her steps became more elevated.

At their next dressage show, only a week after our work together, Keri and Ahot's scores had improved drastically and they just missed reserve champion. Most importantly, continued use of *TTouch* and *Ground Exercises* in the Playground for Higher Learning, combined with attention to saddle fit had made a visible difference in Ahot's willingness and ability to perform in comfort.

Relieving Stiffness and Soreness in the Older Equine Competitor

The Partnership: *Claus Erhorn and Justyn Thyme*

The Problem: I had the opportunity to work with German Olympian Claus Erhorn and his horse Justyn Thyme after they were on the gold-medal-winning eventing team in the 1988 Seoul Olympics. Justyn was 13 at the time, and beginning to get a little stiff in his shoulders and sore in his back.

Tellington Method Solutions: I did *TTouch* on Justyn's topline and observed that he had lost some of the elasticity in the muscles of his back and neck.

His head was always set on the vertical, whether on contact or a completely loose rein. Claus said he had tried many exercises to get Justyn to lengthen his neck, without success.

I suggested riding him without the bridle (using just a *Liberty Neck Ring*) and within 10 minutes Justyn was stretching his neck, extending his head, and swinging through his back.

The Happy Ending: For the next few weeks Claus rode Justyn both without a bridle and with a *Tellington Training Bit* and the *Liberty Neck Ring*. One month later they won the dressage phase at the Burghley Horse Trials in England. It was the first time Justyn had won the dressage phase of an international event in his career.

The work under saddle with Claus and Justyn reminded me how riding with a *Balance Rein*, *Neck Ring*, *Promise Wrap*, and without a bridle could make such a difference to horses at all levels of training. Until that time, I had focused on *TTouch* and *Ground Exercises*, but with this success with an Olympic competitor, I realized it was time to reintegrate riding into my work. And so Ridden Work that I call the "Joy of Riding"— the third component that along with *TTouches* and Ground Exercises makes up the Tellington Method— was reawakened in Germany.

Defusing Explosiveness

The Partnership: *Uri Koushov and Buket*

The Problem: In 1986 I worked with horses at the Equestrian Complex Bitsa in Moscow, Russia, including a Russian Thoroughbred gelding ridden by Olympic dressage rider Uri Koushov. The gelding, named Buket, had been successful and cooperative in training until, without apparent cause, he began bucking under his rider every time he was asked to execute a flying change. An extensive veterinary examination failed to find a physical explanation for his suddenly explosive nature, and because the veterinarians could not diagnose a physical problem, Buket's behavior was said to be caused by a "bad attitude" and it was punished by whip and spur.

When I explored the gelding's body for areas of tension or soreness, I found a tense, tender spot under the left side of the saddle's cantle. In checking the range of motion in Buket's legs, I could not move his left hind in a circle of more than 4 inches in diameter, and his right hind leg was also much stiffer than it should have been. When I watched the horse ridden under saddle, he exhibited stress and pain even at the walk, lathering in sweat within the first five minutes and displaying a dramatically elevated respiration. I found that even when he was ridden on a loose rein, the horse carried himself far behind the vertical: this was the result of too much collected work and little opportunity to stretch and lengthen between exercises.

Tellington Method Solutions: All these pieces of the puzzle added up to a cause of Buket's bucking and rebellion when asked for a flying change: he was tight, constricted, sore, and anxious. I've worked with many cases like his, where riding in an overcollected frame without adequate extension leads to behavioral problems. Classical dressage technique emphasizes allowing contracted muscles in the neck and back to relax periodically. In my travels and when working with horses and riders at the top levels of dressage, I have found that while riders talk about lengthening the horse's frame, in actuality, they often don't allow their horse enough rein or enough time for recovery between collected exercises. This denies the muscles the chance to relax and reoxygenate, and they grow shorter and tighter until eventually circulation and breathing are affected.

For three weeks, I rode Buket using a variety of exercises under saddle and on the ground to soften his tight muscles. Copper Love, a friend and Tellington Method practitioner who was helping me in Moscow, applied *TTouches* all over his body twice a day. Uri also worked with Buket, sometimes in the *Lindell Sidepull*.

The Happy Ending: Nine months after our work together in Moscow, Uri and Buket placed eleventh at the World Championships in Toronto, Canada, with excellent flying changes.

......The Story of Octango: How the Tellington Method Over Time Makes All the Difference

I hope that what has already become clear is that it is possible to overcome resistance and rid horses of the tension so commonly seen in dressage competition today. Using the Tellington Method, you can encourage suppleness and relaxation, and work through fear and resistance without force or confrontation. By stepping back from the pressures familiar to the modern-day pursuit of the sport and acknowledging the horse's need to be "heard" and understood as *you* would wish to be heard and understood, you can apply what you learn in this book to all manner of challenges and expect to see positive results. These are life-enhancing skills.

A wonderful example of how the Tellington Method, used over time, can help guide a fearful and anxiety-ridden horse to a place of emotional and physical Balance, is the story of Octango.

A Troubled Competitor

I first met Octango—a Contango brother to Ravel (three-time member of the US Olympic dressage team, ridden by Steffen Peters)—at Barbi Breen-Gurley's Sea Horse Ranch in Southern California. Barbi has been an active dressage trainer and instructor since 1970. She is a USDF Gold Medalist and has trained several horses to Grand Prix.

A jet-black, handsome and active competitor, Octango was plagued by inconsistent scores caused by extreme reactivity to noise and episodes of sheer terror in the ring: he would randomly shy violently during tests and attempt to exit the arena, running backward. He did not recover well or "learn from" these episodes, and repeatedly spooked at the same unfamiliar object or circumstance. The behavior was limiting his potential and kept Barbi in a state of hypervigilance, which only fed into a cycle of tension. I worked with Octango over three, separate, weeklong trainings, spaced over a year, and it paid off.

Lowering the Cross-Ties

As the first session began, I watched as Octango was tacked up and immediately noticed that the cross-ties in the barn were set too high, in my opinion. Barbi had told me that her horse was very reactive during saddling, sometimes half-rearing or pawing violently. As I will discuss in detail beginning on p. 199, high cross-ties prevent a horse from lowering his head and neck, which contracts the back muscles and creates tension throughout his body. This creates stress before you ever climb into the saddle.

However, teaching Octango to relax was not a simple process of lengthening the cross-ties. In addition I suggested we hold him with a lead and put some food in front of him so he could lower his head to eat while being groomed. This helped, though a preferable option would have been to tack him up while loose in his stall.

Loosening the Noseband and Girth

Octango's anxiety became immediately obvious when Barbi mounted. At the training clinic, he eyed the group of auditors and chairs suspiciously and spooked at a car coming up the driveway.

I loosened his noseband and girth to allow him to breathe more freely, and quietly asked him to *Lower the Head* by placing a hand on his poll. I did some *Ear TTouches* and *Mouth TTouches*, then *Hair Slides* on his forelock to encourage him to continue to lower his head. Physiologically, when a horse's head is level or lower than his withers, the flight reflex is deactivated—something that would be useful in Octango's case (figs. 9.10 A–E).

Bringing out the Balance Rein

I wanted to better understand Octango's spooking, so a chair filled with colorful plastic pool "noodles" was placed on one side of the arena. The goal was for Octango to go past it without concern, first at the walk, followed by the trot and canter. At the first pass, Octango scooted forward and sideways, attempting to bolt.

At this point I asked Barbi to add the *Balance Rein* and *Lindell Sidepull*. As you've already seen in this book, the *Balance Rein* looks like a necklace around the base of the horse's neck, and alone or combined with the *Lindell*, it really helps rebalance horses who have a tendency to come above the bit or behind the vertical. As the rider holds the *Balance Rein* in her outside hand and pulsates it as she might a regular rein, the *Balance Rein* encourages the horse to bring his back up, and lengthen and round his neck, resulting in a "softer," more pleasant horse to ride.

I recommended that Barbi approach the chair sideways rather than face on (remember what you learned about facing an elephant on p. 147!), and ask Octango to step toward the chair in a slight shoulder-fore. By the second pass in the Balance Rein, Octango's flight reflex had decreased dramatically. Barbi noted that he was much freer in his movement and really "through"— usually his back felt "blocked" from tension. The chair was moved in different positions around the arena, and more pool noodles were added. I got on him and rode in and around a variety of obstacles. Octango's confidence increased with every time around the arena and soon he was moving tension- and worry-free, supple, loose, and flexible (figs. 9.11 A–F).

Body Exploration and TTouch Assessment

Our first ridden session together was followed by work with *TTouch*—both a *Flat-Hand Body Exploration* (see p. 104) and an introduction to a full-body *TTouch* session. Octango resisted lowering his head and would not stand square—he stood slightly strung out with his back dropped and his head up in "flight mode." I explored his body, going over his head, neck, back, legs, and hindquarters with my flat hand, interested to find his level of trust in me. I also felt for temperature changes, checking for areas that were too hot or, on the contrary, ice cold, possibly indicating poor blood circulation. I checked the texture of his coat, noting where it was dry and damaged, or shiny and sleek. I found two dry spots in the loin area that led me to suggest the fit of his saddle be checked.

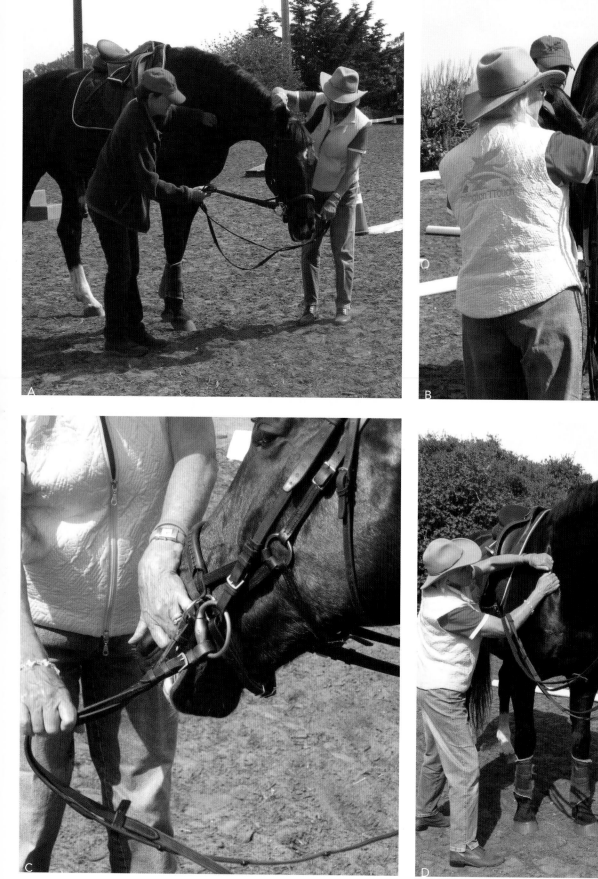

9.10 A–E The first things I do with Octango after seeing his increasing anxiety when mounted are *Lowering the Head* (A), *Ear TTouch* (B), *Mouth TTouch* (C), *Shoulder Release* (D), and *Clouded Leopard TTouch* (E), all of which release tense muscles and encourage a calm, trusting state of mind and body while improving willingness and ability to learn.

9.11 A–F Barbi and I introduce Octango to the *Balance Rein* and *Lindell Sidepull* to encourage him to come up under himself, stride forward, and stretch his neck rather than go behind the bit as his anxiety grows (A & B). These two Tellington Tools helped the horse gain the confidence to go through and around the pool noodles (C), as well as approach a "tunnel" with plastic sides, which at first causes him to stiffen and refuse to go forward before he eventually goes through in both directions on a loose rein that gives him confidence (D–F).

A

B

C

D

E

F

The body exploration also revealed that Octango was sensitive in his shoulder and sacroiliac regions, with tense hamstrings and tender hip sockets. His body reflected the demanding physical work of the Grand Prix horse, but tension throughout had created body sensitivity, which if eliminated, could not only make his work easier for him, but reduce his flight response, as well as increase his muscle symmetry, straightness, balance, and freedom.

To bring Octango into better balance, it was necessary to engage in a variety of *TTouches*, *Ground Exercises*, and *Ridden Work* (figs. 9. 12 A–E). Because of his high head carriage, I began by raising his head from the ground, lifting his head with both hands to encourage him to "release" it and allow it to drop to a lower resting point. This exercise did not work well for the horse as he did not yet trust me enough, so I acknowledged this and let his reaction guide me rather than insisting. I switched to another modality I usually find effective: running the lead rope through the side ring of the noseband and snapping to the upper halter ring, then "milking" the lead rope to ask the horse to lower his head. He remained reluctant, so I added *Hair Slides* on his forelock to encourage him to release his throatlatch. Then I moved his head side to side to release tension in the poll. During the process, Octango threw his head up a few times, so I added *Mouth TTouches* to help relax him further and unclench his jaw.

9.12 A–E To encourage Octango to lower his head, Barbi does *Ear TTouches* to relax him while asking him with her hand on the noseband of the halter (A). *Mouth TTouches* on his muzzle address the limbic system—the seat of his emotions (B) and *Inchworm* along his crest releases tight neck muscles (C). I finish the *TTouch* bodywork session with *Tail TTouches* and *Leg Circles* as the tension in Octango's body decreases and he goes from being reactive and high-headed to standing quietly, ground-tied on his own.

C

D

E

Next, I focused on Octango's hindquarters, using *Jellyfish Jiggles* to release the tension and increase blood flow in the area. This was followed by slow, four-second *Bear Touches* on the muscles of his croup to increase his body awareness, and *Python TTouches* down his legs.

As I worked, the horse's posture began shifting—his neck lowered and his balance changed as he squared up his stance. By the end, his persona had changed: he was no longer in flight mode, but gazing softly ahead and standing quietly ground-tied while I did *Tail TTouches* and completed the session with *Leg Circles*. Octango was unwilling to lift his right hind leg, so I asked him only to rest the toe, which allowed him to release the entire limb from the hip down. This release was accompanied by much chewing and yawning.

Introducing Ground Exercises and the Playground for Higher Learning

After the *TTouch* session I worked with Octango in hand using the *Labyrinth*, one of the *Ground Exercises* in the Playground for Higher Learning. The boundaries of the *Labyrinth* create a "safe space" that help *quiet the mind* and *encourage focus*, both extremely beneficial to horses like Octango. Such work in hand is also a wonderful way to promote straightness, balance, and regularity of gait (figs. 9.13 A & B).

I asked Octango to take deliberate steps through the *Labyrinth*, stop, and turn, so I could evaluate his balance and the regularity of his footfalls. There was some restriction, so I squared him up and asked him to back up, an exercise to evaluate gait purity: when an even diagonal pairing of the steps back is impaired, gait purity will be compromised. Whenever I asked the horse to halt, I did so by touching his chest with the *Wand* and using an accompanying voice command and a light "ask-and-release" stop signal on the lead rope, rather than pulling on him. I did not want to give him reason to assume his old, unhealthy postures by raising his head in alarm, dropping his back, or going behind the vertical.

At the end of the in-hand session Octango was led in the *Journey of the Homing Pigeon* through a small obstacle course, which included a wooden platform, plastic, umbrellas, and spectators standing on bales of hay. *Journey of the Homing Pigeon* encourages the horse to meet new situations with confidence aided by support from a handler on each side.

Octango walked away from the day's session content and peaceful, and I felt so grateful to be working with Barbi, who understood Octango and never resorted to punishing him. It was painfully aware to me how easily such a horse can be misunderstood and labeled "hot" or "spooky" or "uncontrollable," which today too often results in riders attempting to control the "strong" or "scary" horse with techniques such as Rollkur (hyperflexion), and low, deep,

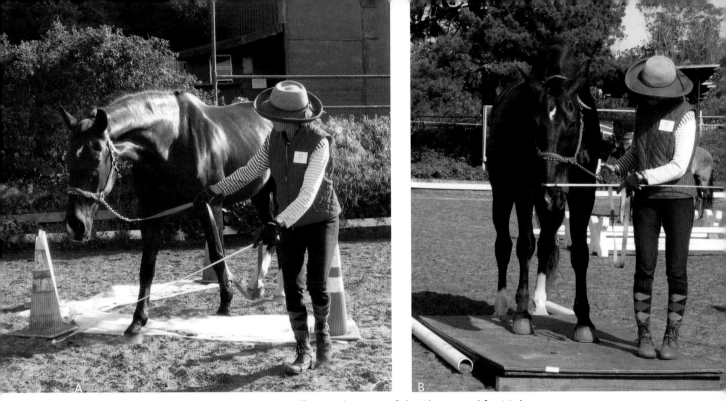

9.13 A & B Barbi introduces Octango to different elements of the Playground for Higher Learning, including traversing plastic on the ground (A) and crossing and halting on the platform (B). I find that when a horse overcomes fear of a specific obstacle it builds confidence in all areas of performance.

and round. I regret that more attention and care is not placed on working with the horse's mind, taking time (see p. 239) to build his trust and confidence so you can teach him to face any situation in a calm and reasonable manner (figs. 9.14 A–D) .

After our work together, Barbi said that Octango really was more confident and less reactive. She incorporated obstacles such as those used in the Playground for Higher Learning in her training on a regular basis, and she said rarely did Octango have trouble with them. She shared a great story from 2010: She and Octango were at a show in San Francisco and as they were in the midst of riding their Freestyle, three loose horses galloped wildly back and forth, multiple times, in a space directly adjacent to the main arena. Adding to the chaos, handlers were on the ground trying to catch the horses, which of course only kept them galloping! Through it all, Octango kept his focus. Although he was disturbed by the neighboring madness, he stayed true to the ride and didn't miss a single one of his 15 tempi changes! They got a 71 percent and won the Sportsmanship Award for keeping their cool in such a tough situation. It was an incredible testament to just how far Octango had come.

D

9.14 A–D It is so easy for a horse to be misunderstood. Octango was considered "spooky," and for good reason, as his anxiety often got the better of him prior to our work together. Here I very much enjoy riding him in the *Balance Rein, Lindell Sidepull,* and *Tellington Training Bit.* By giving him focus in the *Labyrinth* and lateral flexibility in the *Fan* (A & B), and by overriding his flight impulse with a little grain so he learns to *think* rather than just *react* (C), we are able to find the happy, forward horse within, and open the gateway to a new arena of performance potential (D).

175

CREATING AN ATMOSPHERE
OF WELL-BEING

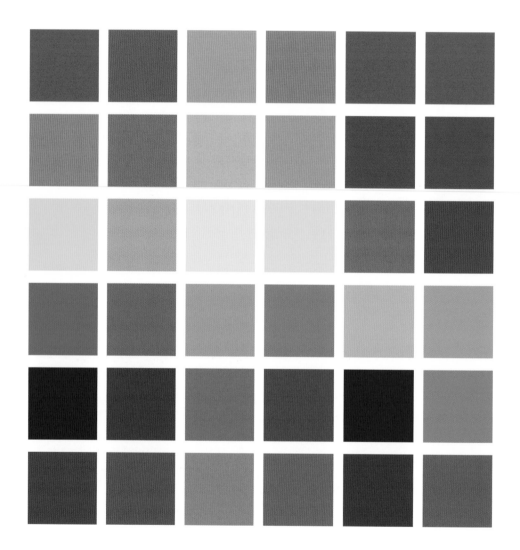

10

AT THE BEGINNING OF CHAPTER 4, I MENTIONED THAT KLAUS
Balkenhol says that giving your horse plenty of love and caring for
him appropriately should be considered as important as abiding by the principles outlined in the Classical Training Scale (see p. 42). I then took this idea
and created a new *foundation level* for my Training Scale called *Balance*, to
illustrate the importance of the dressage horse's physical, mental, and emotional well-being (see p. 47).

I'd now like to offer you some new ways to increase your horse's well-
being and happiness. I say "new" because some of them go against ingrained
habits within the sport of dressage, and are based on recent research that is
just now finding a foothold. You may take an initial glance and shake your
head; you may feel these things are too "simple" or "minor" to make a real
difference in serious dressage work. I ask you to approach this section (as with
others in this book) with an open heart and mind—I assure you, there will be
one or two ideas, at the very least, that could make a profound impact on your
horse's ability to work with you and perform in the dressage arena. I chose
each of these areas as a point of focus because I feel they are particularly
applicable to dressage horses. Amazingly, they are all easy to implement, and
needn't cost you time nor money.

......The Circle of Well-Being

Let's work with the same learning tools we have used throughout this book—
color and *intention*—and a figure I'll call the *Circle of Well-Being*, seven areas
where you can easily make a distinct difference in your horse's general well-
being (fig. 10.1):

- General Health (p. 178)
- Stable Accommodation (p. 189)
- Grooming (p. 196)
- Equipment Type & Fit (p. 208)
- Rider Skill & Attitude (p. 222)
- Use of Music and Sound (p. 228)
- Play! (p. 230)

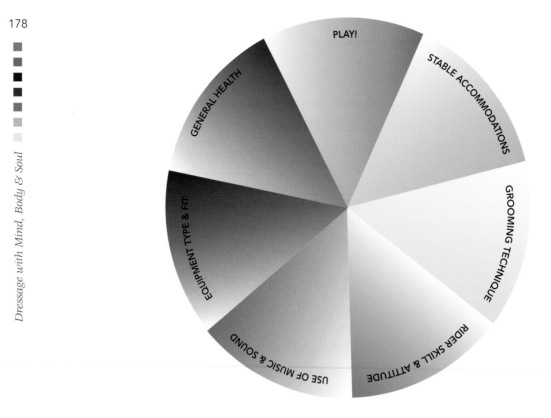

10.1 The Circle of Well-Being.

General Health: Body Soreness, Teeth, Feet, and Nutrition

The Color: The horse's general health is represented by the color *violet*, the color of *Balance* and *Comfort* (pp. 52 and 85).

The Intention: Target your thoughts so you see your horse's body as a wondrous, smooth-running machine at the cellular level.

Body Soreness

One of the first steps to improving your horse's overall well-being is ensuring his physical comfort with a daily (when possible) "hands-on" assessment followed by a few minutes of localized *TTouch* to release tight muscles and ease soreness or sensitivity. I first determined over 30 years ago that soreness or pain was a primary cause for resistance or bad behavior in horses. Body soreness can result from a single episode of work that overwhelms the system, or continuous work without sufficient attention to rest and recovery.

Your horse can be sore virtually anywhere on the body, but common trouble areas in dressage horses include the poll (atlas/axis), shoulder/neck junction, girth area, back, hips, and feet. The causes are many, including problematic training practices, overwork, training in deep or insecure footing, hormonal imbalances, conformation that is unsuitable for the sport (the horse is not built for collected work, for example), or even a rider in pain, as I described in the sidebar on p. 74.

The Five-Minute Horse Inspection

It is useful to discover and monitor specific areas of sensitivity, tension, or soreness that can create resistance in your dressage horse. This knowledge can help you determine how much to ask of your horse in training and in competition, as well as when he may need treatment, be it *TTouch*, acupuncture, massage, chiropractic, or another form of veterinary care or alternative therapy. With the time constraints inherent to the modern-day rider in mind, I recommend developing the habit of using my *Flat-Hand Body Exploration* technique, which I described on p. 104, as often as you can, with the minimum goal of once a week during grooming and prior to your training session.

Alleviating Soreness and Sensitivity

Many of my *TTouches* are ideal for helping ease soreness in specific areas, including *Lick of the Cow's Tongue* and *Belly Lifts* for the back; *Coiled Python Lifts* for the girth area; and *Leg Circles* for the shoulders, legs, and feet. I recommend beginning with the Five-Minute Horse Inspection and then referring to *The Ultimate Horse Behavior and Training Book* for a complete collection of *TTouch* instructions, as well as step-by-step photographs. (Note: If your horse has persistent body soreness or pain, consult your veterinarian.)

The "Mareish" Factor

As noted, a common cause of body soreness or sensitivity is hormonal imbalance. Most of us have been witness to or had to deal with the so-called "mareish" mare at some point in our riding career. This term can refer to different characteristics indicative of the same basic issue—a female horse with physical and mental "blocks" at certain times of the month, or in some worst-case scenarios, plain-old *all* the time.

Mareish "qualities" can include squealing, squatting, squirting, and pinning the ears during estrus. They can involve extreme sensitivity or outright resistance to aids, indicating soreness or discomfort in the body. A mare can be tight, tense, and dramatic prior to ovulation—some even display classic signs of colic, sweating, kicking at their stomach, and attempting to roll. Mares, in general, tend to have more strongly defined feelings and opinions, and their willingness to express them can be amplified by hormonal surges and swings. In other words, the female dressage horse can have a pretty bad day.

Needless to say, delivery and receipt of subtle aiding can be rendered difficult in the face of such physical and mental blocks, often making the execution of a respectable dressage test an exercise in futility. In addition, severe cases of "mareishness" can result in behavior—such as vicious biting, kicking, and striking out—that is dangerous to the rider or handler, and to other horses.

A medical examination may be warranted when a mare's mood changes become extreme, persistent, or limit her ability to perform. An exam can confirm or deny the presence of an ovarian cyst or tumor, retained corpus luteum, or other physiological factors, as well as determine levels of reproductive hormones. Then, consider the following:

1   **Give Her a Break:** Hormones happen. So become familiar with when your mare is in heat—usually between the months of March and October, in the days just prior to ovulation, which can be as frequent as every 21 days. Mark the days off on a calendar and note the most intense days in your mare's cycle. Then, plan accordingly and take some time off or schedule a less demanding schooling session to avoid the likelihood of a spirited debate with your horse. Don't ever attempt to force a mare to perform or punish her when she refuses during this time—this only amplifies her distaste for a task or tasks, regardless of the time of the month, and undermines trust in the long run.

2   **Try the *TTouch* Alternative:** Over the years I have seen numerous mares who suffered extremely during their heat cycles and were thus very reactive under saddle—biting the air, kicking out, and pinning their ears at the slightest pressure on their side, such as the aid to canter. In these cases, *TTouch* has reportedly reduced the intensity and length of hormone-related reactive behavior. *TTouches* I recommend to help alleviate the discomfort that often instigates a mare's poor behavior include:

- *Ear TTouches* from the center of the poll to the base of the ear, and then stroking out to the tip in a slow and deliberate manner. This *TTouch* activates acupressure points over the entire ear and helps to reduce estrus-related pain or discomfort the mare is experiencing.

- *Raccoon TTouches* at the base of the ears to influence the acupuncture site said to activate energy and help balance temperature in the respiratory, digestive, and reproductive organs.

Finding Mare Magic in the Wand

Riding instructor and Tellington Method practitioner Penny Stone of Austin, Texas, shared the story of a Thoroughbred schoolhorse named Lea who had frequent heat cycles, which brought on bouts of extreme reactivity and irritability. During estrus, you couldn't groom the mare on the cross-ties or loose in the stall—she would dance around, pull back, kick out, and pin her ears. Her abdomen was a "no-go" zone, as the lightest brush up against it instigated a kick.

Penny and her students began stroking the mare in a steady rhythm over her entire body with the *Wand* prior to grooming, mounting, and schooling. This seemed to have a soothing effect and Lea stood more quietly. Seeing the positive results, Penny made sure the mare got the full "Wand Treatment" two or three times a week, plus *Ear TTouches* once a month, and a full *TTouch* bodywork session once every couple of months. Nothing else in Lea's life was changed.

The mare has grown steadily calmer. She no longer acts out during estrus—in fact, it is hardly possible to tell when she is in heat. She stands quietly and is more cooperative under saddle. Penny reports that Lea is truly a changed mare.

- *Clouded Leopard TTouches* over every inch of the mare's body.

- *Abalone TTouches* through a warm towel in the flank area, where many mares experience pain.

3   **Take the Heat Out of the Heat Cycle:** A common solution for the mareish horse is to keep her out of estrus with an oral synthetic progesterone, such as Regumate®. Progesterone is the hormone responsible for maintaining pregnancy, and its estrus-inhibiting effect can provide temporary relief from problematic mareish behavior. I also know holistic veterinarians who have had good luck with herbal remedies.

However, when a performance mare's "bad days" outnumber her good ones, and control over her manners is in question, as well as her physical comfort and emotional well-being, then spaying is a valid option.

Spaying of mares—the removal of both ovaries—is not as uncommon as some may think. When a mare is valued as a performer more than a candidate for breeding, and when she regularly falls prey to the hormonal "nasties" or has trouble working during estrus due to extreme discomfort, then it should be considered. Spaying has proved successful in working ranch mares and barrel racers valued for their athletic capability. It can improve focus and consistency of performance, effectively quell dangerous tendencies, and improve a mare's future—particularly mareish horses can have a difficult time finding a human counterpart who is willing to understand and work within their physical and emotional constraints.

According to retired veterinary professor Dr. Robert Shideler of Colorado State University, a pioneer of embryo transfer and author of the book *Management of the Pregnant Mare and Newborn Foal* (Colorado State University, 1984), there are three methods of removing the ovaries: abdominally, through the flank, and vaginally. The three surgeries vary in expense, recovery time, and required technical expertise.

Teeth

Dental issues are some of the most overlooked causes of behavior problems in horses, especially in those who are very young or very old. Many Contact problems, including head tossing; rooting at the bit; letting the tongue flap out the side of the mouth; gaping the mouth; "stargazing"; being unwilling to accept the bit; as well as general behavioral issues such as fidgeting; nervousness or an inability to stand still; and lack of focus are among behaviors indicative of tooth trouble. Scheduling a visit with a competent equine dentist is always one of my first recommendations when dealing with behavioral or training issues. *Mouth* and *Ear TTouches*, for example, can also help in these cases.

Regular dental care is as important for horses as it is for you. Do not neglect this basic component of horse management, as fairly minor (and easily corrected) issues in the horse's mouth can lead to long-term problems with Contact if ignored—detrimental to the dressage horse.

Early in 2011, I worked with Sabrina Deerberg and her hyper-responsive young horse Figo at the Xenophon Society Seminar at Klaus Balkenhol's stable in Rosendahl, Germany. Among other anxiety-driven responses, her horse habitually half-reared at the canter. My immediate thought was of the horse's teeth, but Sabrina assured me they had recently been checked. A veterinarian experienced in dentistry happened to be visiting the stable, so I had the opportunity to ask him to take a second look. Sure enough, Figo had a problematic molar that was obviously causing him significant discomfort.

We proceeded using the Tellington Method with the horse over the course of the clinic, and he improved so much I could ride him with the *Liberty Neck Ring* alone. He focused and relied on me for direction, no longer distracted by a distrust of his surroundings (figs. 10.2 A–I).

Feet

Refusal to stride out, "track up," travel with the desired rhythm, pick up a particular lead, or bend in a certain direction may appear to be stubbornness, unwillingness, or laziness, but can also be caused by a variety of foot and shoeing issues. More serious manifestations result in outright lameness, but subtle shifts in balance over time may go unnoticed and be interpreted as a behavioral issue.

In addition, exercise and turnout are necessary to maintain healthy feet: the more your horse stands around in a stall, the more likely he is to develop contracted heels or tender soles. Movement and regular contact with differing ground surfaces goes a long way in ensuring soundness. (I speak more to the matter of turnout on p. 192.)

Shoeing's Effect On Gait

Shoeing affects the way a horse moves—changes to gait can be subtle or dramatic. According to farrier Doug Butler in the September 2000 issue of *Dressage Today*, the foot's balance (side to side, front to back, and above and below); shoe configuration (how much shoe there is in contact with the ground and in flight, whether or not there is a rocker toe or traction device); and shoe weight (steel versus aluminum) can amplify or inhibit a horse's natural way of going. Finding the right shoeing combination for your dressage horse may be a matter of trial and error, and it may take a number of shoeings for your farrier to discover the combination of factors that ensure your horse can, quite literally, put his best foot forward. The winning formula needs to be consistently applied at regular intervals to keep your horse sound and performing optimally.

I find that stroking the legs and *Hoof Tapping* with the *Wand* are straightforward and effective ways of evening up a slightly irregular gait, encouraging the horse to pick up his feet, and improving his understanding of where his legs and feet are in space and in relation to his body—all of which can lead to cleaner, loftier gaits (fig. 10.3).

Nutrition

Many riders are unaware that nutritional imbalances and feed allergies can cause behavior problems in horses. The most obvious are the results of overfeeding protein or supplements—often coupled with too little exercise or turnout—which can lead to excess energy, bucking, head tossing, and a horse who is difficult to rate. And underfeeding, too, which can cause loss of energy and impulsion and lack of spirit and willingness.

It should be remembered that good-quality forage is the proper foundation of the equine diet. Studies show that grain puts horses at high metabolic

A

B

C

D

E

10.2 A–I Tooth care and health is of the utmost importance to the dressage horse, as the sport in which he competes depends on his ability to accept contact and communicate subtly and efficiently with his rider via the bit and reins, as well as seat, legs, heart, and mind. I worked with a young horse, Figo, in 2011, who expressed his mouth discomfort by rearing at the canter.

We did groundwork in the *Labyrinth* to calm and focus him on the lesson at hand (A). I used the *Wand*, stroking his body while in the *Labyrinth*, as well as his legs, to further develop trust (B). Before mounting him I did *Tail Pull*s to help lower his head and connect him, back to front (C).

I rode at first with the snaffle bridle and a loosened flash, along with the *Balance Rein*. You can see in the photo how Figo is preoccupied with his mouth and the contact with the bit (D). I had his mouth checked by a veterinarian who was attending the seminar, and she agreed with me that his teeth could be the cause of his resistance. In the next session, I introduced Figo to the *Neck Ring*, and practiced the directional aids in the *Labyrinth* (E & F). I followed that by removing the bridle, with a handler on the ground to support the horse, first with a halter, and then a simple loop around the horse's neck (G & H). This usually reactive and nervous young horse was soon moving in a relaxed and willing manner, without a bridle, and with an engaged and interested expression (I). He showed no tendency to rear at the canter as he had done with the bridle on.

risk for gastric ulcers, colic, and founder, and allergies to grain can cause resistance, uncontrollable temperament, and inconsistent performance. I have seen many horses become unmanageable when fed sweet feed, and seen many behavior problems disappear when the feeding program was adjusted.

There are a number of excellent references available for those who want to learn more about the complex science of equine nutrition. My recommendation is to consult an equine nutritionist and have your hay and feed analyzed prior to adjusting types and amounts of grains and supplements. It is easy to forget the profound effect that good nutrition customized for your horse's age, health, and athletic needs can have on his ability to focus and perform his best, and yet it is also one of the most important elements in the Circle of Well-Being to modify and control.

Reduce Occurrence of Gastric Ulcers with Proper Nutrition and Stress Reduction
Today it is no secret that gastric ulcers are thought to be present in over 80 percent of performance horses. Dr. Juliet Getty, equine nutrition expert, special advisor to the Equine Sciences Academy (www.equinesciencesacademy.com), and author of the comprehensive reference book *Feed Your Horse Like a Horse*, says, "For many reasons, a steady, constant supply of forage keeps your horse's digestive system healthy, but it is especially important in ulcer prevention." Unlike in the human, she explains, the horse's stomach secretes acid all the time, even when it is empty. The act of chewing creates saliva, a natural antacid. When without food, horses will chew on whatever is available to neutralize the acid; if there is nothing to chew on, the horse commonly develops ulcers.

Dr. Getty explains that it is the diet and lifestyle we impose on horses that are to blame for this condition—horses in the wild do not get ulcers. She notes free-choice feeding as the first line of defense, but also assures us there is more the owner can do—namely proper nutrition and stress reduction—to protect the horse from this condition.

1 Proper Nutrition

- Offer free-choice forage so the horse can chew as needed to create the saliva necessary to neutralize excess stomach acid.

- Avoid oats and other cereal grains, such as corn, barley, wheat, and rice. Starchy feeds can lead to ulcers by stimulating the horse's stomach cells to produce more acid and encouraging acid production through bacterial fermentation. In addition, cereal grains move through the stomach quickly, leaving it empty and therefore vulnerable to acid.

10.3 Stroking the lower legs with the tip end of the *Wand*, as I am doing here with Dablino, and tapping the walls and soles of the hooves with the knob end, can improve gait regularity and quality, as well as make the skittish horse more "grounded."

- Feed beet pulp as an alternative to cereal grains. It has the same caloric value as oats without the propensity for acid production (see p. 187).

- When you need to feed extra fat, choose the source carefully. Vegetable oils, such as soybean and corn, are the most popular sources of added fat, but they promote inflammation of the stomach lining due to their high omega-6 fatty acid content. The better choices are those high in omega-3 fatty acids, such as flax (meal or oil) or chia seeds, as they actually *reduce* ulcer-related inflammation.

- Provide your horse high quality protein. Legumes such as alfalfa, soybean meal, and clover offer amino acids (building blocks of protein) to allow for proper digestive tract maintenance and healing. Alfalfa should be fed to horses prone to ulcer development (those on stall rest, for example) because it is an excellent digestive buffer.

- "Feed" the horse's hindgut (cecum and large colon) microbial population. Fermentation products and yeast feed the microbes living in the hindgut, making digestion more efficient and promoting B-vitamin synthesis to heal the digestive tract.

- Offer your horse additional B vitamins. Stress, whatever the cause, "uses up" B vitamins at a rapid rate. Consider adding a B-complex preparation that includes all eight B vitamins. Note: make sure the supplement does not include added iron, as there is plenty of iron in forage and additional supplementation is rarely necessary.

 Stress Reduction

- Allow your horse to be a horse. The best way to do this is to give him regular pasture turnout, the more time, the better. It not only provides a steady supply of forage, but encourages movement, a chance to run and buck, and opportunities to socialize with other horses. (See further discussion of turnout on p. 192.)

- Become familiar with what stresses your horse, and be on the lookout for potential additional stressors. Unfamiliar environments, loss of a buddy, stall confinement, training, travel, and competition can instigate increased stomach acid production. A horse that is prescribed stall rest after being accustomed to regular pasture

The Expert

Juliet M. Getty, PhD, has been called a "pioneer in free-choice forage feeding," and her articles and interviews often appear in national and international publications. Dr. Getty runs a consulting company, Getty Equine Nutrition, LLC (www.GettyEquineNutrition.com), that offers consultation services and customized feeding plans to promote horse health, reverse illness, and optimize performance. Dr. Getty's book *Feed Your Horse Like a Horse* is based on the premise that horses (and other equines) should be fed in sync with their natural instincts and physiology.

turnout is likely to develop a gastric ulcer in less than a week. Be sensitive to this and make adjustments to your horse's lifestyle as necessary in order to reduce the possibility of stress.

- In addition to Dr. Getty's recommendations, *TTouches* such as *Ear TTouches* and *Belly Lifts* can help horses suffering from gastric ulcers or a colic episode. I also advise using very light and slow *Abalone TTouches*, with a sheepskin mitt when necessary, over the entire abdominal and flank area. It is important to be patient and find the areas that are acceptable to your horse until you can work the entire barrel area with a 2 pressure (p. 262) and have the horse accept the contact. This may take many weeks, but you will discover increased willingness and performance following this work. (For times of stress, I discuss other *TTouch* recommendations on p. 130.)

Stable Accommodations: Stall Size, Design, Décor, and Turnout

The Color: The horse's living quarters are represented by the color *orange*, the color of *Straightness* and *Confidence* (pp. 53 and 86).

The Intention: Target your thoughts and imagine your horse in an ideal setting that nourishes his mind and body so that nothing is lacking, nothing is amiss.

Horses are herd animals and have been so for millennia. This type of social structure provided stability as well as safety in the wild. However, in modern times, most horses are kept separated from each other for many reasons—they are valuable; there is a lack of turnout space; and sometimes, their owners simply do not realize the importance of horses being allowed social contact and interaction.

When you ensure your horse has time turned out with a "herd"—or, at the very least, with other horses in neighboring paddocks or fields close enough to touch noses when it is safe—he will be happier and healthier. He can scratch and rub on trees, and roll in the grass or dirt or sand, and when turned out with another horse, the two horses can groom each other. If we deprive horses of this environment, we strip away their natural behavior and invite stable vices, such as stall-weaving, nipping, and cribbing.

TTouches such as the *Coiled Python Lift* and *Octopus TTouch* can help release accumulated tension in the stabled horse's body in order to avoid the development of these vices, or lessen their occurrence when they are already present, but in these cases especially, you must also consider changing his surroundings.

Stall Size and Design

It is my opinion that run-of-the-mill, cookie-cutter box stalls don't make the grade for happy, healthy horses. Especially when you consider the number of hours many dressage horses spend within these accommodations (see my thoughts on the need for turnout on p. 192). Many stalls are isolated by solid walls and doors. This setup results in little or no visual or tactile stimulation. You have to think of your horse's housing creatively—if you had to spend 18 hours a day (or likely more) in a cubic space that just cleared your head when you stood up straight and your bottom when you turned around; where you could maybe hear your neighbors but couldn't see them; where little changed day after day after day, wouldn't you get a little cranky or depressed? You'd certainly get bored and stiff.

Many architects who design stables but who don't "know" horses save space for economic reasons without considering the effect on a horse's mental, physical, or emotional health.

The size of the horse and the amount of time the horse spends in his stall should help determine stall size. In addition, how active he is when he is there should also be taken into account. (Is he a lethargic type who dozes in the corner all morning, or a curious, hyper-attentive individual who notices—and reacts to—everything?) Larger horses—and many of today's dressage horses are very large—require more square footage to be able to turn around, lie down, and get up comfortably. A 12- by 12-foot stall has long been the standard recommendation for a 1,000-pound horse, but it is my feeling that in many cases of larger horses this is claustrophobic. I've also seen a lot of stalls measuring only 10 by 10 feet. It should be noted that many commercial stables have stalls slightly smaller than the standard, so if you board your horse and have not checked the size of his accommodation, you should.

I prefer stall partitions that are not solid, but instead have bars or mesh across the upper portion to allow the horse to make visual and even physical (nose-to-nose) contact with his neighbors. This also increases air circulation. Barns are commonly built with a ceiling height of 10 to 12 feet, but open-rafter-style construction (no ceiling) is preferable as again, it maximizes air circulation and decreases the chance of the horse striking his head.

A stall should have as many windows and half-doors as possible, offering different views of the horse's surroundings. A study published in *Applied Behavior Science* (Cooper and McDonald, 2000) showed that chronic weavers (horses who repetitively shift their weight back and forth, swaying their head side to side) who were offered open half-doors on multiple sides of their stalls, providing "multiple visual horizons," showed a significantly decreased tendency to weave. Open windows with differing views offer opportunities for social and environmental interaction, engaging the horse's mind during the course of the day.

Décor

For years I have suggested putting murals in barns with pictures of rolling meadows and trees. This is related to the idea of offering the horse multiple visual horizons (see above) in order to stimulate brain activity during the hours he spends in his stall.

Adding color to the horse's environment is also a way to enrich his "downtime." The debate over equine vision is one of longstanding, but research has found that horses do indeed see some color, rather than black and white only as once believed (see sidebar, p. 193). This indicates that the benefits of incorporating color into the horse's everyday existence might even

Stallions Don't Deserve to Be Isolated

Stallions, who are often isolated simply because that is the way they are traditionally handled rather than by necessity, need to be in a place where they can—at the very least—maintain visual contact with other horses. A "busy" view where a stallion can watch stable activity in aisleways, arenas, and paddocks, provides important stimulation. A stallion needs to feel just as much a part of the daily life in the barn as mares and geldings. Practical and studied use of stall guards and double fence lines should allow for a socialized existence, both indoors and out.

be twofold: not only do you enliven his environment, but you also teach him to accept color as a facet of his surroundings (in other words, no more shying at the brightly colored umbrella near "C"!)

Adding an unbreakable "buddy mirror" to your horse's stall can also alleviate stress and boredom. Research from the Animal Behavior, Cognition, and Welfare Group at the Lincolnshire School of Agriculture in England showed that when researchers placed acrylic mirrors in chronic weavers' stalls, the horses stopped weaving and turned and faced the mirrors for about one quarter of the time they were in the stall (McAfee, Mills, and Cooper, 2002). The mirrors mimicked visual contact with other horses, therefore minimizing the social isolation common in stables, as well as providing additional stimuli in an otherwise visually stagnant space.

Turnout

Dressage riders and trainers will state many reasons why they turn out their horses alone, for only one or two hours a day, or in the worst cases, not at all. The price of a good dressage horse is one reason for this misguided thinking. Dressage horses, especially "made" ones, are expensive, and getting more expensive every day. The time it takes to train one through the levels is another reason—if you're nine years into a 14-year schooling process, you certainly have reason to fear the loss of weeks or months due to injury and related rehabilitation.

But for horses to be healthy, sound, and willing, they need daily exercise and plenty of it. Their body is one built for a roaming animal of the plains, and their feet and metabolic systems fail when their movement is stifled. Stabled horses are at much higher risk of founder, gastric ulcers, and colic. (In one study, colic was virtually unreported in horses kept on pasture full time.) Horses with little or no turnout are prone to developing vices such as stall walking, weaving, cribbing, kicking walls, and biting at passersby.

In addition, confinement affects a horse's ability to learn and perform. If your horse is in his stall 22 hours a day, it's unrealistic to think you can jump on and ask him for advanced collection and difficult movements, without his becoming stiff, sore, spooky, and resistant.

The simple fact of the matter is a horse needs as much socialization, turnout, and free exercise as possible. It is downright inhumane to ignore these needs borne of the animal's basic nature because of our own (again very natural) human desires for success or fame, our competitive drive, and our assumption that the dry, clean barn is far preferable to the damp, muddy pasture. It is high time that dressage riders and trainers *at all levels* acknowledge what is best for the horse and *turn their horses out, with companions, for at least half the day.* It will no doubt surprise many to discover that their horses will

The Equine Color Vision Debate

By Joanne Meszoly

Article originally appeared in the October 2003 issue of EQUUS Magazine and is reprinted with permission.

Studies suggest that horses do, indeed, see color.

Sometime during my earliest dealings with horses, I was told by a now-forgotten authority that horses see only in black and white. I never questioned this version of equine reality, and over the years I've encountered others who shared the same view that most animals—certainly dogs and also horses—inhabit a colorless world.

But how to explain those plentiful barn anecdotes that fly in the face of the black-and-white theory? There's the horse who shies away from orange cones but doesn't take a second look at similar objects in other colors. There's the barrel racer who's startled by red barrels but not blue-and-white ones or the jumper who spooks only at blue jumps. Observant owners sometimes recognize color as the recurring factor in their horses' behavioral quirks. With little true science to go on, these apparent expressions of color perception have been explained away as reactions to the shade, the shape or the placement of the object rather than the color itself, if not purely random outbursts of flightiness.

Yet the anatomy of the equine eye suggests that some color perception is possible, and in the last 25 years, a few behavioral studies have attempted to test color recognition in horses. Using color as the distinguishing characteristic to mark the rewarded choice, some studies determined that shades of red are visible to horses, while others found that blue, not red, is a recognizable color. The inconsistent results may have arisen from flaws in the studies' designs, causing the horses to respond to the darkness or brightness of the color, rather than to the color itself.

More recent research has examined equine vision in a new and more objective light by monitoring horses' physiological reactions to the range of colors. In addition, more carefully designed behavioral tests have produced convincing support for the physiological findings that suggest horses do possess color vision.

COLOR PROCESSING

Eyeballs vary in shape and size throughout the animal kingdom, but the color-sensing process is the same among all mammals. Two types of photoreceptors operate in the eye: rods, which are responsible for seeing in darkness or dimly lit conditions, and cones, which are sensitive to color. The well-studied human eye is known to contain millions of cones grouped into three classes that react in different ways according to wavelengths in the light.

"Light is made up of a lot of different wavelengths, just as sound is made up of a lot of frequencies," explains color-vision researcher Jay Neitz, PhD, a professor in the department of cell biology, neurobiology and anatomy with the Medical College of Wisconsin. "We recognize different frequencies when we hear different pitches. Light frequencies—what we call wavelengths—work the same way."

When light passes through the pupil, it is directed toward the retina, which consists of several layers of nerve cells—including rods and cones—lining the back of the eyeball. Light stimulates the pigments in the photoreceptors, which encode the information about each wavelength and send a message to the brain. Although each cone class responds best to a small range of wavelengths, they all respond in some way.

"With each wavelength of light, each of the receptors reacts to a different degree, and certain receptors prefer one wavelength," says Brian Timney, PhD, a researcher of mammalian vision who is dean of social science at the University of Western Ontario. In the human eye, the cones register short wavelengths as blue, medium wavelengths as green, and long wavelengths as red. Horses' eyes have just two types of cones, and until recently, the visual effect was not known.

THE EQUINE PALETTE

To evaluate horse color vision, Neitz tested six anesthetized ponies by exposing their eyes to individual colors and measuring the neurological responses using an electro-retinogram. The instrument, which has also been used to examine cone pigments in cattle, goats, and sheep, shines a narrow band of light into each eye. "It's like taking all the colors of the rainbow and showing each of them, one at a time," says Neitz.

When a photoreceptor responds to a wavelength, it sends out a nerve signal, which the testing equipment senses and records. "[The electrode] is a very thin thread that sits on the cornea and picks up electrical signals like a little antenna," says Neitz. "Those signals are processed by the computer. Basically, we're measuring the amplitude of the signal in response to different colors of light."

With only two types of cones in their retinas, horses have more limited color perception than people. Neitz found that the ponies' eyes responded to blue and green but not to red. Using the computer data, he constructed an equine color wheel showing that the horse's version of green is different from ours. "They have cones like our blue-sensitive ones," says Neitz, "and they have a cone [class] that's similar but not identical to our green-sensitive ones. Those cones perceive more of a yellow color."

When viewing red, horses see an earthy color with a faint yellow and blue hue. Magenta and its blue-green complementary color are seen as gray. "Basically, there are certain colors that the horse can't tell from gray," Neitz explains, "and there are certain colors that are not like gray but that can't be distinguished from one another."

Although horses can see blue and yellow as separate colors, when presented with blue-yellow, the image is perceived as gray or white. "When both types of cones are stimulated equally, you don't get an intermediate color, you get no color," says Neitz, "and they don't see its complementary color. It's the same for people. If you stimulate red and blue, you get purple. But put in green as well, and you get white."

Neitz's findings indicate that horses probably see the world similarly to people who suffer from red-green color blindness. Color-vision deficiencies vary greatly in

continued from page 193

people, but even those with severe abnormalities probably see more color variations than horses do. "Since horses have just two color receptors [to begin with], there will be several combinations of wavelength and light intensity that will induce equal response ratios in the receptors," says Timney. "As a consequence, various colors will appear similar to one another."

COLOR IN ACTION

Timney has conducted two behavioral studies confirming that horses are able to discriminate among colors. In his first study Timney trained two horses to press on a trapdoor to access a feed treat. With two trapdoors set side by side, Timney projected a colored square on one door and a gray square on the other. The horses had to access the colored door to get the treat. To reduce the chance that the horses were responding to shading or brightness rather than color, Timney matched the color hues with the gray.

"The horses behaved more or less like red-green color-deficient people," says Timney. "A person who's red-green deficient doesn't have a problem with blue and yellow, and some red and green are okay. The horses responded similarly."

Timney found that the horses were able to distinguish red from gray, but the ability to differentiate between them doesn't mean that horses perceive the color red as we do. "We didn't have the horses judge between red and green," he says, "so we don't know if red looks distinct to them."

In a second study, Timney tested how different levels of brightness affected the horse's vision. "We measured the lowest intensity of light that a horse could see," he says. Again, the task was to locate the lighted trapdoor concealing the food reward, but this time the light became gradually dimmer. As the light dimmed, the rate of correct responses fell from 100 percent to only 50 percent. "In this study, the horses were most sensitive to green and yellow in the middle range of light," he says. "It doesn't necessarily tell you what they see. It just means that they respond better to those colors. Color vision is not required for either successful foraging or reproduction, so it's not an essential survival tool for horses as it is for some other species.

"Old-world monkeys have color vision similar to people, and you could say that monkeys need to find bright red fruit from green trees," says Timney. "As grazing animals, horses don't have the pressure to be very selective between the colors. They see what they need."

Yet the fact that equine vision has evolved with a degree of color capability indicated some survival advantage to seeing beyond black and white. More than likely, it's a function of their niche as a prey animal.

"[Color] breaks up the world, separating things on earth and things in the sky," Neitz says. "Blue is distinctly different. Even though they can't distinguish between brown and green, horses watching for predators can see them especially well against that background. If a lion suddenly appears against a blue background, that's a very salient thing for a horse."

continued from page 194

Dressage Judge Cindy Sydnor Takes a Stand on Turnout

Cindy Sydnor, a United States Equestrian Federation (USEF) "R" judge and a United States Dressage Federation (USDF) Certification Examiner who trained with Egon von Neindorff, Karl Mikolka, and Colonel Bengt Ljundquist, and was long-listed for the US Equestrian Team in the 1970s, stated the following in *EQUUS Magazine*:

"Turning out all of my dressage horses—Grand Prix horses included—has made all the difference in my success as a dressage rider and trainer, as well as my horses' performances, their overall health and their happiness. They are much more relaxed. They're more trustworthy and understanding and calm about the environment. Nervousness in the show ring is reduced as well...Since I began turning out my horses about 25 years ago, I've never had one single case of colic."

be more willing, more supple, more energized, and overall better performers under saddle with this simple change in management.

For those horses who are confined many hours of the day, I recommend using *TTouch*, which has been proven to help relax stall-bound horses and substitute for social contact in situations where horses cannot, for one reason or another, be turned out with others. Find out which *TTouches* your horse enjoys most and alternate them. For starters, I recommend *Ear TTouches*, *Tail Pulls*, *Neck Rocking*, *Tarantulas Pulling the Plow*, *Lick of the Cow's Tongue*, *Rib Releases*, and all the leg *TTouches*.

Grooming Technique

The Color: Grooming technique is the color *yellow*, which stands for *Impulsion* and *Capacity for Learning* (pp. 53 and 86).

The Intention: Target your thoughts and imagine each stroke of the brush "opening up" the horse's cells so they can absorb new lessons and release forward energy.

Due to a number of lifestyle issues (many of which I've already discussed), dressage horses today are often highly stressed and hyperreactive. I have seen evidence of more dressage horses made uncomfortable and tense by pre- and post-workout rituals than almost any other cause. Some greet you with pinned ears or swinging hindquarters when you enter their stall (to me, a sign of discomfort and unhappiness, likely related to the workout the horse senses is ahead); some grind or snap their teeth and switch their tail when you brush them. Others demonstrate residual effects of inappropriate grooming technique when worked under saddle—they are unwilling to stride out, stiff, or resistant in other ways, both physically and mentally.

I have found that many of these symptoms lessen considerably or disappear altogether when grooming technique is conscientiously analyzed according the horse's body, sensitivity, and character, and when the cross-ties (if used) are appropriately adjusted to allow for a natural headset and physical stance while being groomed and tacked (see Avoiding Detrimental Effects of Cross-Tying, below). I call this "Grooming with Awareness."

It is amazing to me how much time and money dressage riders and trainers are willing to put into their horses—purchasing them, transporting them, feeding them, housing them, and dressing them—and yet something as integral to good horsemanship as a patient and sensitive grooming technique is not given sufficient attention. In my opinion, it must be remembered that everything else builds on the foundation of well-being that we are discussing in this part of the book—of which grooming is a major contributor.

It is extremely easy (and perhaps tempting) to disregard "currying," "brushing," and "tying" because they are considered "elementary" acts of horsekeeping, and once learned early in one's evolution as a horseperson, rarely revisited for critique or improvement. But I ask you to consider this in your grooming routine: If you knew that altering the speed that you (or your groom) brush your horse, changing the order or type of brushes, or incorporating five minutes of simple bodywork would not only clean your horse but also relax him, warm up his muscles, and shorten your pre-workout preparation time in the saddle significantly, wouldn't you do it? In addition, Grooming with Awareness increases your ability to read your horse's mood and state of physical health, and improves horse-human communication. To me, making this part of the Circle of Well-Being a priority makes all the sense in the world.

Avoiding Detrimental Effects of Cross-Tying

When grooming a horse, it is common, I find, for the base rings for cross-ties to be positioned high on walls (or posts, depending on stable design). This is often combined with very short lengths of rope or flat nylon, usually only just long enough to reach and clip to the side rings on a standard halter with little sag or "give" on each side.

While the intention here may be to ensure the handler's (relative) freedom of movement; the horse's safety by preventing a low or "looping" cross-tie over

Rampant Resistance to Grooming

I've told you about the symposium in February of 1999 where I was a guest of seven-time German Olympian Dr. Reiner Klimke at a four-day symposium at the Los Angeles Equestrian Center in California (see p. 21 for more about this). I was present at ringside to comment on each horse, and I had 18 of our Tellington Method Practitioners working on horses between their rides. During the symposium, the most common characteristic we found among the 12 horses (working at various levels) was resistance to grooming. This was characterized by tossing heads, switching tails, and shifting bodies during the most basic of grooming activities.

Every professional groom I know has been taught that vigorous brushing and currying are the order of the day. Often, horses are cross-tied fairly tightly at a height that keeps their head in the air, which then causes their back to drop (see more about this on p. 197). This causes a horse to tighten his back and hold his breath so that he is already tense before the rider is even in the saddle.

A key to success is the understanding of the value of quiet, soothing grooming techniques that seek to relax the horse, deepen his breathing, and increase his circulation, as well as get him clean. Rather than "strictly business," grooming sessions should be thought of as part of the warm-up or cool-down, with the horse secured in a way that is comfortable for him while still safe for you. Best is when you can work with your horse free in his stall so he is well situated to teach you just what pressure and tempo he likes the most.

I recently read Dr. Allan Hamilton's book *Zen Mind, Zen Horse* (Storey Books, 2011). He likens grooming to the traditional "tea ceremony" performed in Chinese, Japanese, and Korean cultures. The tea ceremony is practiced to foster harmony with nature while disciplining the mind and quieting the heart as one seeks enlightenment. As every step of preparation of tea for honored guests should be lingered over and "blessed," in a sense, with your full attention, so should every stroke of your brush transmit the love you feel for your horse—indeed an "honored guest" in your life and deserving of such respect each time you interact with him.

which he can hook a leg; and to keep him relatively motionless during routine care that requires his security and obedience, this practice holds most horses in an unnatural position. The horse's head is held so the neck is above the parallel (or almost parallel) line from the withers commonly seen in the horse at rest. This results in tension from the poll to the croup and encourages an "upside-down" neck and hollow back—the opposite of what is desired in the dressage horse. Over time, this habitual positioning has a bad effect on the musculature necessary for the horse to round and work over the back—the muscles in key areas of his body are shortened, tense, and sore.

I was recently in a barn with several upper-level dressage horses who were routinely groomed and saddled in this state of high tension on the cross-ties. They all pawed excessively, threw their heads, and half-reared while being groomed. Some of them received regular chiropractic treatment but still exhibited a sore back and hindquarters and tended to stand "stretched out" when on the cross-ties—in my opinion, an attempt to relieve the discomfort in their body. The "annoying habits" of pawing and head-throwing were the horses' attempts to communicate their pain in the only way they knew how.

I can't imagine that anyone would see much sense in intentionally taking three steps back before trying to take one forward, but in essence, that is what improper cross-tying (and grooming) technique does in the case of the dressage horse. When Grooming with Awareness, it is possible to warm the horse up and relax him so he is receptive and on the aids when you get in the saddle. Causing tension from poll to tail and irritability with high or tight cross-ties (and rough or rushed brushing) increases the time you need to take to warm up in the ring and the likelihood of a distracted, stiff, riding partner. Over time, the tension and discomfort can build, causing extreme reactivity and spookiness, to the degree the horse might be labeled "dangerous" or "unrideable."

I recommend that cross-ties, when used, be secured with breakaway ties (knotted strands of baling twine work well for this) to a base ring that is located approximately a foot above what would be level with the side rings on the horse's halter. While they certainly shouldn't be loose enough for the horse to get a leg over, they should have enough "give" to allow the horse to lower his head to its natural resting position, typically with the poll at or below the level of the withers.

Ideally, you should work toward grooming your horse loose in his stall or another enclosed space clear of safety hazards. Grooming him while he is free to stand as he is most comfortable encourages him to become involved in the process, relax, and enjoy your touch and attention. Eventually, Grooming with Awareness (which I discuss on p. 202) should make this scenario possible.

When grooming your horse loose is not possible, using my single-handler "containment" technique called *Taming the Tiger* (I describe this on p. 204), is preferable to using cross-ties.

Adrenaline (epinephrine) is a hormone and neurotransmitter (a chemical from within the body that fires neurons in order to activate receptors) that is commonly triggered as part of the short-term stress reaction in both horses and humans. The release of adrenaline into the bloodstream increases heart rate and blood pressure, while dilating air passages, readying the body for immediate "fight or flight."

Noradrenaline (norepinephrine) is very similar to adrenaline, and it too is released when physiological changes occur in the horse due to a stressful event. Along with adrenaline, noradrenaline underlies the fight-or-flight response, directly increasing heart rate, among other changes. The two hormones balance each other in the body's preparation for and recovery from muscular action. Further, noradrenaline affects the parts of the brain that control attention and focus.

Cortisol (hydrocortisone), the "primary" stress hormone, increases sugar (glucose) in the bloodstream. It also inhibits "nonessential" bodily functions in a fight-or-flight scenario, such as the immune, digestive, and reproductive systems.

Studies have shown that in humans, common stressors that lead to the release of stress hormones, such as physical threat, excitement, noise, bright lights, and high temperatures, to name a few, have grown to include psychological stress, pain, and even memories. The problem is that with most of these stressors, fight or flight is not actually necessary. Therefore, the activation of the sympathetic nervous system caused by the release of adrenaline is, in fact, not needed, and only results in adrenaline "sensitization" in pathways in the brain—that is, the adrenaline is not "used up" (Kanji, G.). In humans this can result in insomnia, hair loss, high blood pressure, and digestive issues. In his book *Why Zebras Don't Get Ulcers* (Holt Paperbacks, 2004), primatologist Robert M. Sapolsky states that the fight-or-flight reflex can actually be deadly in modern society. Long-term stressors—such as searching for a job or dealing with a lengthy commute in heavy traffic—keep stress hormones circulating in the bloodstream far longer than is healthy, setting us up for any number of chronic disorders.

Various causes are known to cue the release of stress hormones in horses, including transport, isolation, and confinement, to name just a few. According to veterinarian Dr. Nancy Loving in her book *All Horse Systems Go*, stressed horses demonstrate symptoms such as viral illness (due to a compromised immune system); diarrhea, dehydration, impaction, or colic (due to a cortisol-inhibited digestive system); and the development of stereotypic behaviors, such as cribbing, weaving, kicking, and striking out.

I find that grooming and cross-tying technique are huge contributors to the accumulation of stress (and thus the increased—or even what could be

Chewing: Overriding the Fight-or-Flight Reflex

The ancient fight-or-flight response was critical for survival of horses and other mammals of the plains. Those who did not react to a perceived threat with the appropriate stress-related response would no doubt soon fall prey to one of many predators.

My aim in this book and via the Tellington Method is to teach riders and their horse to override the fight-or-flight reflex and replace it with the response to *think* rather than just *react*. One very effective way to override stress-related reactions is by feeding your horse when he is tense or nervous.

The act of chewing activates the *parasympathetic nervous system (PSNS)*, which along with the *sympathetic nervous system (SNS)* that I mention in my discussion of stress hormones (see p. 200) makes up the *autonomic nervous system (ANS)*. The ANS regulates the function of internal organs and glands: the PSNS stimulates what are termed the "rest and digest" activities, such as salivation and urination, while the SNS handles the fight-or-flight response. The PSNS and SNS function in opposition to each other—when one is activated, the other is usually dormant. Thus, intentionally activating the PSNS during training through the use of food, especially with anxiety-ridden or nervous horses, helps override their impulse to flee.

In addition, chewing instigates relaxation of the muscular attachments in the tongue and underside of the neck, as well as the muscles of the poll.

thought of as "constant"—release of stress hormones) in the dressage horse's existence. The short-term results are both behavioral (the "crankiness" and unwillingness I described earlier) and physical (tense muscles, increased pulse and respiration). And I have seen evidence of detrimental long-term effects as well—inability to perform, unsoundness, and depression.

In 1989, Tellington Method Practitioner Annegret Ast gave a grooming demonstration at one of our Advanced Training Clinics. There she shared the stories of several horses brought to her after being deemed "unrideable" by veterinarians. In all cases the horses hated being groomed, some displaying "negative" behaviors and others becoming so upset during the process that their heart and respiratory rates rose dramatically and then stayed elevated (beyond what would be considered "normal" for their level of conditioning) while they were worked under saddle. With careful attention to each horse's body type, skin sensitivity, and handling preference, Annagret showed how positive change in each horse could be brought about in an amazingly short period of time.

Introduction to Grooming with Awareness

Step 1 Gather your grooming tools. Final choices will vary depending on your horse's sensitivity, so to save time, first lay them all out together to allow you the opportunity to test different brushes and find those your horse likes best. With the very sensitive and hyperreactive dressage horse in mind, I like to have a soft rubber mitt or gentle curry (Grooma® products work well), a sheepskin mitt, brushes of different degrees of softness and bristle type, a hairbrush, a bucket of hot water, and some clean towels. In addition, a *Tellington Wand* can provide a good introduction to the process and help ground your horse before you begin (see Step 3).

Step 2 Take your horse's pulse and respiration before you begin (see sidebar, p. 207).

Step 3 The ultimate goal is for your horse to enjoy being groomed enough

A Russian Study

In 1985, 20 sport horses were involved in a 14-day study at the Equestrian Complex Bitsa in Moscow, Russia (where the equestrian events were held during the 1980 Olympic Games). Eight veterinarians from the Department of Standard Physiology of the K.I. Skryabin Moscow Veterinarian Academy, along with numerous riders and trainers, took a practical course in the Tellington Method under my direction. All 20 horses were worked daily in either dressage or jumping. The participants used the Tellington Method on 10 of the horses each day; the other 10 did not receive additional bodywork or training. Each day, blood samples were taken and the levels of stress hormones recorded.

It was found that stress hormone levels were indeed reduced in the group of horses that received *TTouch* and groundwork training. In addition, the attending veterinarians noted a general improvement in these horses' outward appearance, that their ability to work increased, their behavior calmed, and prior movement issues—whether caused by injury, trauma, arthritis, or something else—disappeared, in many cases.

to stand quietly without being tied or cross-tied. Initially you may need someone to hold him, as this process is most effective if you can use both hands on your horse's body. When assistance is unavailable, I recommend using the tying technique I call *Taming the Tiger* (fig. 10.4):

Run a 15- to 18-foot rope through the bottom ring of your horse's halter, through a ring on the wall or a post (this should be about the height of your horse's nose when he stands in a relaxed and "natural" position), and clip it to the side ring on the halter closest to the wall or post. Clip a standard lead rope to the other side ring (closest to you). Hold the long rope and lead in your left hand when on the left side of the horse (and vice versa), with your index finger between them, and use your opposite hand to groom. When the horse is standing quietly, the ropes should have a slight slack to them. *Taming the Tiger* is about "containment" rather than "restraint."

Step 4 Start by stroking your horse with a *Wand* (or standard *white* dressage whip—horses seem to respond very differently to white rather than black) all over his body. Stroke firmly to avoid tickling the horse—there should be a slight "flex" to the *Wand* as you move it against his body. Pay attention to the rhythm and quality of your breathing. Note how your horse is standing during this pro-

10.4 When the horse does not yet stand quietly on his own during grooming, and when you do not have an assistant available to hold him, I recommend using the tying technique I call *Taming the Tiger,* demonstrated here.

cess: Is he in balance over all four feet? Is he fidgeting? Watch his eyes, ears, and skin—how do they look as the *Wand* moves?

Step 5　I like to follow the *Wand* with a sheepskin mitt. Many sensitive horses react to even the softest brush, especially if their grooming experience has been unpleasant in the past. The sheepskin mitt, or another soft and "unexpected" grooming tool, can break this pattern of reaction and the negative behavior that can go along with it, including adrenaline release and poor performance under saddle in the workout ahead. Let the horse look at the mitt.

Rest one hand lightly on the halter and do *TTouch* circles with the mitt on the horse's face, muzzle, and up around his ears. Watch the horse's response and monitor your own breathing. With a nervous or headshy horse, it may be best to start at the neck or shoulder after showing him the mitt.

Step 6   Move the mitt slowly over the horse's body, going with the hair, and make a connection with your horse with your other hand. Watch your horse's body and expression for signs of concern—a turn of the head, twitch of the ear, stamp of the foot, swish of the tail. Acknowledge these signals and pause, quietly and mindfully. This pause tells the horse you are listening to him and are aware of his uncertainty or discomfort. Note: You do not want to overreact; just acknowledge. After the pause, change something about how you are moving the mitt—for example, try the *Python TTouch* or *Abalone TTouch*.

Step 7   Choose a soft brush with a flexible bristle. If your horse is very sensitive or reactive to grooming, place one hand between the brush and your horse's skin, and move them slowly and gently over the horse's body. Occasionally let your "support" hand precede the brush, and sometimes, let it follow the brush. Keep the tempo of the strokes and the rhythm of your breathing *very slow* as you move over the hair. Be aware of your own balance and breathing as you move, as well as your horse's. Notice how one affects the other.

As before, pause and change when your horse reacts negatively or with concern to your brushing—change the pressure or speed of your brush strokes, or the type of brush, and again gauge your horse's reaction to brushing in the same area. Does the change help? And what does this tell you about where your horse is most sensitive or (possibly) sore? What does this tell you about how your body position and movement impact his mood and stance? How could these affect him in the arena when under saddle?

Step 8   I like to use a human hairbrush on the horse's mane and tail. Working *Hair Slides*—from the root of the hair out to the end—into your grooming routine is very relaxing to most horses. The *Forelock Slide* is one of the most rewarding means of relating to your horse and deepening trust, while at the same time achieving a relaxed, peaceful state in both horse and human.

Step 9   Next, use a damp towel or cloth, soaked in very hot water and wrung out so it is barely wet. Start with the horse's nostrils, gently clean them, then slowly move the towel up the horse's face. Proceed to wipe the horse all over his body, ending with the dock and tail, rewetting and wringing out the towel as it cools. I find this leaves the horse clean and relaxed.

Conscientious Mane-Pulling

Pulling the horse's mane—a necessity for most dressage competitors who need to braid on a regular basis—needn't be stressful or painful for the horse. I like to use *Inchworm* along the crest, along with *Hair Slides* to prepare the horse for mane-pulling.

Pull the mane only a few hairs at a time, and pull the hair straight up as it grows out of the follicle, rather than across it. Try to pull the mane regularly, a little at a time, rather than only occasionally and in one long session.

Step 10 Especially in the case of a horse who tends to be very reactive to grooming, take your horse's pulse and respiration again. If they were high when you began, the goal is for them to have settled. If they are high, then your grooming technique—and what you internally and externally bring to the "grooming table," such as stress or anxiety—is potentially decreasing your horse's ability to perform his best and connect with you to the degree necessary for artful, joyful dressage. When you are grooming in preparation for riding, end the session with *Flick of the Bear's Paw* to "wake up" your horse. This warms *you* up prior to mounting, as well.

Once your horse learns to enjoy the grooming process, rather than fear or fight against it, you will find that the amount of time you need to groom him will decrease. Rushing the process to begin with, because of your own stress or time constraints, only results in problems in the ring, and thus real wasted time, later. Grooming with Awareness is truly one of the best gifts you can give your horse and yourself.

Note: When you have a groom who regularly works with your horse, I advise working with him or her through this process, at least a few times. It is important for you as your horse's rider or trainer to experience Grooming with Awareness because it will improve your ability to communicate with your horse in the saddle.

Learning to Listen

Even if your dressage horse is not super-sensitive; even if you see little evidence of grooming technique affecting his attitude and way of going, taking the extra time to consider your technique and how he reacts to it, to go slowly and *pay attention to your horse*, teaches you to listen to him. It provides another means of "reading" his heart, mind, and body, and opens another channel of communication.

Easy Instructions for Taking Your Horse's Heart and Respiratory Rate

It should become a habit to check your horse's pulse and respiration on a regular basis. It is an excellent gauge of stress level and can tell you a lot about your horse's state of mind and body. It is necessary to be able to do it quickly and accurately in times of injury and illness.

To check your horse's heart rate: There are several ways to do this, but the easiest place to take your horse's heart rate is via the mandibular artery located just under the jaw. Slightly curl the fingers of one hand and place them in the groove between your horse's mandibles (jawbones). Pull your fingers back toward the mandible closest to you until you feel the horse's mandibular artery. Press the artery slightly against the mandible and you will feel the horse's pulse—the blood flowing in response to the heart beating. Count the number of "beats" in 15 seconds and multiply that number by four to get the horse's heart rate. The horse's average resting heart rate should be between 32 and 44 beats per minute.

To check your horse's respiratory rate: Count the number of times the horse's flank moves in and out (each inhale or exhale is one breath) in one minute. Note whether the horse is taking shallow or deep breaths and any abnormal sounds or signs of blockage. His respiratory rate should be between 12 and 24 breaths per minute.

You can reduce pulse and respiration with *Ear TTouch* from base to tip of the ears. When either (or both) heart and respiratory rate is very high, your horse may be suffering acute trauma or pain, and you should call your veterinarian and do *Ear TTouches* until he arrives. *Ear TTouches* have been proven to control pulse and respiration, reduce discomfort, speed healing, and calm a distressed horse to allow for treatment (see p. 130).

You and your horse speak different languages, and to truly move as one with him, to "dance" with him, you need to listen to him in every way possible. Think of how you "talk" to each other when you ride a test. Think about the subtle changes in his body, the muscle motion you feel between your legs and seat, the movements of his tongue and mouth that you can sense through the reins. The better in tune you are to these movements, the better able you are to anticipate his reactions to your requests, the better the test. In the

Mutual Grooming

Horses groom each other as a show of companionship. Have you ever watched two horses in the process? They progressively work their teeth up and down their partner's mane, neck, or withers, seeking out itchy spots, softly moving over sensitive areas, and giving firm attention to others. It is rare for one horse in a grooming pair to show discomfort or displeasure. If possible, watch your horse in such a mutual grooming scenario. Note his reactions and preferences. Think of yourself as his equine grooming partner as you are performing intriguing *TTouches* on his body. Imagine being able to bestow, and thus receive and enjoy, the same kind of companionship and benefits as he experiences in the pasture with his buddies.

past 20 years, we've heard a lot about horse "whisperers," but I believe, as my sister Robyn Hood has often pointed out, that it is the horse who is constantly whispering to us. We have to learn to hear what he has to say.

In a sense, as a dressage rider you are the "director" in a film about your horse's beauty, power, and grace. A good director sees the big picture, and yet has his finger on the pulse of the minutia. A good movie isn't just what fills the screen, it's what's in the details—the expressions on the extras in the background, the color of the flowers on the table in the corner, the light glinting off a building, the pitch of the actor's voice when he speaks a particular word. And in the same way, a good dressage test isn't just about an astounding extension and a fabulous passage. It is about the expression in your horse's eyes, the movements of his ears and tail, the softness of his mouth, the fluidity with which he accepts your touch. All these details are literally "at your fingertips" when you Groom with Awareness. If you "see" such details and "hear" what they are telling you on the ground, you can better communicate with your horse when in the saddle. The result? A great test. A superior "film." Dressage with "heART."

Equipment Type and Fit: Boots and Wraps; Nosebands and Girths; Saddles

The Color: Equipment type and fit is the color *electric indigo*, the color of *Rhythm* and *Coordination* (pp. 53 and 88).

The Intention: Target your thoughts so you see your horse's body moving with tick-tock regularity, uninhibited by the tack he wears.

It is not new that we "dress" our dressage horses—that we blanket them, wrap them, and girth them up tight (fig. 10.6). It is in our nature to protect what we value, and as we might carefully pad and wrap fine china between holiday meals, so we pad and wrap our horses between competitions and during training workouts.

It is my feeling, however, that in an effort to protect the horse from damage, we in effect wreak havoc on his *vestibular* and *proprioceptive systems*—the integral systems that control balance and spatial orientation in most mammals.

The Sixth and Seventh Senses

The *vestibular system* primarily controls movements of the eyes, head, and body through receptors in the inner ear. It transmits positional changes of the body to the brain so the body can compensate in order to stay upright.

The *proprioceptive system* is made up of proprioceptors (specialized sensory receptors) located in joints, tendons, and muscles that detect changes in body part position far more quickly than other sensory organs. This provides both a conscious and unconscious body awareness and a sense of knowing just where the body is in space, which is called *proprioception*. It is the physical feeling of the moving body, of knowing where your feet are without looking at them. In the horse, proprioception not only helps with basic physical navigation, it is integral to physical expression, beautiful gaits, and athletic prowess.

Moreover, the vestibular and proprioceptive systems impact the horse's ability to learn and perform new movements. In studies of student performance in the classroom, it has been shown that those with healthy vestibular and

10.6 When misused, wrapped incorrectly, or applied too tightly, boots and wraps can cause problems with the horse's balance and spatial orientation.

Finding "The Spot" and Learning the Horse's Language

Kristen McDonald, groom former Technical Advisor of the US Dressage Team Anne Gribbons, grew up a member of the US Pony Club, competing in amateur eventing, dressage, and hunter shows. She began at Anne's training facility, Knoll Dressage, as a working student before working her way up to becoming Anne's personal groom. Here Kristen shares her thoughts on the role of the groom in the dressage horse's life.

10.5 Kristen McDonald, groom for former Technical Advisor of the US Dressage Team Anne Gribbons, with Anne and Alazan in 2010.

"There is an old Irish tale that depicts the island of Inishnills, where unicorns run free. Only those who believe in the magic power of the unicorns could ever be lucky enough to witness their purity and beauty, and perhaps earn their companionship. The man who acknowledges the unicorn as sacred and treats him with love and respect will have an ever-faithful friend and partner of unparalleled magnificence.

"A good partnership works both ways. Like the unicorn who devotes himself to the man who believes in his magic, the horse will willingly carry his rider safely if, in return, the rider does everything within his means to make the experience as comfortable and safe as possible.

"As riders, we must listen to the horse and learn his language, just as the horse strives to learn ours. I believe that learning to hear what the horse is telling you starts long before you are ready to get on his back.

"As a professional groom the very best advice I can give is to know your horse and his body. Not only does this ensure you catch small physical problems (strains or injuries) before they become bigger, more painful, and more expensive to deal with, but it also helps you discover the methods of handling the horse that keep him happy and sound.

"For example, the stallion I ride loves a metal curry rubbed gently but firmly all over his back. How do I know he loves it? When I begin to use the curry in slow, circular motions, he sighs, drops his head, and sticks out his nose, indicating I found 'The Spot.'

"Another horse in my care is incredibly sensitive to any grooming. I must move really slowly, using only the softest brushes in my kit as I try to find the places he enjoys being touched before I move on to the areas that cause him anxiety—his back and underbelly. This horse is an excellent example of one who directs me to potential health problems by using body language—he now receives chiropractic treatment for his lower back, which is sometimes sore, and is on a special diet and medication for a mild tendency to develop stomach ulcers. As I am his only groom, I am very in tune to when his ailments may be flaring up: his behavior changes in his stall, on the cross-ties, and under saddle.

"When I ride, I like to use lots of praise to reward good work. I want the horse to know he has performed well so he is happy to do it again in the future. Once mounted, I always begin by giving the horse a sugar cube before he steps off. This helps teach your horse to stand still while you mount (he's waiting for the sugar cube!), but I also have a friend who calls the practice 'putting a quarter in'—I'm setting my horse up for an enjoyable ride by beginning with a positive moment.

"Working for Anne Gribbons has been the experience of a lifetime. She is one of my best friends, as well as my boss and trainer, because she knows that I love her horses as much as she does and will stop at nothing to care for and protect them. I feel we owe it to our horses to treat them fairly and provide for them. We expect them to grant us a ride on their back, pull a heavy load, or breed with another horse of our choosing. More often than not, they are willing and compliant to do our bidding. Only when we have attempted to learn the language of the horse can we even begin to repay him for his service and obedience."

continued from page 210

proprioceptive systems are more attentive, better able to orchestrate movements, and thus more successful in learning scenarios than those inhibited in either area (Wells-Papanek, 2006). It makes sense that when the student—whether child or horse—is secure in his spatial relationships and comfortable in basic navigation, he is more receptive to lessons and more able to perform in response to physical and verbal cues.

Sensory Integration

Sensory integration is the process that deals with how the brain regulates and organizes multiple "inputs" from our senses and turns the information into effective use of the body within the environment. Sensory integration is essential in enabling human or horse to comprehend his or her surroundings. In addition, its regulatory role ensures that the brain tunes out sensory information that is not important, while honing in on what deserves action or reaction. Without efficient processing of sensory information, it would be very difficult to learn and very difficult to perform athletically—we are, quite simply, overwhelmed by sensory input.

Interference in the vestibular and proprioceptive systems leads to *sensory integration dysfunction,* making the processing of direction difficult, if not impossible, and dressage training at any serious level a struggle for both horse and rider.

The Effect of Improper Leg Wrapping on Proprioception

Too tight leg wraps or poorly fitted protective boots can not only damage tendons and ligaments, they can prevent the proprioceptors in the horse's lower legs from transmitting accurate data to the brain, effectively resulting in a disconnect between the horse and his feet—that is, he doesn't know where they are in space in relation to the rest of his body.

When a horse experiences such dysfunction, he may have difficulty telling his body what it needs to do in order to move a certain way (to complete a movement, for example); he may stumble and trip often; he may dislike changes in footing, crossing bridges, and going up ramps; and he may have a hard time preserving postural stability, which is the ability to maintain the position of the body (the center of balance) within specific boundaries of space. The latter is of particular interest because one of the goals of dressage training is to shift the horse's center of balance (naturally occurring toward the forehand) back so that more of the horse's weight is borne by the hindquarters. This feat is only accomplished with years of careful training and conditioning. Therefore, the possibility of disrupting the strategically developed postural stability of the dressage horse through the improper use or overuse of leg wraps and protective boots seems all the more troublesome.

The Tellington Body Wrap and Body Rope

When a child suffers from *sensory integration dysfunction*, he often craves the feel of tight clothing—fully zipped sweatshirts in one-size-too-small, turtlenecks, knee socks, and long sleeves. The light pressure touch the tight clothing provides soothes him by helping his nervous system decipher his body's boundaries and where it is located in space.

10.7 A & B I worked with this mare at a clinic in Middleburg, Virginia. Her rider was trying hard to collect the mare, but I thought physical discomfort was making it difficult for the horse to round up and come "through." The *Body Wrap* in a figure eight around her shoulders and hindquarters, in combination with the *Tellington Training Bit*, worked wonders, encouraging the mare to step under herself behind, and reach forward in front.

Years ago I developed the *Tellington Body Wrap* (shown here) and *Body Rope*, as well as the *Promise Wrap* and *Promise Rope* to provide the same sort of support to the horse suffering from a lack of proprioceptive data. For the *Body Wrap/Body Rope*, use elastic bandages, wraps, or a 21-foot-long nylon rope arranged in a figure eight around the shoulders and hindquarters of the horse, to reinforce the horse's "internal body picture," improving his body awareness and his ability to move in a smooth and coordinated manner (figs. 10.7 A & B). The *Promise Wrap/Promise Rope* is again a bandage or rope, this time wrapped round the horse's hindquarters and attached to the saddle billets on either side of the horse (see figs. 6.5 A & B).

If leg protection is absolutely necessary when you turn out and work your dressage horse, I prefer dressage boots that fasten with Velcro to wraps. In addition, the following *TTouches* can enhance your horse's proprioceptive system and improve his ability to know where his feet are in space: *Coiled Python Lifts, Octopus TTouches, Rainbow TTouches, Front and Hind Leg Circles,* and *Hoof Tapping*.

Tight Nosebands and Girths

It has become commonplace to ride dressage horses with a very tight noseband (cavesson) and girth. Sometimes riders even use mechanical levers to crank the noseband or girth tighter when their own strength fails. This creates a major conundrum. A dressage horse is expected to be flexible and move fluidly, but the tight noseband and girth prevent free movement of the jaw and restrict the ribs. When any joint in the body is restricted, the movement of all joints is affected so that the horse cannot bend, flex, and achieve free-flowing gaits as expected.

In her seminal book *Centered Riding* (Trafalgar Square Books, 1985), Sally Swift described a simple exercise that illustrates this phenomenon: Take one hand and shake it. Now, continue to shake the hand and tighten one finger. Notice what happens to your hand...and what happens to your breathing. When you tighten one finger, you tighten the other fingers of the hand, as well as your wrist, on up into your arm, eventually limiting your breathing. One tight finger results in the larger part of your body becoming stiff.

For decades I've hoped that prominent veterinarians and trainers in the international dressage world would speak out against the practice of cranking nosebands and girths so tight that sometimes I have found my hands are not strong enough to release them. In 2007, 12 years after I had first visited his farm and worked with him and Goldstern, Klaus Balkenhol taught a clinic during Equitana in Germany in which he recommended that riders loosen the traditionally tight nosebands and girths, mentioning that I had brought the matter of such restrictive tack inhibiting a horse's freedom of movement to his attention. At the time I was both surprised and elated, hoping that the riding community would prick up their ears and pay attention. Unfortunately, I do not feel that enough change has come to pass in this area, even with the support of such prominent and successful individuals.

Two Veterinarians Weigh In

It was a number of years ago that veterinarian Dr. Joyce Harman, author of several bestselling saddle fit books and DVDs (see p. 274 for more information), first stated in one of my newsletters that "a comfortable mouth is as important to a horse's happiness and performance as saddle fit, good shoeing, and tooth care."

"For years," she wrote, "in my quest to help riders improve their horses' comfort and performance, I have asked them to loosen tight nosebands. When one part of the horse is tight, the rest of the horse cannot move freely—just clench your own jaw and feel how far down your back and shoulders the tension travels.

"The key to understanding the effect of tight nosebands (and bitting, too) extends far beyond the mouth. It begins with the anatomy of the horse's tongue, head, and neck, and expands to include how the front part of the body affects movement of the whole horse. The tongue lies partly between the bones of the jaw (bars of the mouth) and above the jaw. Some of the tongue muscles connect to a small set of bones in the throat called the *hyoid bones* (figs. 10.8 A & B and see p. 216).

"Originating from the hyoid bones are two major neck muscles. One attaches to the sternum (*sternohyoideus*); the other to the inside of the shoulder (*omohyoideus*). Thus, there is a direct connection from the tongue to the sternum and shoulder along the bottom of the horse's neck. Consequently, if you have tension in the tongue, you have tension all the way down to the sternum and shoulder along the bottom of the neck, where you actually want suppleness. Once you have tension to the sternum, the horse cannot raise his back and use the commonly cited 'circle of muscles' that allow for collection and the self-carriage desired in dressage.

"Small muscles also connect the hyoid bones to the temporomandibular joint (TMJ) and the poll. The TMJ is an important center for nerves that control the horse's balance and proprioception (see p. 209). And the poll—its ability to bend and flex—is of central concern to the dressage rider. Because of the small muscles connecting them, there is a very close relationship (which few riders know about) between the horse's tongue, hyoid bones, TMJ, poll, head, and neck.

"When the horse's tongue is free and soft, all of this translates into a horse who is better able to move well, with coordination, improved balance, and a significantly lengthened stride."

Dr. Renee Tucker, a veterinarian certified in equine acupuncture and chiropractic and author of the book *Where Does My Horse Hurt* (Trafalgar Square Books, 2011) concurs with Dr. Harman. "The super-tight noseband," she says, "what I not-so-fondly refer to as 'STN,' not only keeps the horse's jaw from opening, but in a lot of cases prevents the lower jaw from moving forward and backward. When a horse is flexed at the poll, the lower jaw needs to move forward—just bend your own neck to bring your head toward your chest, and notice how your lower jaw moves forward to accommodate the movement.

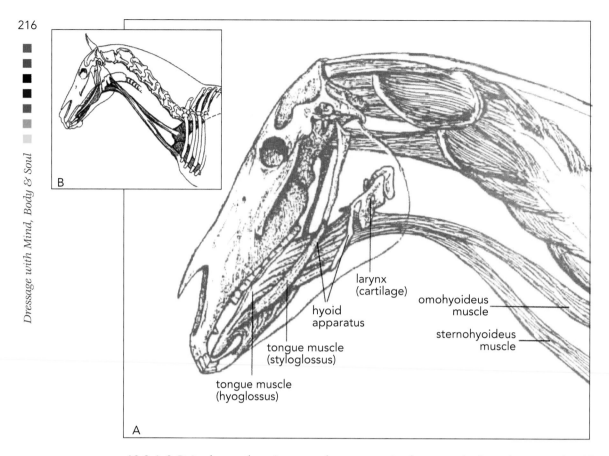

10.8 A & B As shown, there is a very close connection between the horse's tongue, hyoid bones, temporomandibular joint (TMJ), poll, head, and neck: some of the horse's tongue muscles attach to the hyoid bones from which stem two major neck muscles, one attaching to the sternum and the other to the inside of the shoulder.

"When the lower jaw is prevented from moving forward, the horse's tongue gets 'bunched up' in his mouth. The amount of 'bunching' depends on tongue size and the arch above the roof of the mouth (both of which vary from horse to horse). I believe this is why we see many horses with STN trying to stick their tongue out the side of their mouth—there is no room in there! Especially for breathing!

"The joint with the most proprioceptive nerves in the horse's entire body is the TMJ. When the horse's lower jaw cannot move, it cannot, therefore, 'transmit' accurate positioning data to the horse's body, which results in poor movement and performance.

"A tight noseband means the horse cannot breathe, cannot flex at the poll comfortably, and doesn't know where he is in space. I feel justified in saying that this is not desirable when trying to attain optimal performance from any horse, and is especially problematic in the case of the dressage horse."

"Freeing" the Hyoid Bones with the Tellington Training Bit

The *Tellington Training Bit* is a loose-shanked, stainless steel bit with a copper roller set in a high port that I use in training scenarios to help improve transitions, self-carriage, balance, and engagement, as well as soften the back and encourage flexion at the poll (figs. 10. 9 A & B). Dr. Joyce Harman (see p. 219) says that two of the reasons the *Tellington Training Bit* is so effective is because the high port and loose shanks free up the horse's tongue while the roller encourages tongue "softness." As I've explained, some of the horse's tongue muscles attach to the hyoid bones, from which two major neck muscles stem, attaching to the sternum and the shoulder (see fig. 10.8 B). Therefore, a "free and soft" tongue relieves pressure on the hyoid bones, translating into less tension in the neck muscles, and carrying all the way through to the horse's shoulders. A "free and soft" tongue enables the horse to carry himself better within minutes, with little or no input from the rider.

While I do not recommend that dressage riders use the *Tellington Training Bit* on a daily basis, it is a great tool for introducing the horse to an improved carriage, increased suppleness, and less dependence on contact. In addition, it helps break old "bad" patterns of behavior and way of going to make way for new, better ones.

Note: *The Tellington Training Bit* cannot be used with a closed-fist hand (fingertips touching your palms) or with your wrists "broken" inward. To work, it must be used by those with fine motor skills and a rein style similar to the method of the French school and espoused by riding master Captain Vladimir Littauer, with both reins held lightly over the top of the index finger and stabilized with the thumb, and with all fingers "alive and listening" so an elastic connection is established. I like to ride with the bottom rein (the "curb" rein as if in a double bridle) between my ring finger and pinky, and the top rein (the "bradoon") below my pinky and back up through my hand, exiting between index finger and thumb as described. Rein length and width also play an important role: both reins must be the same length, the top rein should be 1½ centimeters wide, and the bottom rein 1 centimeter wide. The ½ centimeter's difference makes it possible for you to tell when you are influencing the top or the bottom of the bit.

Riders new to the bit should work with someone on the ground who is familiar with it so they allow enough rein to enable the horse's neck to "telescope" forward and out, and thus his back to "swing."

Girthing Is Similar

Ideally, the horse's girth should have equal give on both sides to allow the horse to breathe freely and his rib cage to move evenly. The girth only needs to be

10.9 A & B It has been found that the *Tellington Training Bit* improves balance and engagement because it frees up the horse's tongue, and thus the muscles that attach to the hyoid bones. This mare responds favorably to the bit (A). I ride with the top rein on the outside of my little finger and with a longer rein than when using a snaffle (B).

The Experts

Dr. Joyce Harman graduated from Virginia Maryland Regional College of Veterinary Medicine in 1984 and became a member of the Royal College of Veterinary Surgeons in 1985. She is certified in veterinary acupuncture and chiropractic, and has completed advanced training in homeopathy, herbal, and Chinese medicine. Dr. Harman is a world-renowned saddle-fitting expert with several books and DVDs on the subject (see p. 274) and operates a holistic veterinary practice in Washington, Virginia (www.harmanyequine.com).

Dr. Renee Tucker received her doctorate in veterinary medicine from the University of Tennessee in Knoxville, Tennessee. She added her Certification for Animal Chiropractic (CAC) in 1998, and acupuncture certification in 2000. She is the author of the book *Where Does My Horse Hurt?* and runs a private veterinary practice specializing in equine acupuncture and chiropractic work in Redding, California (www.wheredoesmyhorsehurt.com).

tightened enough to secure the saddle in place—two large fingers should fit comfortably between the girth and the horse's ribs. As long as your saddle fits correctly (see more on this subject on p. 220), this is sufficiently tight. If you need to tighten your girth further because your saddle rotates or slips, then you have a serious saddle fit problem—or a very fat horse with low withers!

Overtightening the girth restricts the horse's breathing—undesirable in an athlete as reduced oxygen intake compromises performance. It causes discomfort that can range from acute to chronic, including sore muscles and accumulated scar tissue along the girth line, which can inhibit shoulder movement and thus cause gait deviations, such as shortened foreleg stride, poor extension, and lack of impulsion because it "hurts" to go forward and because tightness in the shoulders prevents hind limb engagement. Horses suffering from chronically overtightened girths may take a long time to warm up and exhibit discomfort while doing so, with a swishing tail, grinding teeth, or pinned ears. They may resist leg aids due to sore and constricted ribs, or buck when mounted or asked to go forward.

Front Leg Circles and *Shoulder Release* can help free up constricted shoulders due to past girthing practices and allow your horse to come "through," fully engaging from behind.

Saddles

It never fails to amaze me how often saddle fit is overlooked as a cause of spookiness, bucking, bolting, and a generally sour attitude. Many common horse behavior problems can be traced to pain or restriction as a result of an incorrectly fitting saddle. A pinching saddle restricts freedom of movement from the poll to the pelvis, creating discomfort, shortening stride, and causing imbalance, unsoundness, and incorrect movement. In addition, the dressage rider's goal is to encourage the horse to move "over the back" and essentially "round" up *into* the space beneath her seat. The saddle's gullet must allow the horse's back freedom of movement while the seat provides the rider a means of maintaining correct balance—unfortunately a characteristic not often achieved by dressage saddle manufacturers.

A saddle can be too narrow or set too far forward, jamming the shoulders and withers and inhibiting movement. Pressure from the pommel crowding the withers can be exacerbated when the horse tends to be high-headed, has a dropped or swayed back, or travels downhill. Some saddles do not have enough gullet clearance and compress the horse's withers, causing soreness. "Bridging," in which the front and back of the saddle make contact with the horse but the midsection does not, is a common cause of discomfort. A saddle that is too big for the horse is not stable; one that is too long may jab into the loins. The potential problem areas are numerous and complex, to say the least.

In addition, although there are more saddle-fitting "experts" available to the riding public today than ever before, saddle fit is truly a difficult science. It must take into consideration horses with challenging conformation (such as a dropped back or asymmetrical shoulders). It must include rider variables, as weight and balance change where and how pressure points occur. I've also seen horses wearing expensive, custom-made saddles that no longer fit properly, although they may have at one time, because when the horse gained or lost condition or weight, it impacted the way the saddle sat on the horse's back and the way the rider sat in the saddle.

In chapter 4, I discussed how Contact is one of the principles of the Training Scale, and also how—to me—it means more than rider's-hand-to-horse's-mouth. It means contact in all physical senses (as well as mental and emotional). In order to truly connect with your horse on all these levels, you need as little coming between you and your horse as possible. What *does* separate your seat and legs from direct contact with the horse—your saddle—must be a means of transmission of your aids, your feel, and your "heART." It must fit your horse comfortably; it must fit you comfortably. And it absolutely must not interfere with the horse's physical, mental, and emotional Balance as so many do.

When working toward a dressage goal with an athletic partner—your horse—it is imperative you have your saddle's fit analyzed and properly adjusted by a knowledgeable individual. Without an expert's assurance that your saddle is indeed right for your body, and right for your horse's, it may be holding you both back, causing unnecessary discomfort for your horse and unnecessary struggle (in maintaining a correct and balanced seat) for you. I list several sources of further information regarding saddle fit at the end of this book (see p. 274).

Just Think About Yourself for a Moment

Veterinarians' opinions aside, just take a moment to think about your own athletic body and how you ensure its ability to perform as you need it. The common analogy compares tight nosebands and girths and poor fitting saddles to a pair of shoes that are too small for you—perhaps trying to walk all day or dance all night in them. But this analogy has been around a long time and has inspired little change that I can see in the dressage community. (Perhaps because many of us sacrifice comfort for fashion—at least when it comes to footwear!)

Instead, I'd like you to think about how you dress for a training session, riding lesson, or show. Do you show up to ride your best in the brand new pair of riding boots you just purchased and have worn only once before? Not likely, as you know the top edge of the stiff new boots might bite into the back of your legs behind your knees when your feet are in the stirrups. This will be annoying and potentially painful after warming up, proving a distraction during your test and maybe causing you to hold your legs tensely in a way that eases your discomfort, sacrificing your position and ability to aid.

Do you wear the britches from three years ago that perhaps are too tight in the waist, digging into the flesh there, possibly leaving a mark on the skin when you unbutton them? Again, the discomfort caused would certainly prove problematic, inhibiting your ability to focus and to aid your horse correctly. Do you wear the too-small sports bra that makes it difficult for you to breathe? Do you wear the helmet that is too tight and causes a headache?

I feel confident saying that given the above, all of you would choose clothing and equipment for yourself that is the most comfortable and least distracting during your time in the saddle. In fact, millions of dollars are spent each year by manufacturers to develop such apparel—boots and britches and undergarments that promise comfort and freedom of movement as you ask your body to perform its athletic best, both in obvious and subtle manners.

It is then most egregious that many people expect differently of their horses. They wrap them tightly, constrict their tender flesh, bind their middle...then warm them up and tighten it all some more, sometimes with the help of mechanical cranks.

After all this, the horses are asked to extend and collect smoothly, bound lightly over the ground, focus on the most subtle of aids, and perform difficult collected movements for extended periods of time.

This is the equivalent of dressing you in stiff new boots, britches that are too tight, a too-small sports bra, and a helmet that doesn't fit, and then asking you to sit the trot for 45 minutes (without sacrificing proper position) while reciting the alphabet backward. To add to the stress of the scenario, someone will poke you in the ribs with a piece of metal every time you start to slouch or lose track of which letter you last stated aloud.

Sounds a little like a refined form of torture, doesn't it?

I have said it many times, in many places before, and I will say it again here. The trend that insists that dressage horses must be trained and competed in tight nosebands and saddles "clamped" in place with extremely tightened girths is unnecessary and unkind. As I have demonstrated, it goes against the recommendation of veterinary science and your own commonsense as an athlete. It is your responsibility as a dressage rider to develop your horse from the ground, and develop your seat through proper training, in order to control your horse from the saddle. When properly done, the techniques I've discussed in this book can provide an alternative to constrictive devices used in an attempt to achieve the highest level of cooperation.

Rider Skill and Attitude

The Color: Rider skill and attitude is the color *green*, the color of *Contact* and *Cooperation* (pp. 53 and 90).

The Intention: Target your thoughts to focus around your horse's willing and cooperative nature melding with your own stable, centered seat and positive attitude to establish an ideal connection at all points of horse-human contact.

Dressage is not alone with participants who demonstrate insufficient skill and a poor attitude. You can find examples throughout the horse industry, regardless of discipline. Quality instruction needs to be more affordable and easier to find in order to better nurture young and aspiring riders as they choose dressage as their passionate pursuit in life. Without an appropriate example set, many riders are at sea, overwhelmed by the sheer amount of information, methodology, tricks, and techniques presented. Where to turn? How to counter a difficult moment in the saddle? When to move up and move on?

More than anything else, aspiring dressage riders today need mentors they can count on for solid advice that has the horse's best interests at heart. One of the reasons for the suffering we see on the part of the dressage horse, one of the reasons so many people are resorting to forceful tactics, is quite simply that riders do not have the skill necessary to control their mount. Neither do they have the attitude to achieve that skill easily.

Skill

Any training technique used excessively can cause repetitive-motion stress in a horse. This has long been apparent in dressage, as well as other horse sports that emphasize repeated drilling of patterns and lateral movements, such as reining, cutting, and barrel racing. In particular, a heavy or unyielding hand and a driving seat leading to "chin-to-chest" positions on the part of the horse can contribute to tension and soreness throughout the horse's body, especially in the poll, shoulders, back, loins, and pelvis.

Earlier in this book I mentioned my concern with the modern trends of training dressage horses—namely Rollkur (hyperflexion) and LDR. Why do some dressage riders force their horse into these uncomfortable frames? I believe it is often because they simply can't restrain their horse any other way. The horse may be considered "hot" or "reactive"—and throughout this book I've provided a litany of reasons why this could indeed be the case. It is my opinion that usually, hot and reactive are symptoms of some other problem, and attempting to "contain" or "mask" the symptom with devices or abusive training techniques does not suit the goals that dressage has a "heART."

Using *Flat-Hand Body Exploration* (p. 104) and Grooming with Awareness (p. 202) and your powers of observation (p. 240), be on the alert for symptoms such as body soreness, uneven gait, a tight neck, a sour attitude, explosive or resistant behavior, stocking up, and pinned ears. All of these problems, and others, can be avoided by alternating your training schedule with trail rides, ground driving, or other types of cross-training. My *TTouches*, *Ground Exercises*, and *Ridden Work* offer many opportunities for expanding your horse's training routine, and keeping him interested and engaged in his work (figs. 10.10 A–G).

Attitude

I feel strongly that a rider's attitude is more important than his or her raw skill or technical ability. The best technical rider in the world will limit a horse's potential if her attitude doesn't recognize and honor the horse's individuality. On the other hand, if you have a compassionate attitude toward your horse

10.10 A–G Adding variety to your dressage training is integral to keeping your horse interested and willing in his work. *TTouches* from the saddle can provide you a positive work session where training goals are being met while at the same time feeding the physical, mental, and emotional needs of the horse. Riding with the *Lindell Sidepull* can also give your horse a break from the normal routine. I worked with French dressage rider and former star of Cavalia, Magali Delgado and her stallion Nacarado in 2009 (A). Here, I ride Nacarado in the *Lindell Sidepull* while performing *TTouches* from the saddle on his neck and shoulder (B & C). I use the back of my fingernails in the *Baby Chimp TTouch* and then the side of my hand on his head (D & E). When you can't reach easily, use whatever part of your hand is able to make a circular *TTouch*. The combination of *Lindell Sidepull* and *TTouches* encourage Nacarado to stretch beautifully forward and down (F) and find a happy balance (G).

that allows him the freedom to be comfortable and express his "side of the story," you're well on your way to a rewarding relationship.

Change your mind, open your heart (allow yourself to feel gratitude and to achieve heart coherence—see p. 71), and you can transform your horse.

Remember your potential for perfect functioning—and your horse's. This takes you back to the idea of *intention* (see p. 60) and how holding a positive picture of what you want for your horse's behavior, performance, and health, and for the relationship you share with him, can provide a meaningful path to the realm of success.

I've already mentioned some of the ideas I feel hold the most power when training and riding horses. The truth of the matter is, rider attitude is probably the first thing I should have mentioned on the first page of this book. Without a mind open to the possibilities presented by the next fresh new idea; without an attitude of willingness to embrace something that might deviate from your "norm" or push you out of your comfort zone; without a sense of excitement at the thought of change, rather than gloom, resistance, or trepidation; without these things, you may become a technically skilled rider, and you may be very successful indeed—but you will never be as successful as you really could be. The sky is not your limit, your attitude is. You will only climb as high as the positive *intention* you project before you. Dreams shouldn't be constrained by reality. Reality should subsist of the dreams you make come true.

What's in a Name?

The attitude you bring to the barn and into your horse's world affects the horse in myriad ways. In wild herds, horses communicate with each other via body language and a kind of *intent* that is so subtle as to defy the human eye. These forms of "silent language" preserved the equine species for thousands of years, and so the skills have been honed and sharpened over time.

This means the horse senses whatever you carry with you, be it joy or sadness, anxiety or excitement. He reads the way you carry your body and the inflections in your voice. Whether you are aware of it or not, certain words and phrases cue your mouth and tongue to behave in certain ways—and so, for example, curse words almost always sound "bad," even when you use them laughingly. There is even a modern movement called "creative swearing" that substitutes words that are acceptable by societal standards for those that are not, and uses only context and inflection to get the meaning across. Believe me, the system is just as effective in voicing anger and frustration, and just as hurtful.

This leads us to the words you use around your horse every day, how you say them, and how they ultimately affect him. To me, one of the most important concepts on this list is the horse's "barn name."

Whatever the breed and whatever the sport, it is common to provide the horse an "easy" name—whether an abbreviated form of something longer, or a term of affection completely unrelated. Generally, I'd say not a whole lot of thought goes into choosing a horse's barn name—after all, it has no official capacity and may even change upon the lease or sale of the horse to a new rider or owner. However, the barn name wields great power, and I'll tell you why:

1 **The Barn Name's Baggage:** Let's say your registered Hanoverian goes by "Joe" in the barn. He came with that name, and honestly, you haven't thought much about it. The thing is, "Joe" was also the name of the first man you ever loved—a relationship that ended badly and with you hurt and angry. All of that may have happened a long time ago, but whether you are conscious of it or not, every time you say "Joe," some little bit of you, deep inside, feels hurt and angry again. And that little bit of feeling seeps out into the greater energy you project— in this case, almost always when you are with your horse. Poor Joe the Horse. He doesn't understand why you are always hurt and angry when you are with him.

I've met horses with other kinds of barn names—silly ones that actually detract from their stature and in effect demoralize them, and others that infer a troublemaking nature, or a "dark side." A name like "Mouse" implies meekness or a lack of courage, while "Diablo" argues for explosiveness and temper. The barn name is a lesson in self-fulfilling prophecy—a prediction that, directly or indirectly, causes itself to become true. So give your horse a name he can be proud of, and one that you can use without hesitation, only in conjunction with him and the joyfulness you share as riding partners.

2 **What Water Tells Us About the Power of Words:** In 2001, Japanese scientist Dr. Masaru Emoto's book *The Hidden Messages in Water* (Atria Books, 2001) became an international sensation. Using high-speed photography, Dr. Emoto showed how crystals formed in frozen water reveal changes when specific thoughts are directed toward them.

Dr. Emoto and his team wrapped paper with words in different languages typed on it around frozen bottles of water, then captured images of the crystals formed on the surface in the 20 to 30 seconds after the temperature rises enough to cause the ice to melt. "Thank you" in different languages resulted in beautiful crystals of different shapes, while "Fool" produced crystals that were malformed and fragmented. "Let's do it!" created attractive crystals, while "Do it!" formed hardly any crystals at all.

In the brief moment of time between states of being—frozen and liquid—water exposed how the "vibration" of good words has a positive effect on the world, whereas the vibration from negative words has the power to destroy. (Dr. Emoto also used music in his experiments, the results of which I mention on p. 229.)

It is argued that because our cells are made up of almost 90 percent water, words have a similar effect on us. Since learning this more than a decade ago, I have become very aware of the words I select because I know they can affect my health and that of the horses and friends around me.

Use of Music and Sound

The Color: The use of music and sound is represented by the color *blue*, the color of *Suppleness* and *Connection with Rider* (pp. 53 and 90).

The Intention: Target your thoughts so your favorite piece of music provides the soundtrack to a fantastic riding session, where your horse is elastic and listening and "one" with you.

It has long been common to use music in horse and livestock barns around the world, both to entertain and relax farm staff and the animals within. In recent years, music has been shown to have both a *physical* and a *mental* therapeutic effect on human subjects. Research reported at the American Society of Hypertension in 2008 showed that listening to classical, Celtic, or Indian music for just 30 minutes a day could significantly lower blood pressure. In fact, studies have shown that "music therapy" is extremely effective in many areas, including physical rehabilitation and facilitation of movement, motivation, emotional support, and expression of feelings.

I feel that the right kind of music can indeed add interest to and be a soothing influence in the horse's environment. It can provide companionship to the horse stabled alone. It can calm the reactive or anxious horse when stalled, help a horse focus during training, encourage relaxation or stimulation during warm up and cool down, and take the edge off a nervous equine athlete before competition. On the other hand, scientific studies have shown that cows exposed to noxious noises have decreased milk production and increased presence of stress hormones in milk obtained (Guttman, H.). I have no doubt "noise pollution" has a similar effect on the horse.

I have found music to be very useful in relaxing horses with stereotypic behaviors when confined—stall-walkers, for example. A number of years ago, I secured a small cassette player with classical guitar music onto the halter of a stall-walking stallion in Germany, and taped headphones near the base of his ears. Amazingly, the horse stopped his pacing and stood quietly with a relaxed neck. When you watched his eyes, you could see them change as the music altered in rhythm, tempo, and volume. As long as the music played, the stallion did not stall-walk.

Sounds That Influence Brain Waves

Dr. Helene Guttman is a former university professor and researcher, with extensive publications in areas of neuroscience, immunology, biochemistry, nutrition and microbiology. Dr. Guttman was one of the first to examine

Musical Preferences: Plants and Water Have an Opinion

In the early 1970s, Dorothy Retallack's book *The Sound of Music and Plants* (Devorss & Co., 1973) detailed an experiment she conducted at the Colorado Women's College in Denver. Using separate laboratories containing the same species of plants, Retallack piped in different types of music then recorded the daily growth of each plant. She also had one control lab where there was no music playing. Results showed the plants in the laboratory where music was played daily for three hours a day grew twice as large and became twice as healthy as those in a music-free environment. When different types of music were compared, it was found that the plants that heard rock and roll (for example) turned out sickly and small whereas the group listening to "soothing" music (such as Indian sitar music) became large and healthy, and actually grew bending toward the speakers just as they might bend toward sunlight.

In the New York Times Bestseller *The Hidden Messages in Water*, Japanese scientist Masaru Emoto demonstrates how molecules of water are affected by our thoughts, words, and feelings (further evidence of the interconnectedness of all life on this planet—see where I delve into this idea on p. 60). Emoto also shows the impact music can have on the formation of water crystals, with photographs of crystals formed when a water bottle was placed between two speakers. Beethoven resulted in fanciful, detailed crystals; Mozart in great beauty and circular patterns; Bach in melodious complexity; and heavy metal in no crystals at all. (See more about Dr. Emoto's work with water crystals on p. 227.)

documented studies of the use of sound to modify behavior in humans, and then apply it to horses.

Of interest to the dressage rider, and indeed all horse owners, is Dr. Guttman's research in conjunction with the The Monroe Institute—an organization that provides experiential education programs and research facilitating the exploration of human consciousness. Robert A. Monroe was the founder of Hemi-Sync® (www.hemi-sync.com), an audio-guidance technology that uses complex, multilayered audio signals acting together to create a resonance that is reflected in unique brain wave forms characteristic of specific states of consciousness—deep relaxation or focused attention, for example. The result is a focused, whole-brain state known as hemispheric synchronization (Hemi-Sync), where the left and right brain hemispheres work together in a state of coherence (see more about the left and right brain hemispheres on p. 29).

In controlled studies, Dr. Guttman found that horses, as well as humans, respond to Hemi-Sync signals with brain synchronization. In one of her studies Dr. Guttman used music developed by the composer to fit the tempo of 50 to 70 beats per minute—a rhythm found to promote relaxation and enhance learning and retention skills in humans. Hemi-Sync signals were embedded under the music, and resulted in similar effects in the horse. This suggests that Hemi-Sync technology, along with music, could indeed be used to reduce stress during travel, calm or gear-up prior to competition, enhance sleep or rest, and enrich the stable environment.

Play!

The Color: Play is represented by the color *red*, the color of *Collection* and *Change* (pp. 53 and 92).

The Intention: Target your thoughts so you envision a fantastic transformation before you, as if your horse is emerging from a cocoon and finding himself a joyful ball of energy and impulsion.

Part of establishing a means of caring for and training the horse that improves his well-being in mind, body, and soul, is acknowledging that "Drill, drill, drill," may get you an efficient soldier who obediently follows orders—but don't you want more than a soldier for a partner? Dressage as *art* requires inspiration, enthusiasm, and my favorite word—"sparkle." This means practice and preparation must be infused with joy every day, and every step of the way.

How best to make dressage fun for your horse and fun for you? The secret ingredient is simple, really.

Play.

That's right. Incorporate games in your training regimen. Intersperse lateral movements with brief moments of frivolity. Juxtapose several days' hard work in the ring with a relaxing afternoon stroll on the trail. Surprise your horse with a morning where you hand-graze him and treat him to some soothing, recuperative *TTouches* that you know he loves.

It may be hard to imagine a top-tier dressage barn where smiles and laughter reign, despite ambition and serious application to riding study. But in fact, it is just such a scenario that might ensure dedication to equitation and proper training of the horse would some day add up to the glorious partnership of which dressage dreams are made.

Of course, *play* isn't simply an alternative to your usual schooling routine—it is in some ways the alter ego you want to invite to Sunday dinner. As I mentioned at the very beginning of this book, you can transform what you think of as dressage *work* into dressage *play*, by simply changing the way you think of your workouts. Your horse will sense your shift in attitude, and you might be surprised to find how much more quickly you conquer training goals when "have fun" is your priority instead of an unusual side effect.

Tricks, Games, and Agility

French riding master Philippe Karl spent years as a member of the French national riding school in Saumur, becoming an *Ecuyer* with the prestigious Cadre Noir. Today he is known and respected for his many books and DVDs, as well as the *École de Légèreté*—his "school of lightness," which offers a three-year training course based on the principle of "absolute respect for the horse."

Those in the dressage world may very well know of Philippe Karl and the mark he has made spreading the French style of classical equitation around the globe; however, they may not know that he says, "Trick training may not seem 'serious enough' for 'serious riders,' but it is the means of helping humans make more of their horses than athletes or beasts of burden—it is one of the best ways to make your horse your friend."

Of course, the kinds of "tricks" we see in dramatic stage shows or performed by horses in films are far from what some of us might desire to spend our limited time and energy doing. It can take just as much time to teach a horse to sit, kneel, or lie down as it can to teach him tempi changes. Really, what Philippe Karl is saying is that there are lots of "little" games you can play with your horse that can add an element of fun to your training while engaging his mind fully and still having a practical application.

A few good examples are my *Ground Exercises*, some of which incorporate obstacles in the Playground for Higher Learning. They offer a refreshing change from the 10- and 20-meter circle routine, while building the horse's sense of self and security and increasing his Confidence and Capacity for Learning along the way. Working your horse from the ground through the *Labyrinth,* over the *Platform, Teeter-Totter,* or *Star* may feel like a deviation from the school figures you depend upon to help you ascend the Classical Training Scale and climb the rungs of the dressage levels. But, in fact, this kind of groundwork goes a long way to shoring up what you've already built— that is, it buttresses your foundation for a more solid end structure. (I talked about what the Tellington Method can do specifically in terms of the Training Scale on p. 95.)

You might even consider teaching your horse some agility movements to give you a fun and engaging activity to do together on your "days off" from your regular dressage schooling. Horse Agility is a relatively new sport that began in the United Kingdom and is now becoming popular in Europe and the United States. Involving the successful navigation of specific movements and obstacles, either in hand or at liberty, Horse Agility requires the same unique partnership between horse and rider, and the same precision and discipline that enhances your performance as a team in the dressage arena. You can find out more about Horse Agility at www.thehorseagilityclub.com.

"Dancing"

Magali Delgado and Frédéric Pignon—the founding (and married) stars of the stage show *Cavalia* that took the world by storm when it began in North America in 2003—have become my very good friends since I first met them in Los Angeles on tour eight years ago. In my opinion they are two of the finest horsemen in history. Their unique ability to relate to the heart and mind of their horses has astounded and inspired. Their repeated displays of artistry with stallions at liberty, usually in front of large crowds in cramped quarters, are legendary.

I have been lucky enough to spend a lot of time with Frédéric and Magali at their home in Southern France, and to witness how they interact with their horses in both training and performance scenarios (figs. 10.11 A & B). I love the way Frédéric always "waits" for his horse to be ready before expecting him to perform—he always gives the horse a few moments to romp before inviting him to stand beside him, where Frédéric likes to start their work together with some *Mouth, Nostril,* and *Ear TTouches* (figs. 10.12 A–C). The muzzle has a direct connection to the limbic system, the part of the brain that controls emotions, and *Ear TTouches* have long proven to instill calm in nervous or frightened animals. And so, beginning this way allows Frédéric to make an immediate connection, build trust, and help the horse relax (very important when performing in front of a crowd of thousands, as Frédéric and his horses

10.11 A & B I have been lucky enough to spend a lot of time with Frédéric Pignon (A) and Magali Delgado (B)—liberty trainers, dressage riders, and the original stars of Cavalia—at their home in Southern France. They both regularly incorporate *TTouch* in their work with their horses, on the ground and in the saddle, in training and during performance.

234

10.12 A–C *Mouth TTouches, Nostril TTouches,* and *Ear TTouches* have long proven to instill calm in nervous or frightened animals. Frédéric uses them with his horses in order to make an immediate connection, build trust, and help them relax.

often do!) Then, he will suggest a little game, something he knows the horse enjoys and something to ensure the horse remains interested in the learning process and intended lesson.

In the book he wrote together with Magali, *Gallop to Freedom* (Trafalgar Square Books, 2009), Frédéric says: "The essence of a brilliant performance by two people is not just that they do dance steps perfectly and in time to the music, but that they add an emotional quality that lifts the performance into another realm. I strive to achieve this emotional element with my horses. We both have to be totally concentrated on what we are doing. I can suggest games and sometimes the horse will show me he wants to try something... My job is to create the background, the mood, the feeling of security, and a readiness to respond and to reward with my approval. The 'dances' are not always the same...at any time, a horse can come up with something new, unexpected, and wonderful."

Grand Prix to Liberty

In addition to being a stage performer, Magali is a superb rider and top dressage competitor. "I never have long sessions of work without introducing periods of play," she says. "My aim is to make the sessions a pleasure for both of us."

Magali has shared many stories of her wonderful Lusitano Dao, but the one I remember most, and that best demonstrates the importance of incorporating play in day-to-day training, is featured in *Gallop to Freedom:*

Over the years, Magali actively competed Dao in Europe although Dao was also involved in the various stage shows and "spectaculars" Magali and Frédéric choreographed and performed on a regular basis. A pinnacle moment was when Magali and Dao won second place amongst top company at a Grand Prix—the winner that day was the French champion at year's end. It was a huge honor, and one not easily attained in the case of a Lusitano competing at the country's highest level against primarily Warmbloods.

After the awards ceremony, the show organizer asked if Frédéric would be willing to give a demonstration of liberty work during the evening's special programming. Frédéric hesitated, explaining that the horses he usually used for such performances were at home and only Dao, who had performed a strenuous test earlier that day, was available. As the organizer was persisting, an eavesdropping competitor remarked that a serious dressage event was neither time nor place for foolish games. So, of course, Frédéric immediately agreed to do the demonstration!

That evening, Frédéric and Dao gave an astounding liberty performance, with the stallion rising to the occasion—sitting, kneeling, lying down, galloping, bowing, and doing the Spanish walk, piaffe, and passage. The judges from the afternoon's competition told Magali how utterly refreshing it was to see a horse like Dao—happy, relaxed, and not showing any signs of the stress so commonly seen in Grand Prix dressage mounts. He joyfully demonstrated the same movements required in the top levels of international dressage competition, but naked of tack, free of restraint, and by his own impetus. He was vibrant proof that horses can love what they are doing and be willing to do it at the slightest invitation.

Magali and Frédéric always finish the story by mentioning how after the liberty show, they led Dao to an available paddock so they could turn him out for a romp and a roll (figs. 10.13 A & B). Another trainer approached and urged them not to because Dao was "far too valuable" to be set loose to his own devices. Of course, the very reason for Dao's value—his spirit and willingness and top performance that day—was that Magali and Frédéric always let him be a horse, before and above everything else. It says much about the world of competitive dressage that this trainer could not see how stifling that spirit, as he urged Magali and Frédéric to consider, could easily sap the horse of his "worth," transforming him from a sparkling vision to just another obedient soldier.

Pondering Play

Dao's story is an example of what could be. Yes, he is a particularly talented animal. Yes, his rider and trainers are blessed with remarkable intuition and ability. But mostly, they respect the horse for being a horse. Regardless of education level, the educated dressage horse gets bored. Regardless of general domesticity, the once wild equine gets stir crazy. Regardless of age and temperament, the social equine enjoys a game or two, every now and again. By allowing for these entirely natural behaviors and engaging your horse in play, you effectively nurture his instinctive spirit rather than tamping down the embers and effectively putting out his flame.

In order to be successful in this effort, you have to be clear in your own mind about what is "work" and what is "play." In other words, your *intention* must delineate between what is the horse's "lesson" for the day, and what is a treat or reward. This can vary from horse to horse depending on his likes and dislikes, strengths and weaknesses. And it can range from trail riding to trick training. The important thing is that you allow time for your horse to play a little *every time* you work—like practicing piaffe while he is wearing a *Liberty Neck Ring* only. In this way, the "work" (piaffe) is associated with the "play" (riding bridleless) and so it, too, becomes a pleasurable experience, free from stress, and one in which the horse is more willing to participate.

10.13 A & B Magali and her Grand Prix stallion Dao at the extended trot early in his dressage career (A), and Dao at home, just "being a horse" (B). I love working with Magali and Frédéric because their horses have wonderfully social lives and freedom.

If you do integrate little games and tricks into your training repertoire, maintain your horse's enthusiasm for the activity and acknowledge his intelligence by restricting the number of repetitions you request. In fact, this rule should apply to your dressage schooling, as well. It is important to recognize when your horse "gets" the lesson. Repeating a move 50 times in a row is no longer considered ideal teaching methodology. Studies of equine learning at the University of Pennsylvania School of Veterinary Medicine in Philadelphia recognize that a horse is still digesting a lesson up to three days later.

Note that play requires mutual respect and the same "boundaries" necessary in your day-to-day interaction with your horse (see p. 18). Even when engaging in a moment of affection, a hug, or a fun-filled game, clear and fair boundaries ensure that you and your horse stay safe.

THE TELLINGTON METHOD AND YOU

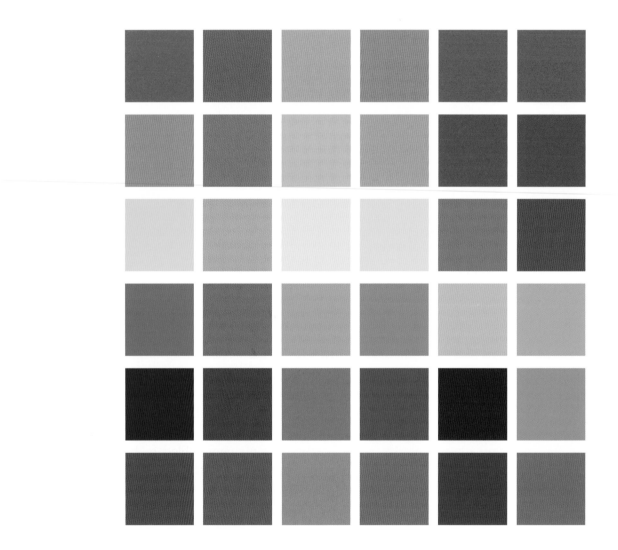

11

.......What You Can Do to Improve Your Horse's Performance

In reality, I've already given you a choice of many different avenues that can lead to the same desired end result. The nice thing is, some of these roads closely parallel each other, so you can travel two, three, or more at once. With all the tools you now have at the ready, you are primed and positioned to become a better dressage rider who better deals with her horse—and if you can better deal with your horse, then you will handle all manner of life circumstances with patience and positivity. Your children, your friends, your career—all will benefit from the pursuit of dressage with "heART."

That said, there are a few major themes that should be considered distinct from the other material we have already covered.

Time

One of the most important elements of dressage with mind, body, and soul is your use of *time*. I have already acknowledged the fact that today's society does not allot time as it should, and neither does it breed and then nurture humans with a sense of time "on their side." The result is a state of "perma-urgency," that constant activation of stress hormones I mentioned on p. 200, which leads to "too much" adrenaline, and a number of physical and mental side effects.

Regardless of their state of domesticity, horses have not been subject to the "shortening" or "quickening" of time as we have. They have not evolved to "keep up" with modern technological demands. They require pacing and patience. This is one of the most important things you can bring to your dressage training, and indeed, to your regular, day-to-day handling of your horse. Time.

When I work with a horse, I take my time introducing myself, whether for the first time ever or for the first time that day. I take the time to Groom with Awareness (see p. 202) and allow myself the mental and emotional space to devote all my attention to the horse. I lead by example—remember, horses "mirror" our thoughts and actions—so with my relaxed and attentive movements, the horse can walk or stand with a long neck and lowered head, a learning and trusting posture, from the start. I do not compartmentalize the time "before I ride" and "when I ride"—it is all fluid.

You need to allow and encourage the horse to listen to his body. Do not constantly interact or distract him, or prevent him from looking back over a shoulder or reaching down to scratch his nose on his foreleg. It is not lost on the horse that he is expected to obey all the time—especially in the sport of dressage, where still in many texts you can find the word "submission" used as a main goal and a testament to the quality of the horse's training. When you allow the time to read the horse's responses, using them to inform and guide your work, then you make the horse feel understood by a considerate fellow being, one who gives him time to feel, to react, to integrate, to be seen, and to be respected.

Today it is often professed that you need a training plan, that the horse responds best to routine, much like a two-year-old child. I do not necessarily feel that this is true. It is not that your work with your horse should be aimless and without purpose—on the contrary, you should have goals that you visualize (see p. 245) and as we've discovered, you need to handle and ride your horse with clear intent (see p. 60). However, you do not need a set routine in attaining your goal, you need to take the time to observe and listen, and let the horse's reaction to your touch, your posture, and your connection via seat, hand, legs, and heart, lead you.

> "Time is not absolute: what we call linear time is simply a reflection of how we perceive change."
>
> —*Deepak Chopra*

Observation

As a horseman, as the "keeper" of the powerful four-legged animal we know as the horse, it is your responsibility to hone your powers of observation so that you can tell your horse is trying to tell you something. You speak a different language from the horse, and while certainly, you and your horse may find common ground and a means of understanding each other, that doesn't negate the fact that sometimes he doesn't understand what you want, and sometimes you don't know what is bothering him.

The horse is *always* talking to you. He is constantly conveying signs of stress, fatigue, lack of understanding, and lack of ability. As I shared earlier in this book, I distinctly remember the evening session of the symposium with Dr. Reiner Klimke (see sidebar, p. 21) when my sister, Robyn Hood, publicly stated that while most riders have heard about "Horse Whisperers," with *TTouch* we are interested in "listening to the whispers of the horse."

Avoiding Overfacing

In addition to noting signs of stress or fatigue, it is the rider's responsibility to sense when a horse is incapable of performing at a certain level. Sometimes resistance appears only because a horse is truly not built in a way that enables him to move in the way you, your trainer, your level, or your current test, requires.

Many years ago I was giving a clinic at the US Equestrian Team headquarters in Gladstone, New Jersey, and a rider asked me to have a look at a mare she intended to compete at Grand Prix. The mare, a 16.2-hand Warmblood, was angry and reactive when asked to perform upper-level movements. The rider felt the mare was intentionally resistant to avoid work and so pushed her, which only exacerbated the problem.

This particular mare, although well conformed in many ways, had a short, heavy neck with a stiff, rigid crest—and upon examination, it was very sore. Her neck was simply not made for the collected frame required at the highest levels of dressage. I recommended the owner sell her to a lower-level rider who would require less from her, competing the horse at a level where she'd be more comfortable.

I remember a similar situation with an Irish Thoroughbred who was being ridden in an overcollected dressage frame. The rider rode him with heavy contact on a short rein with a strong driving seat to "pull the horse together." The problem was, in several ways this horse wasn't built to take this degree of collection, so he would literally bolt in an attempt to flee from the psychological stress and physical pain.

When your horse exhibits problematic behavior, both a veterinary examination and careful consideration of his conformation should precede the label of sour, lazy, or resistant. It may be that, in fact, your horse really can't do what you're asking of him. Open your eyes and your ears; observe and listen.

Breathing in Rhythm

Breath is communication and sends a message to your horse whether you are tense or relaxed. Unless you have practiced breath-awareness exercises off the horse, you may find yourself unconsciously holding your breath when you concentrate. Holding your breath creates stiffness and tension in your body.

Many people tend to breathe shallowly, into the upper chest area, stopping the inhalation there. Instead, take a full breath into your chest and continue to breathe down into your belly, and even lower, as if you are expanding a balloon. I often imagine my breath going down my legs and into the earth so it can mingle with the rhythm and breath of the planet—this serves to ground me. Develop an awareness of your breath, experimenting with it until it feels even, rhythmic, and easy. Conscious breathing will aid in stilling and focusing your mind, relaxing your neck and shoulders, and softening your hands. I frequently practice breathing in through my nose and out through pursed lips, emitting a a light "chhheeewwwuuu" sound as I send the sound upward from my tongue. The horse can hear this and it will help *him* to breathe more deeply. Any time you work with your horse to change his behavior, remember to breathe slowly. With practice your horse will mirror your breathing.

One trick I use when working with nervous riders and horses is singing. Singing to yourself not only keeps your mind from traveling down the path of negativity, it also keeps you breathing. When you feel your horse start to tense under you, or you are approaching a corner of the arena where your horse habitually shies, sing a little song to yourself, and *visualize* (see p. 245) your horse maintaining focus on you and your aids and trotting quietly through the problematic space.

How to Breathe

As I mentioned early on in this book, breathing exercises are integral to find *heart coherence* and *forming intention* (see pp. 71 and 60). My *Method* has long primarily focused on slow, rhythmical breathing, in through the nose and out through the mouth, using your diaphragm so that your belly slightly protrudes on the "ins," and pulls in toward your spine on the "outs."

In 2011, I had an intense travel schedule that took me all over the world and allowed me to meet some amazingly wonderful people, along with their delightful companion animals. When I came home to Hawaii for some time off the road to work on a number of books I was writing and to prepare for the beginning of the New Year, I was as tired as I had ever remembered being. One afternoon, I felt I simply could not work at the computer for another moment. I usually do a walking/breathing exercise to relax and rejuvenate my cells, but on this occasion, I actually didn't feel I had the energy to walk, so I settled down for my standard 12-minute power nap.

However, I sensed I needed to "give my cells" a special boost, that I should do some deep breathing instead of napping. I've been practicing and teaching breathing techniques for more than 20 years. I have a ritual of sorts to help me focus, energize, and "cleanse" my body, and I felt at that moment more than any time prior, I needed to "empty out" the carbon dioxide and "welcome in" the oxygen. So, while lying in my bed, I performed the following four steps—an easy breathing exercise that I call *Orca Breathing*:

Step 1 Breathe in through your nose, long and slow, really feeling your lungs expand from the top of your chest to your pubic bone.

Step 2 Hold your breath as long as you comfortably can.

Step 3 Slowly and consciously breathe out through pursed lips, creating "back pressure" to ensure that you empty the lungs completely of carbon dioxide. I find it helps to picture the alveoli in your lungs like little "balloons" deflating completely, exuding the carbon dioxide they've acquired via "gas exchange." The alveoli are in essence tiny interlinking "pockets" that provide a location for oxygen absorption into the bloodstream. They have thin walls surrounded by capillaries that allow them to "swap" oxygen for carbon dioxide.

Step 4 "Hold" the empty space in your lungs, for the same amount of time you held your breath in Step 2, before breathing in through your nose again.

The result of this easy breathing exercise was dramatic and almost immediate—within five minutes I was no longer tired. I felt exuberantly reenergized. My cells were reoxygenated and my capability to concentrate and tap my creativity was rejuvenated. I sprung from my bed and got to work!

Since that moment, I have found this simple exercise to be invaluable as a centering and energizing technique. You can perform it in the car on the way to the barn, before you mount, and even on your horse. In clinics I often have riders perform the breathing exercise in rhythm with the horse's walk: breathe in for four steps, hold it for four steps, breathe out through pursed lips for eight steps (to create that "back pressure"—see above), hold the empty space in your lungs for four steps, then breathe in again. The number of walk strides you use for each step of this breathing exercise can change according to your wind and your cardiovascular conditioning.

Creating "Peak Performance"

I introduced you to Anna Wise and the work I did with her back on p. 31. Wise analyzed her studies of brain-wave patterns and developed a means of cultivating ways for humans to increase their emotional health and well-being, improve their communication skills, and become better leaders and problem-solvers. In her evolutionary book *The High Performance Mind,* she explains how to recognize moments of "peak performance" and then train your brain to attain this state of enlightenment, clarity, or incredible athleticism (aka "being in the zone), and have it, in effect, "on call," that is, at the ready when you need it most.

So how do you do this? Wise says you must begin by developing your Awakened Mind—as you discovered on p. 31, using the Tellington Method in your work with your horse stabilizes your brain-wave frequencies and engages both brain hemispheres. Meditative practices are also beneficial (and useful in regular visualization techniques, as well—see p. 245). You need to learn to set an *intention* before beginning an activity, and then focus and concentrate during it. Finally, you must be able to recognize the state of peak performance and reward yourself with positive feedback every time you experience it, no matter how brief the moment, and regardless of where in life it appears. It may appear in a moment of clarity as you are preparing dinner, addressing the recipe with feel and intuition rather than following the instructions on the page of the cookbook. By recognizing this state and validating it in your kitchen, you can harness that moment of power and transfer the confidence and clarity you experienced to a training session in the riding arena.

Tips for Attaining Peak Performance on a Regular Basis

- Whenever you attain a peak moment, notice how your body feels and how your mind feels: How are you sitting, moving, or breathing? On what are you focusing?

  For example, during a rock-solid canter depart perhaps you notice that your weight is settled just a little to the left, your chest lifted only so slightly before you ask, and your breath exits through pursed lips as you feel your horse's inside hind reach under you. Your eyes are focused softly ahead of you on the corner coming onto the short side of the arena.

- Attach symbols, images, colors, or words (remember our Mind Map of the Tellington Training Scale—see p. 55) that describe how your mind and body feel.

  In their respective books, Sally Swift, creator of Centered Riding, and Jane Savoie, Olympic dressage rider and coach, do a wonderful job providing ideas for images you can attach to how your mind and body feel during moments of peak performance. Do your legs feel long and strong like the roots of tree? Are your hands quietly holding two glasses of water without spilling a drop—even at the trot? Or, perhaps, in your mind, you picture your lower body as blue and supple and your torso as violet and balanced. Use the tricks and techniques that best help you build body awareness.

- Notice exterior variables during your moments of peak performance: what time it is, where you are, how warm or cold it is, how full or hungry you are, how tired or rested. These allow you to set up the right conditions to encourage peak performance when and where you want it, however often, and even for sustained periods.

  For example, record the surrounding details present when you regularly have riding breakthroughs—moments of synchronicity when you feel yourself unite and "meld" with your horse as you understand exactly *what your instructor is saying and how to perform a movement, without even thinking through the order and intensity of multiple aids. Perhaps they always happen during early morning lessons when the sun is just coming up, the air is a little crisp, your nose is a little cold, and all you've had is a single cup of coffee and a granola bar.*

  This provides a number of factors you can try to recreate at different times and places in order to experience the same sense of peak performance. It also gives you a base for changing *the variables you seem to need to ride your best—say, working to perform just as well late in the day as you do at first light (after all, you have little control over when you are scheduled to ride your test in competition).*

Visualization and "Sensualization"

The power visualization and imagery can have in sports and on athletic performance is no secret in this day and age. Huge numbers of books have been written on the subject, for all manner of pursuits, whether involving the mind, body, or soul. Reserve rider on the 1992 US Olympic dressage team and coach at three Olympic games Jane Savoie has even written two books specifically for riders that explore the use of visualization and imagery in cultivating your "winning attitude," and thus your ultimate success in the saddle (see p. 274 for more about her books).

Horses "read" our mental pictures, and visualization is inextricably intertwined with your power of intent; therefore, it is an important facet of the Tellington Method. I firmly believe that you cannot achieve better performance and better behavior on the part of your dressage horse unless you are capable of picturing what it is you want of your horse—the rhythmical half-pass, the square halt, the quiet tail during a canter transition, the supple circle at a medium trot. Many riders have a hard time with visualization; in fact, they write it off because they feel they are "logical thinkers" or "too left-brained" to indulge in "such nonsense." But as I've addressed in this book, visualization is part of an important element of "hemispheric balance" currently missing from the performance of many dressage riders. Cultivating your ability to use imagery is a part of the big picture in a big way.

In *The High-Performance Mind*, Anna Wise admits that a great many individuals have a very hard time effectively visualizing. She explains that she feels this is because we don't realize we have *all of our senses* to use in the process—that "visualization" would be far more attainable for many more people if it were called "sensualization."

In other words, you don't just see the picture in your mind, you hear it, touch it, smell it, taste it, and experience related movement in time and space. Let's say you're "sensualizing" your opening halt before the judges during your last test of the season as you try to earn the score you need to win the year-end championship:

- You *see* the halt, square and straight, on the centerline.

- You *hear* the jingle of the curb chain as your horse gently mouths the bit, the connection soft in your hands.

- You *smell* the faint odor of sweat emanating from beneath the saddle, where you know his coat is damp following your warm-up.

- You *taste* the cherry chapstick you applied to your lips as your groom wiped off your boots prior to hearing the judge's entry bell.

- You *feel* the muscles in the triangle of your seat tensing, your fingers closing, and your back tightening, all almost imperceptibly as you ask for the halt, and then the slight release you offer when your horse responds with immediate willingness and fluidity.

Using your senses in your visualization increases clarity and vividness, and Anna Wise found it actually improved alpha brainwave production—the brainwaves associated with daydreaming and fantasizing. The stronger the imagined image, the more senses you involve in your visualized *intention*, the more successful your outcome.

Ho 'oponopono

Ho 'oponopono (ho-o-pono-pono) is an ancient Hawaiian practice of reconciliation and forgiveness, traditionally used when a friend or family member is physically ill. I discovered it when I read the book *Zero Limits* by Joe Vitale

(Wiley, 2008). Vitale tells the story of Dr. Ihaleakala Hew Len, a therapist in Hawaii who cured an entire ward of criminally insane patients without ever seeing any of them. The psychologist studied each inmate's chart and then looked within himself to see how who he was could have created that person's illness. As he steadily improved himself as a person, each patient's state of mind also improved. "I was simply healing the part of me that created them," he told Vitale.

Dr. Len was working via the idea of total responsibility (that wherever you are and whatever your life is like, you created it through who you are and the choices you have made) but with a twist that makes this "pop psychology" concept less about "me" and more about "you" and everyone else, for that matter. Dr. Len thinks that total responsibility for your life means that everything in your life, simply because it is in your life, is your responsibility. Big or small, distant or local, everything you experience and feel is bad or that you do not like, it is up to you to heal, because they simply exist as you know them as projections of something within yourself.

"Healing" others, for Dr. Len, meant looking inside and healing himself. The Hawaiian practice of *ho 'oponopono* was his means of doing so. Loving yourself is the greatest way to improve yourself, and as you improve yourself, you improve the world around you.

I have already found how powerful this can be. Since reading this story of Dr. Len, I have incorporated a four-line mantra—it can serve as positive self-talk, or even prayer—in my life. If I feel frustrated, or without hope, even for a moment, I simply repeat the following lines, aimed "inward" toward my soul, over and over:

"I love you."

"Please forgive me."

"I'm sorry."

"Thank you."

Surprisingly, these words can be very difficult for people to say to themselves. "I love you," especially, is almost impossible for many women to aim inward. But it is this simple chant, four lines only, that can in its simplicity remind you of the constant potential for change that exists in this world. When you are frustrated with your riding, your trainer, or your horse, it can be as easy as four short sentences to change your mind about the situation, and thus change the reality.

If you forgive yourself for feeling your horse is incapable of nailing lead changes every third stride, you can change the outcome by changing your expectation of the movement. If you love yourself even when you immediately recognize a mistake you have made, the mistake is easily made up for and avoided in the future. I stopped saying, "Gosh Linda, that was really stupid," when I read the research from the Institute of HeartMath that demonstrates how your cell function is adversely effected by a negative attitude toward your body. I started to think about the 50-trillion-plus cells that make up my body and are on the receiving end of that sentiment. Today, sometimes that derogatory statement might rise to my lips, and even escape part way, but I am now practiced at stopping mid-sentence, and replace it with *ho 'oponopono*. My body, mind, and soul are much happier for it, and I feel the world reflected back to me is a better place, as well.

In this book, I have already talked about Dr. Emoto's work demonstrating the effect of words on the appearance of water crystals. And, I've talked about the power of *intention*, and of heart coherence. Now you will see again how whenever you want to improve anything in your life, there's only one place to look: inside you. It is a very Gandhian belief to understand that "you must be the change you want to see in the world." Some might feel overwhelmed by the responsibility this implies; however, I find it comforting to know that in some small way, we can effect change—we can be the tide rather than a shell caught in its swell. "Change your mind, change your horse" is a tenet of the Tellington Method. "Change your mind, change the world" can bring new meaning to your life with dressage. Think about it. Why do you do what you do, and love what you do, and spend the money and time to do and love what you do? It doesn't have to be meaningless. It can be about something bigger.

TTouches for the Rider

When I worked with Ingrid Klimke in May of 2008 in order to prepare her and her horse Abraxxas for the upcoming Olympics (see p. 121), we also explored a few of the different *TTouches* the rider can use on herself prior to competition.

Ear TTouches

Self-applied *Ear TTouches* on the rider have a similar effect as they do on the horse, calming and creating focus. After a strenuous test or riding lesson, 5 to 10 minutes of rather swift strokes in a slightly upward direction from your folded thumb and forefinger on the ear, starting at the lobe and working toward the top, can assist the rider in recovery of her strength and well-being (figs. 11.1 A–C). In the case of injury or exhaustion, 10 to 15 minutes or more of *Ear TTouches* applied with a rhythmical stroke, will aid recovery and prevent shock, or help to bring a rider out of shock.

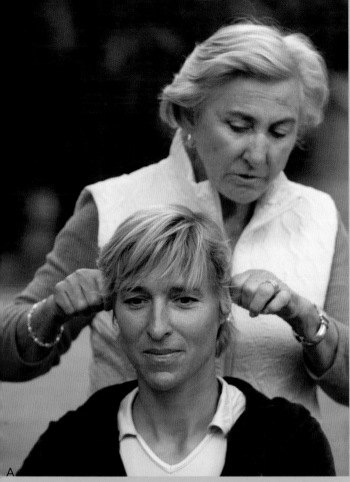

11.1 A–C I show Ingrid Klimke what *TTouches* for the rider can feel like, and how they can help her riding. Here we do *Ear TTouches* to calm, create focus, and assist in recovery after a strenuous test.

A

B

C

Heart Hugs

To help calm a rider before competition, the *Heart Hug* has a meditative quality that helps you focus and eases anxiety (fig. 11.2).

11.2 Ingrid performs *Heart Hugs*, which help you become calm, find focus, and reduce stress.

Step 1 Place one hand on top of the other with slightly cupped hands on the center of your chest. (Some people prefer the feeling of one hand with the fingers folded back lightly, almost to the base of your thumb, and the other hand cupped over it.) Visualize the face of a clock on your chest, under your hands, with six o'clock at the bottom of the circle, closest to the ground.

Step 2 Beginning at six o'clock, inhale and exhale while slowly, gently, and lightly moving the skin in a circle-and-a-quarter (in whichever direction feels best to you) with a consistent rhythm, stopping again at nine o'clock (or three o'clock, if you prefer to move counterclockwise: try both directions to find your preference).

Step 3 Take another deep breath, in and out, with your hands remaining quietly at the nine o'clock position.

Step 4 Take a few normal breaths and focus on the air moving in and out of your lungs.

Step 5 Repeat the *Heart Hug* several times, followed by quiet focus on your breathing. When you feel a sense of peace, send a prayer or thoughts of thanksgiving for all the beings on the planet, along with the message "Remember your perfection."

The Body Blessing

This is a simple, two- to four-minute *TTouch* session done on yourself in a standing position. Apply the lightest *Abalone TTouches* from the top of your head and moving down, thanking your ear, neck, shoulder point, upper arm, elbow, forearm, wrist, and hand. Begin a second time at the top of your head on the same side and repeat to the shoulder, then continue thanking your chest, ribs, hips, pelvis, thigh, knee, calf, ankle, and foot. Be sure to really say, "Thank you," out loud to each of your precious parts as you move your hand all the way down your body, to the tips of your toes. Then repeat on the other side.

You can do this when you get up in the morning, in the shower, or just before you mount your horse. With each butterfly-light *TTouch*, "smile at your cells" and thank them for running the physical "vehicle" that houses your soul. This simple form of meditation promotes awareness of your entire body, "wakes you up," and promotes a positive energy that you can then share with your horse, and indeed with all those you come into contact in the course of your day.

DRESSAGE IN THE TWENTY-FIRST CENTURY—A CONCLUSION

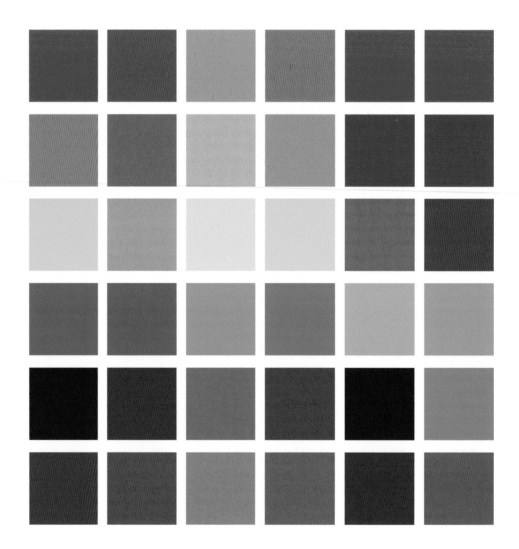

12

I QUIT THE HORSE WORLD IN 1974 BECAUSE I THOUGHT I DID NOT HAVE A specific teachable alternative to the abuse and lack of understanding I was seeing at that time. Having since then developed the "role model" of the Tellington Method approach for a compassionate relationship between horse and rider is what today keeps me inspired and excited. I believe that it is time we all acknowledge that loving our horses as beings is an acceptable, desirable attitude, which leads to a happy, successful athletic partnership—and even greater things, if we are willing to open our heart and mind to the possibilities.

Working with horses and riders to achieve a level of excellence in competition while deepening their mutual trust, self-confidence, and sense of "oneness" leaves me with a deep sense of gratitude. Each time we replace fear with harmony and resignation with joy in our day-to-day dealings with both our horses and with each other, we make a difference we cannot begin to imagine.

Without a doubt, the Tellington Method can improve horses who compete at the very top levels of dressage by reducing stress and tension—qualities that go against the very core of the dressage ideal, and yet are rampant in the sport today—and by developing trust and athletic ability beyond what can be achieved with the best classical riding. As I noted early in this book, I feel strongly that the tenets of classical riding are imperative and pure, and there is no moving forward without conscientious attention paid to all that has been learned and proven in horsemanship's past. However, move forward we must, with the intent of achieving something better in the decades ahead and a common goal of alleviating the prevalence of pain, anxiety, and depression in the wonderful, talented sport horses with whom we are so lucky to pursue our dreams. This intent is a responsibility to be shared equally by all dressage riders, at all levels, in all nations of this world.

The "Classical" Objective

The "classical" goal to develop a horse who is calm, keen, confident, attentive, "loose," flexible, and supple, which encapsulates the Objective of Dressage in

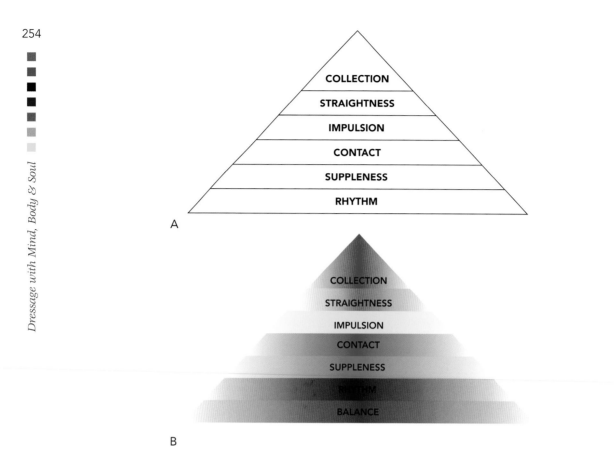

A

B

12.1 A–D The Classical Training Scale (A); the Tellington Training Scale (B); the Seven Cs (C); and the Circle of Well-Being (D).

the FEI Rule Book Article 401 (see sidebar, p. 256) can seldom be achieved from the saddle with the level of horsemanship that we see in the twenty-first century. These classical concepts took hundreds of hours of patient preparation when riders expected to take many years to develop a horse, mentally, physically, and emotionally. Because, as we have discussed in this book, patience and time are no longer the accepted norm nor are they particularly valued in today's fast-paced world where instant gratification rules, riders resort to devices and extreme training methods (overfacing, LDR), which seek to subordinate the horse rather than develop a partnership with him. We can change this with the incorporation of the Tellington Method in our horse training and management practices. What I have described in this book offers you a proven, humane, comprehensive approach to developing not just your horse's physique, but his mental, physical, and emotional Balance, as well—that new and fundamental foundation to the Tellington Training Scale (p. 47).

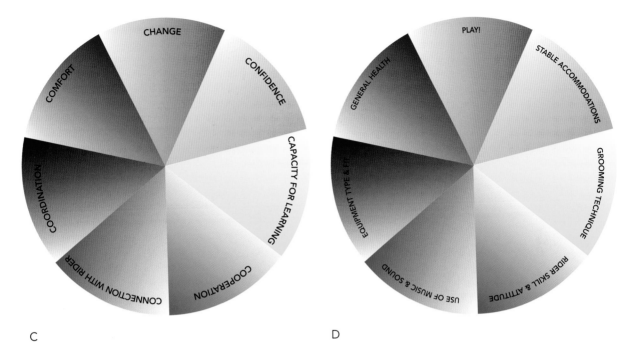

C   D

It also cultivates the trust in his rider the horse needs to be able to enjoy the training process as much as you do.

The Tellington Method places the health and welfare of the horse first and adheres to the spirit of FEI Article 401, which recognizes that a good horseman is one who cares about his or her horse's body, mind, and heart, and ensures that in every aspect of his care, management, and training, every effort is made to promote the horse's well-being, first and foremost.

......Looking Back, Looking Ahead

In the preceding chapters of this book, I reviewed the principles of the Classical Training Scale (fig. 12.1 A), a time-tested guide that remains well regarded and present in today's sport of dressage. I also described how the Training Scale could be improved upon by adding the additional element of Balance—meaning mental, physical, and emotional well-being—which together with color gives you the Tellington Training Scale with seven elements, the original six made stronger by the presence of a stable base missing in the formation of many competitive dressage horses (fig. 12.1 B).

I also described the Seven Cs to which the Tellington Method has been proven to contribute in terms of the care and training of the horse (fig. 12.1 C). And finally, I explored seven areas where you can ensure potential sources of stress and discomfort are alleviated or avoided altogether—the Circle of Well-Being (fig. 12.1 D).

From FEI Rules for Dressage Events, Effective January 1, 2012

Article 401: Object and General Principles of Dressage

1. The object of Dressage is the development of the Horse into a happy Athlete through harmonious education. As a result, it makes the Horse calm, supple, loose and flexible, but also confident, attentive and keen, thus achieving perfect understanding with the Athlete.

   These qualities are demonstrated by:
   - The freedom and regularity of the paces.
   - The harmony, lightness and ease of the movements.
   - The lightness of the forehand and the engagement of the hindquarters, originating from a lively impulsion.
   - The acceptance of the bit, with submissiveness/throughness (*Durchlässigkeit*) without any tension or resistance.

2. The Horse thus gives the impression of doing, of its own accord, what is required. Confident and attentive, submitting generously to the control of the Athlete, remaining absolutely straight in any movement on a straight line and bending accordingly when moving on curved lines.

3. The walk is regular, free and unconstrained. The trot is free, supple, regular and active. The canter is united, light and balanced. The hindquarters are never inactive or sluggish. The horse responds to the slightest indication of the Athlete and thereby gives life and spirit to all the rest of its body.

4. By virtue of a lively impulsion and the suppleness of the joints, free from the paralysing effects of resistance, the Horse obeys willingly and without hesitation and responds to the various aids calmly and with precision, displaying a natural and harmonious balance both physically and mentally.

5. In all the work, even at the halt, the Horse must be "on the bit." A Horse is said to be "on the bit" when the neck is more or less raised

→

and arched according to the stage of training and the extension or collection of the pace, accepting the bridle with a light and consistent soft submissive contact. The head should remain in a steady position, as a rule slightly in the front of the vertical, with a supple poll as the highest point of the neck, and no resistance should be offered to the Athlete.

6 Cadence is shown in trot and canter and is the result of the proper harmony that a Horse shows when it moves with well-marked regularity, impulsion and balance. Cadence must be maintained in all the different trot or canter exercises and in all the variations of these paces.

7 The regularity of the paces is fundamental to Dressage.

continued from page 256

When the Classical Training Scale (where it all begins) becomes the Tellington Training Scale and comes together with the Seven Cs and the Circle of Well-Being in the training of the dressage horse, you have accomplished something new and exciting for the future of dressage as sport, and dressage as art. You have a complex architectural figure that is strengthened and stabilized by the support offered by buttressing elements on all sides. You have, in effect, looked both to the past and to the future, taking what horsemen of ancient times imagined, tested, and perfected, and injecting it with a dose of "right now."

Take a look at your new Training Scale, now a fortified pyramid of possibility that can withstand the sands of time (fig. 12.2). Roll it about in your mind's eye. Consider its durability. Consider its balance. This figure is representative of all that you could want for your dressage horse.

Turn this new Training Scale diagram into a Mind Map, using the steps you learned on p. 55. Note how the elements interconnect, how one inspires the next. Use imagery and color to help your mind trace its steps from origin to destination, and back again, via various routes. Dressage with "heART" is no more a linear pursuit than the Training Scale is a one-dimensional list of accomplishments to tick off; it is an exploration deserving of tangential wanderings and lengthy pauses, depending on the emotional and physical needs of both horse and rider.

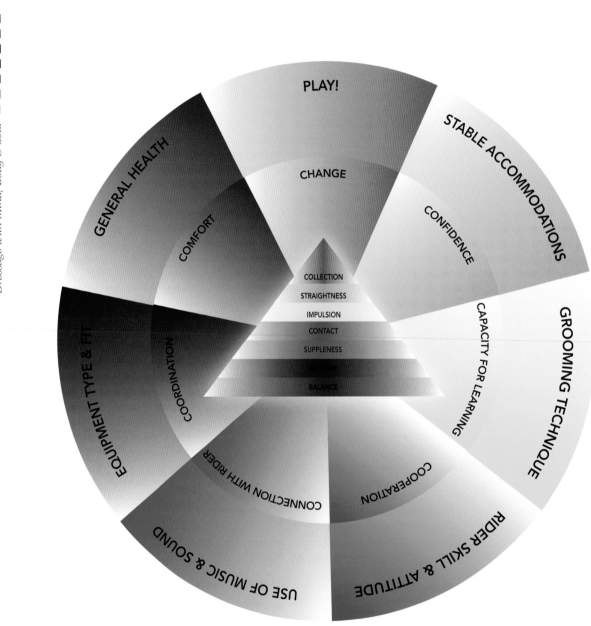

12.2 The Tellington Training Scale is supported and strengthened by the Seven Cs and the Circle of Well-Being. The result is a solid and vibrant image that visually pulses with positivity and possibility.

.. ....All That Surrounds Us

Throughout this book I have tried to share the evidence that suggests we are all interconnected. Whether a cellular connection, a shared energy, or a common belief, whether you lean toward the scientific explanation or the spiritual one, the fact remains you and your horse inhabit one miniscule microcosm of space that affects the millions of like spaces around it. How you inhabit that space with your equine partner, how you dwell in it, breathe in it, move in it, and grow in it, manipulates the experiences of those around you, whether they attend to similar pursuits or something altogether different.

In chapter one I suggested that how you practice and ride dressage can impact other facets of your life—your interactions at work, with your family, with your friends. Perhaps when I first mentioned this belief you found it a bit silly or farfetched, but now that you have familiarized yourself with my ideas and the Tellington Method, I hope you will reconsider. When you attend to your horse's most elemental needs and tune yourself into (what is to us) his silent language, you gain an awareness of what those around you might be experiencing at any given moment. It matters not whether they are horse or human—we are all cells and water. Tuning in excludes no one, and nothing. Mindfully apply it to your pursuit of dressage, and it will filter into other parts of your life.

As I have discussed, using the Tellington Method with your dressage horse incorporates both brain hemispheres. This is like calisthenics for your left and right brain. You will ride your best when you have a balanced use of left and right hemispheres, and that hemispheric synchronization leads to optimal (peak) performance. Just think of how you can apply peak performance in other areas of your life, and how your energy and innovation will generate ripples of ideas and "aha!" moments spanning in every direction.

The same balance which you aim for via hemispheric synchronization is within reach when you appeal to both your scientific and spiritual sides. As I've said, you can have both proof and belief in your life with horses, and your riding will be the better for it. Science and spirituality can potentially be the glue that holds your world together, if you are open to the possibility that there is more than room for both—that there's a *need* for both (fig. 12.3).

.. ....And Then, There's Your Horse

It is gratifying to acknowledge that dressage needn't be considered a selfish sport devoid of relevance in terms of the "bigger picture." By conscientiously recognizing that we all make our impact on this world, that we create our reality, in whatever it is we choose to do, then we can take responsibility for

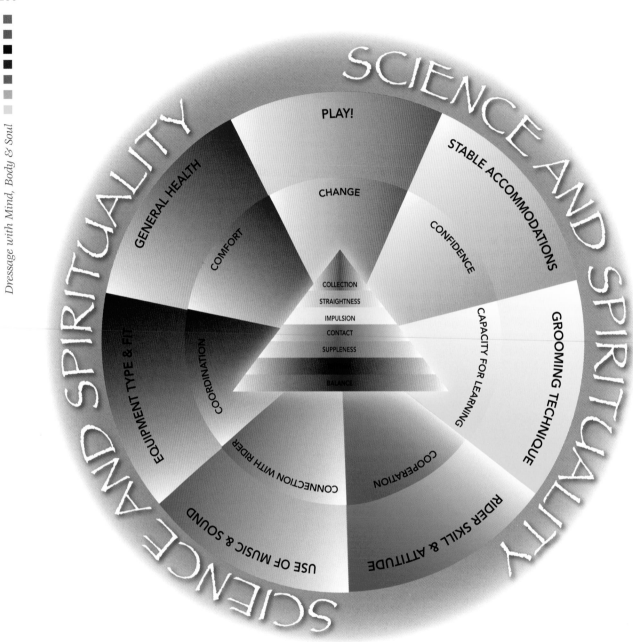

12.3 Science and spirituality are potentially the glue that holds together all that you strive for—*if* you are open to the possibility that there is room for both in the pursuit of dressage.

ensuring that our time is time well spent. That the results of hard work and devotion are not only beneficial to your own ego or pocketbook, but that they, in some small way, contribute to the greater good.

If all this feels a bit beyond you, if perhaps you move forward best with your feet stepping firmly on solid ground, then remain satisfied in the assurance that the Tellington Method can make your horse more comfortable physically, less stressed psychologically, and more open to your presence in his life. We receive from the horse as much, or more, than we give. It has always been this way. It is our responsibility as man, the being who domesticated the horse, wrested him from the open plains, stalled him, harnessed him, and made him do our bidding, to now make him as "happy" as we can determine possible. For the horse, this amounts to a living situation as close to what "comes naturally" as can be had in modern civilization. This includes turnout, socialization, light, and good air to breathe—and care that what we demand of him is asked fairly, at the right time, with a sufficient amount of preparation. In addition, the equipment we use and how we use it, and the different ways we attend to the horse's physical and mental health needs—farriery, veterinary attention, alternative sources of bodywork, and mental stimulation—are paramount to ensuring we give back to the horse what his species has given to us over time.

......Dressage with "HeART"

My wish for every dressage rider is that she may come to a place where she delights in her horse's brilliance, whatever the level, whatever color the ribbon or medal. If you change your mind, and open your heart, you can transform your horse. Horses touch our hearts—it is my hope that this book provides the guideposts we need to touch theirs.

The Tellington Method is not about being a "fixer" or a "healer" or a "trainer" as much as it is about merging with the horse on a cellular level, allowing your "borders" of self to melt and meld together with your horse's. The result is a form of congruency, of joined meditation, if you will. And it is exactly this that is the aim and ideal of classical dressage.

When you take the time to acknowledge the miracles, small and large, that occur in your life, when you count your blessings—in and out of the saddle—you bring a new sense of appreciation, of gratitude, of humanity, and of community to the sport of dressage, and to the world of horsemanship. Indeed the reach extends out into other parts of your life, impacting your family, friends, and career. And ultimately, the littlest ripples in the river meet the ocean.

Let's join together to make a difference.

TELLINGTON METHOD QUICK REFERENCE CENTER

Introduction

There are many words and concepts used to define bodywork techniques, movement exercises, and the tools that are part of the Tellington Method. Since many of these are exclusive to my *Method*, not everyone will be familiar with them. This Quick Reference Center is intended to help you become familiar with the terminology that I and my practitioners use. In addition, it provides summaries of how to perform the *TTouches*, *Ground Exercises*, and *Ridden Work* you learned about in this book. As I explained earlier, it is not possible to include detailed instructions in these pages. However, for those intending further study, step-by-step instructions can be found, along with photo series, in my book *The Ultimate Horse Behavior and Training Book*.

The Nine Elements of the Tellington TTouch

There are nine important elements that will ensure success with *TTouch*.

1 THE BASIC TTOUCH CIRCLE

Imagine the face of a clock drawn on the body of the horse, with six o'clock at the bottom of the clock, nine on the left side, twelve at the top, and three on the right. Place your fingers (or hand, depend-

ing upon the *TTouch*) at six o'clock and smoothly move the horse's skin in a circle-and-a-quarter (from six o'clock once all the way around past six o'clock to nine o'clock). At the end of the circle-and-a-quarter, release the pressure, slide your fingers lightly to another spot, and begin the next circle-and-a-quarter. Be sure to move the skin rather than just sliding across the hair. Begin your circles in a clockwise direction, but note that if your horse does not seem comfortable, counterclockwise may be preferable (or he may need a different tempo, pressure or *TTouch*).

2 THE PRESSURE SCALE

The pressure of each *TTouch* is rated on a scale from 1 to 10. Most of the time, a 2 to 4 pressure is used when working with horses. Remember, the intention of *TTouch* is *not* to massage your horse and work with the muscular system, but rather to support cellular function and enhance communication (see p. 36 for more).

You can learn the difference between light and firmer pressures of *TTouch* by trying them on yourself. Support your right elbow with your left hand. Rest your right thumb on your cheek, curve your fingers lightly, and with your middle finger leading, move the delicate skin below your eye lightly enough so it just moves the skin in one-and-a-quarter circles. Move the skin clockwise and counterclockwise to see which direction feels better to you. Repeat this same light circle on your arm between the wrist and elbow. Notice that there is almost no indentation of your skin. This pressure is your baseline: a Number 1 pressure.

To feel the 3 pressure, return your fingers to your cheek, but this time move them about an inch lower, then make firm contact with your cheekbone with your curved middle-finger pads all the way around the circle-and-a-quarter. Repeat the same pressure in a circle-and-a-quarter on your arm and note the indentation in your skin, and the difference between the Number 1 and Number 3 pressures. The Number 2 pressure is between 1 and 3, and a 4 pressure is slightly more. (In some cases I do use up to a 6 pressure on a horse's neck, but only when the horse seems to enjoy the deeper work by relaxing the neck, lowering the head, and half-closing the eyes.)When you are working with an injury or a sensitive horse, use less pressure: Number 1 or 2 is enough. Number 3 is best for a horse who is confident in your touch all over his body.

3 TEMPO

Tempo is the time it takes to move the horse's skin around the circle-and-a-quarter. Tempo can vary from one to three seconds. To *activate* your horse, use one-second circle-and-a-quarters. When you want to *calm* him or *bring focus*, use two-second circles with a "Mindful Pause" after three or four of them (see below). Note: one-second circles are most effective for reducing swelling and relieving acute pain.

4 A MINDFUL PAUSE

After making several circles on the horse's body, hold the connection at the end of the circle-and-a-quarter

TTOUCHES BY CATEGORY

TTouches for Trust

Abalone TTouch • Coiled Python Lift • Connected Circles • Ear TTouch • Front and Hind Leg Circles • Lick of the Cow's Tongue • Llama TTouch • Lying Leopard TTouch • Mouth TTouch • Owl TTouch • Snail's Pace • Tail TTouch • Troika TTouch • Turtle TTouch

TTouches for Awareness

Back Lift • Chimp TTouch • Clouded Leopard TTouch • Hoof Tapping • Inchworm • Jellyfish Jiggle • Mane and Forelock Slides • Neck Rocking • Noah's March • Octopus TTouch • Sponge TTouch • Tarantulas Pulling the Plow • Tiger TTouch • Zigzag TTouch

TTouches for Health

Belly Lift • Ear TTouch • Raccoon TTouch

TTouches for Performance

Bear TTouch • Flick of the Bear's Paw • Neck Bending • Neck Release • Pelvic Tilt • Rainbow TTouch • Rhino TTouch • Rib Release • Shoulder Release

TTOUCHES BY TYPE

Circle TTouches

Abalone TTouch • Bear TTouch • Chimp TTouch • Clouded Leopard TTouch • Llama TTouch • Lying Leopard TTouch • Raccoon TTouch • Rhino TTouch • Sponge TTouch • Tiger TTouch

Lifting and Stroking TTouches

Coiled Python Lift • Inchworm • Lick of the Cow's Tongue • Jellyfish Jiggle • Noah's March • Octopus TTouch • Rainbow TTouch • Tarantulas Pulling the Plow • Troika TTouch • Zigzag TTouch

Other TTouch Bodywork

Back Lift • Belly Lift • Ear TTouch • Front Leg Circles • Hind Leg Circles • Hoof Tapping • Mouth TTouch • Neck Bending • Neck Release • Neck Rocking • Pelvic Tilt • Rib Release • Shoulder Release • Tail TTouch

GROUND EXERCISES & RIDDEN WORK

Dancing with Your Horse

Boomer's Bound • Cha Cha • Cueing the Camel • Dancing Cobra • Dingo • Dolphins Flickering through the Waves • Elegant Elephant • Grace of the Cheetah • Journey of the Homing Pigeon • Peacock • The Statue

The Playground for Higher Learning

Barrels • The Fan, Cavalletti, and Pick-Up Sticks • Freework • Labyrinth • Neckline and Ground Driving • Work with Plastic Sheets • Platform • Teeter-Totter • Tires

The Joy of Riding

Balance Rein • Half-Walk • Liberty Neck Ring • Lindell Sidepull • Tellington Training Bit

TELLINGTON TOOLS

Balance Rein • Chain Lead • Liberty Neck Ring • Lindell Sidepull • Promise Wrap and Promise Rope • Tellington Training Bit • Tellington Wand • Zephyr Lead with a "Mindful Pause," which many meditation teachers define as "a pause that allows a wondrous stillness." The Mindful Pause is what allows you to make an important connection with your horse at the cellular level.

5   CONNECTIONS

When using a variety of *TTouches* on different areas of the horse's body, it can be better to work in lines with a slide of the fingers (keeping contact with the horse) between the *TTouches,* rather than skipping from place to place. Note: When working on painful, sensitive, or injured areas, *do not* connect the circles with a slide. Instead, lift your fingers off the body and make a smooth move through the air to connect with the body again in the area of the next circle. I call this "weaving."

6   BODY POSTURE

When *TTouching* your horse, stand with your weight more over the balls of your feet than on your heels, and make certain your knees are not locked. Standing with one foot a few inches behind the other allows you to turn and move away quickly should the need arise, and it also helps maintain your balance. Use both hands when *TTouching* your horse: one hand to apply the *TTouch* and the other hand to keep the horse listening to you and make him feel supported.

Your horse's posture is just as important as yours. For instance, a spooky or flighty horse is often high-headed and ewe-necked with a dropped back. Use *TTouches* to lower his head, release his neck, and raise his back. You may be surprised how changing his posture will change his behavior.

7   MINDFUL BREATHING

It is a common human trait to hold the breath when concentrating. Mindful breathing—inhaling through your nose and exhaling slowly through pursed lips—will keep you calm, focused, and energized. Exhaling so your horse can hear your breath often causes him to take a deep sigh and relax noticeably.

8   INTENTION

As we've discussed in this book, a fundamental principle of *TTouch,* and the Tellington Method as a whole, is to hold a positive image of how you would like your horse to behave, perform, and relate to you, knowing that you can influence behavior and health by the *intention* you hold (see p. 60).

9   FEEDBACK: OBSERVE THE HORSE'S BODY LANGUAGE

TTouch has been described as an interspecies language. Since your horse can't use words, learn to read his body language. Watch for small changes of posture that indicate a negative response—such as throwing or turning the head; moving to the side or backward; switching or clamping the tail (when there are no flies); stomping a foot; grinding teeth; pinning the ears; pinching the lips and nostrils—as all are indicative of the language of the horse. Learn to "listen to the whispers of your horse" and you will find another level of understanding and relationship.

The Tellington Method A to Z

ABALONE TTOUCH   In this most soothing *TTouch,* the whole hand is lightly cupped and placed softly on the horse with the palm and fingers making contact, depending on the contour of the muscle. Use just enough contact so that you can push the skin in a circle without sliding over the hair. The center of the circle is the center of your palm. Use a 1 to 2 pressure for this *TTouch,* which quiets horses reactive to grooming, releases tight neck muscles, and soothes "girthy" horses, to name just a few benefits. (See photos 8.10 C & E.)

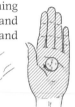

BACK LIFT   A method of raising a horse's topline, the *Back Lift* aims to get your horse to contract his abdominal muscles so that he lifts his back. To feel this, press into your own belly muscles with your fingertips—most people suck in their breath and move away from the pressure, your back moving away from your fingers. This is the equivalent of the *Back Lift* on a horse. To perform it on your horse, place both hands under the horse's belly, about 6 inches from the midline, on your side of his body. Your palms should be up and the fingers curved and snugged tightly together for stability as

you apply pressure. You should see the back rise and the ribs fill out. The amount of pressure you use depends on your horse; he may need a very light pressure while others require a firmer pressure. With some horses, you will need to use your fingernails to get a response. The *Back Lift* helps relax sore or stiff back muscles, lengthens and relaxes the neck, and encourages engagement of the hind legs, among many other benefits. (See photos 9.9 B & C.)

BADGER RAKE   Once your horse learns to consistently respond to the *Back Lift*, you can often get the same result with a raking motion from your fingertips, pulling them across the bottom of the horse's belly toward your body, and part way up the barrel. You can also use *Zigzag TTouch* with both hands under the belly to encourage the horse to lift and stretch the topline (see p. 273).

BALANCE REIN   This braided nylon rope is like a "necklace," or a second rein draped around the base of the horse's neck. Its steady contact helps to round and rebalance the horse through transitions; overcome the habit of coming above or behind the bit; lengthen the horse's neck; and encourage the horse to become less spooky and/or shy. (See photos 2.3, 6.1, 6.4 A & B, 6.5 A & B, 7.7, 9.1 B & C, 9.2 A & B, 9.11 A & B.)

BEAR TTOUCH   This name was inspired by the fingernails being compared to a bear's claws. Place your hands on the horse's body in a claw-like position, the first phalange perpendicular to the body, with your fingers snugly together for stability.  Hold your wrist raised several inches off the horse's body and maintain a steady connection with your thumb as you move your fingers together in a circle-and-a-quarter (see p. 262). This allows you to go in deep, without discomfort for your horse or your hands. The recommended pressure ranges between a 1 and 5. *Bear TTouch* promotes circulation in deep muscles, releases tightness in the neck and croup, and increases range of motion, to name just a few benefits. (See photo 3.6 B.)

BELLY LIFT   The intent of this *TTouch* is the opposite of the *Back Lift* (p. 264). You want the horse to *relax* the abdominal muscles rather than *contract* them. This occurs when you support the belly with a slow lift, then steadily release the pressure. The *Belly Lift* can be done with two people—one on either side of the horse—or one person can manage alone by using a long beach towel, folded and wrapped around the horse so both ends are held on one side. You can also use a wide cinch,

a wide elastic bandage, or your arm under the horse's ribs. Starting behind the horse's elbows at the girth area, lift slowly until you can't lift anymore; then hold from five to fifteen seconds and slowly release. Move back on the horse's barrel about 6 inches and repeat. Continue until you reach the horse's flank. If the horse moves or shows discomfort, lift less. The *Belly Lift* relaxes back muscles in horses with a sore back, helps raise a low or sway back, and eases colic signs, among many other benefits. (See photo 7.2.)

BODY ROPE   This *Tellington Tool* is a 21-foot nylon rope wrapped in a figure eight around the shoulders and hindquarters of the horse. Place the rope around the base of the horse's neck, crossing one end (the shorter one) over the withers toward you, wrapping it several times around the longer end of the rope to allow movement. Bring the long end of the rope around the hindquarters, allowing it to settle at the top of the gaskins; then tie it and the shorter end in a bow on one side of the back, just behind the withers. Like the *Body Wrap* (see below), the *Body Rope* gives horses a sense of connection and fosters a sense of security and safety, calming those who are tense, shy, or spooky.

BODY WRAP   The *Body Wrap* is comprised of two or three elastic bandages (Ace bandages or elastic leg wraps) tied together and "wrapped" around the horse, most commonly in the same figure-eight pattern as described for the *Body Rope* (above), although there are many variations and, in fact, an entire book on the subject (*All Wrapped Up* by Robyn Hood with Mandy Pretty, www.ttouch.com). Like the *Body Rope*, the *Body Wrap* gives horses a sense of connection and fosters a sense of security and safety, calming those who are tense, shy, or spooky. (See photos 10.7 A & B.)

BOOMER'S BOUND   When standing on the near side of the horse, hold the lead line in your left hand and the *Tellington Wand* in your right. Move the wand slowly in a large arc from the horse's withers over the area above the horse's ears, down to the tip of his nose. Practice at the halt and the walk. This exercise is useful for horses who are afraid of move-  ment around their head or above them, and is good preparation for trailer-loading and/or entering coliseum-type arenas with grandstands.

CHA CHA A leading exercise that asks the horse to take one step back and then one step forward, moving diagonal pairs of legs. Use the *Tellington Wand* to stroke and tap as you give verbal commands and light signals on the lead. This helps lighten the horse while improving responsiveness and coordination.

CHAIN LEAD A 6-foot soft nylon lead with a 30-inch chain, which is attached to the halter in a specific configuration so that the chain goes over the noseband of the halter, remaining effective while preventing uncomfortable pressure on the horse's nose. This tool is essential for a horse who is hard to control as it encourages the horse to listen to precise, subtle signals without pressure.

CHIMP AND BABY CHIMP TTOUCH Curl your fingers so they are softly folded in toward the palm of your hand, and use either the first knuckle joints or between the first and second knuckle joints to make contact with the horse's skin. *Baby Chimp* is a similar curl of the fingers but your fingernails are what make contact with the horse's body. These *TTouches* are generally less threatening and less invasive for more sensitive horses, and the position is a better one for people with arthritis or stiff fingers who are trying to apply *TTouches* to their horse. Use a 2 to 3 pressure. (See photos 10.10 D & E.)

CIRCULAR TTOUCHES The *TTouches* using the basic *TTouch* circle, which is a one-and-a-quarter circle generally performed in a clockwise direction on the skin of the horse (see p. 262 for more details).

CLOUDED LEOPARD TTOUCH This *TTouch* is the basic *TTouch* position for activating the horse's mind and body. Hold the fingers together and slightly curved, and use the pads of the fingers to push the skin in a circle-and-a-quarter. The heel of the hand does not come in contact with the horse's body. Use pressures 1 to 5. *Clouded Leopard*  *TTouch* builds confidence and trust, enhances coordination and suppleness, and improves willingness and ability to learn. (See photos 3.6 A, 6.2 B, 8.10 A, 9.10 E.)

COILED PYTHON LIFT This *TTouch* is a combination of either an *Abalone TTouch* circle or a *Lying Leopard TTouch* circle with a lift of the skin. Begin at the top of the leg, using both hands flat around the horse's leg with just enough contact with the skin so your hands

do not slide over the hair. Use either hand to lightly push the skin in a *TTouch* circle, then with both hands, gently push the skin upward, hold four seconds, and support the skin as it returns slowly to its beginning position. Slide several inches lower and repeat. Work from the top of the legs down to the fetlock joints, using a 1 to 3 pressure. To be effective requires only a small move. If your horse shifts away, you're squeezing too hard or pushing the skin upward too much. This *TTouch* releases tense or tight muscles in the body, increases circulation and proprioception in the legs, and revitalizes tired legs after a long trailer ride or a hard workout. (See photos 9.3 A & B.)

CONNECTED CIRCLES Each circular *TTouch* is complete within itself; however, connecting the circles with a short, clear slide over the hair, about 2 to 3 inches between circles, gives the horse an enhanced sense of the body—an improved self-image—and develops confidence, coordination, and balance (see p. 262 for more information).

CUEING THE CAMEL While standing on the near side of the horse with the lead in your left hand close to the side ring of the halter, and the *Tellington Wand* in your right, bring the *Wand* to the front of the horse's chest and apply three light taps on the chest, signaling to the horse with your voice and the lead to shift his weight back and stop. This is a useful exercise to enhance balance.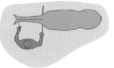

DANCING COBRA Stand about 3 feet in front of the horse, facing him. Hold the lead between both hands, with the *Tellington Wand* in the hand that is on the end of the lead. Give a light signal and release with the lead, crossing the *Wand* over the lead and sweeping it toward you as you shift your center backward and step back, asking the horse to follow you one or two steps. Then, point the *Wand* toward the horse's nose as you bend your body toward him and ask him to stop. This exercise improves balance, focus, obedience, and response to aids.

DINGO This leading position is a four-step move: 1) With the *Tellington Wand* in your right hand (when 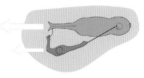 you are on the left side of the horse) and the lead in your left, give a light signal on the lead to get the horse's attention; 2) stroke the horse's back firmly with the *Wand* two or three times, from the withers to the croup; 3) give a light signal and release with the lead, asking the horse to go forward; 4) and apply a "scooping tap, tap" with the *Wand* on the top of the croup while giving the verbal command to walk. *Dingo* teaches the horse to stand still and listen, step forward from a signal when asked, and is especially useful in trailer-loading scenarios. (See photo 8.8.)

DOLPHINS FLICKERING THROUGH THE WAVES

This exercise is used to teach the horse to respond to your aids for walk, trot, and halt, while maintaining a steady 6- to 8-foot distance from you out at the end of the lead. Start in *Dingo* (above) and then slide out on the lead, lightly tapping or "flicking" the horse in four differ-

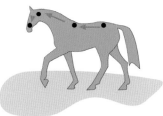

ent places with the tip of the *Tellington Wand* as you go: the hindquarters to move forward; the side of the withers keep the horse from moving in toward you; the neck just behind the ears to keep him out on the line and encourage him to accept contact in this area; and very lightly on the side of the nose to keep him focused. The idea is to be active with the *Wand*, but not hard. The movement of the *Wand* makes me think of dolphins leaping in the ocean. The exercise is called *Baby Dolphin* when the horse is just halfway out—about 4 feet—and it becomes *Joyful Dolphin* once the horse is out on the end of the lead and no longer needs the *Wand* taps to respond willingly and confidently in this position.

EAR TTOUCH
Slide from the middle of the poll over the base of the ear all the way to the very tip emphasizing contact with the tip as you slide your hand off the ear. If the horse allows, fold the ear together to give him a feeling of the inside of his ears. Some horses enjoy having your finger sliding or circling on

the inside of the ear, as well as the outside. Use a 1 to 5 pressure. *Ear TTouch* invigorates the tired horse, calms a nervous or frightened one, and alleviates pain and shock from illness or injury. (See photos 8.12, 9.4 B, 9.10 B, 9.12 A, 10.12 C.)

ELEGANT ELEPHANT
This is my *Method's* basic leading position. Standing on the near side of the horse, hold the lead about 4 inches from the halter with your right hand, and hold the end of the lead and the *Tellington Wand* in your left. Balance the *Wand* in your hand near its midpoint, with the "button" end

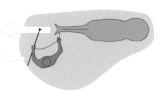

toward the horse. Use a soft stroke of the button end on the horse's muzzle, and a sweep of the *Wand* forward, to ask your horse to walk forward. Then move the button end along the path you'd like your horse to follow.

EXPLORATION
I use two forms of exploration to assess the degree of trust, tension, fear, discomfort, and/or pain in a horse's body. I often begin with a flat-hand exploration, using either the front or back of my hand to slide lightly over every inch of the horse. The primary purpose of this form of exploration is to observe the degree of trust the horse has in being touched over every inch of the body. The second type of exploration I do is intended to access reactivity and/or pain or soreness. For this form of exploration, the fingers are held together and curved as the fingertips apply a press-and-release rhythm into different muscle groups. It is a distinctive technique that takes time to master. (See photos 8.9 A & B.)

FLICK OF THE BEAR'S PAW
This *TTouch* is a sideways flicking motion done with a cupped hand, usu-

ally performed on the barrel in lines running parallel to the horse's spine. The *TTouch* can be done quite actively to give confidence and energize, or very lightly with a "feathering" motion, your fingers making a brief, light contact in the direction of the hair, as if you were brushing off dust (used with horses who are hypersensitive).

FRONT AND HIND LEG CIRCLES
A series of circular movements done with front and hind legs to increase range of motion; free up the shoulders, back, and hindquarters; improve balance; and lengthen stride. Position your-

self facing the hindquarters and pick up the front or hind leg, supporting the fetlock joint with one hand, the hoof with the other. Circle the leg in both directions and at different heights by moving your pelvis, knees, and feet, rather than your arms. (See photos 3.4 C, 8.6, 9.3 E, 9.4 C, 9.12 D.)

GLIDE OF THE EAGLE Standing on the near side of the horse, face forward and hold both the button end of the *Tellington Wand* and end of the lead in your right hand. Point the *Wand* toward the horse's hip to ask him to go faster; toward the horse's shoulder to ask him to stay out; and

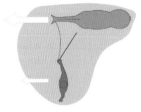

toward his nose to ask him to slow down. This is an advanced movement that tests the horse's willingness to stay level with you and is useful in such exercises as trotting over cavalletti in hand.

GRACE OF THE CHEETAH In this leading position, when standing on the horse's near side, the *Tellington Wand* is transferred from the right to the left hand while you continue to hold the end of the lead in the left hand and slide the right hand about 14 inches up the lead toward the halter. Make very small motions with the *Wand* about 3 feet in front of the horse's nose, followed by a very light tap of the *Wand* on the nose or chest and a verbal command to ask him to halt.

HALF-WALK This exercise teaches your horse to take short, precise steps with you either leading him from the ground or riding. From the ground, bend slightly forward and take small steps, giving subtle signals on the lead between your thumb and forefinger as you make small up-and-down movements with the *Wand* several feet ahead of the horse's nose. From the saddle, raise your horse's head to shift his center of gravity back and lighten your seat slightly as you squeeze and release your fingers on the reins. (See photo 8.3.)

HEAD WRAP This *Tellington Tool* is like a *Body Wrap* (p. 265) for the head and neck. Wrap an Ace bandage or elastic leg wrap across the horse's forehead or in a cross between the ears to encourage focus, calm nervousness, and increase general relaxation. Think of it as a "thinking cap"!

HOOF TAPPING Tap gently around the perimeter of the outer hoof wall with the "button end" of the *Tellington Wand*. Make three rows of taps to cover the hoof, tapping firmly enough for the horse to feel it but not so hard he moves away. This "connects" a skittish horse to the ground, improves an irregular gait, and helps eliminate stumbling.

INCHWORM This *TTouch* is done along the crest of the neck, and helps release tension in the neck and tightness in the shoulders. Place both hands on the top of the horse's neck, about 4 to 6 inches apart, with the thumbs on one side of the neck and fingers on the other. Hold the crest firmly as you push your hands toward each other, moving the skin an inch or so, holding it a few seconds, and then slowly moving it back to the starting place. Move both hands to another area on the crest and repeat. This *TTouch* can also be done on the back and along the ribs running parallel to the topline. Use a 2 to 3 pressure. (See photo 9.12 C.)

JELLYFISH JIGGLE This wavelike, jiggling *TTouch* is used to soften and loosen muscles, often in a horse's neck, back, or hindquarters. Place both hands on the horse horizontally with your fingertips nearly touching, and jiggle the skin upward with your fingers and palm to send a wave of movement upward. Use a 3 to 4 pressure. (See photo 9.3 F.)

JOURNEY OF THE HOMING PIGEON This *Ground Exercise* requires two handlers, one on each side of the horse, and both holding a *Tellington Wand* and a lead. The position quickly teaches a horse to focus, balance, keep a distance, travel straight, and perceive and process information coming from both sides of the body/brain. Each person holds the end of the lead line and the *Wand* in the outside hand (away from the horse), with the inside hand (closer to the horse) about 14 inches away from the halter. One handler is in charge and decides direction, as well as when to give commands to stop, go, and turn. (See photos 7.3 A & B, 8.7.)

LABYRINTH Six 12-foot ground poles arranged in a basic maze pattern, with about 4 feet between the poles. You can lead your horse or ride him through the *Labyrinth*. This is a key exercise for promoting focus, attention, and balance in the horse. (See photos 3.1 B, 3.5, 7.4, 10.2 A.)

LEADING POSITIONS The Tellington Method uses a variety of ways to lead the horse, such as *Grace of the Cheetah* and *Journey of the Homing Pigeon*, just for example. These ground exercises are like Tai Chi for horses. The movements are mindful and intended to show horses what you want; to give them new experiences and influence their posture.

LIBERTY NECK RING This stiff, adjustable ring made of lariat rope is placed around the horse's neck and held with two hands or one, with or without the bridle reins. It is easy for the horse to feel and it's an effective aid for the rider who uses it for stopping and turning, instead of—or along with—the bridle reins. The *Liberty Neck Ring* improves the horse's balance, sense of movement, trust, and cooperation, and increases rider balance and confidence in her seat. (See photos 9.4 I & J, 10.2 E–I.)

LICK OF THE COW'S TONGUE These long, smooth, diagonal strokes across the lay of the horse's hair are generally used to give the horse a stronger sense of connection from belly to back. Apply this *TTouch* with your flat hand, palm against the horse, beginning under his belly on his midline and raking across and up the barrel. Mid barrel, rotate your hand so your fingers are pointing up and continue on to the spine. You may need to vary pressure and the part of the hand you use for this *TTouch*, depending on the horse's sensitivity. *Lick of the Cow's Tongue* enhances suppleness, increases awareness of and response to leg aids, and improves the horse's sense of connection through the core of his body. (See photo 8.4.)

LINDELL SIDEPULL The *Lindell* is a kind of bitless bridle with a flat leather nosepiece and a soft, adjustable, leather strap under the horse's chin that can be left loose. A jowl strap keeps the cheek pieces clear of the horse's eyes. The *Lindell Sidepull* helps horses who are overbent or behind the vertical; allows horses with dental issues or a mouth injury to continue to be ridden; and provides a gentle alternative for starting young animals. (See photos 9.1 B & C, 9.11 A & B, 10.10 A–G.)

LLAMA TTOUCH Use the back of your hand, with the hand softly open (a less threatening way of making contact), to push the horse's skin in a circle-and-a-quarter or to stroke. This *TTouch* builds confidence in timid horses, soothes nervous ones, and

helps when you are approaching a horse you don't know for the first time. Use a 1 or 2 pressure, most commonly on the face, ears, or neck.

LOWERING THE HEAD This is the single most important lesson to earn your horse's trust. Teaching your horse to lower his head from a signal from the halter or your hand on the top of the neck relaxes the anxious horse, fosters cooperation, and relieves muscle tension in the neck and back. Begin by stroking the horse on the neck and chest with the *Tellington Wand* while "milking" the lead rope with a light pulsating pressure. When your horse lowers his head, be sure to reward him with the "release" of pressure on the lead. Next ask with one hand on the noseband of the halter and the other on the lead, and finally repeat the exercise with one hand on the noseband and the other on the horse's crest near his poll. (See photos 1.3 A & B, 7.8 A–C, 8.10 B & D, 8.11 B & C, 9.10 A.)

LYING LEOPARD TTOUCH This is a more diffused, less direct *TTouch*, using contact from the first two phalanges of your fingers to move the skin in a circle-and-a-quarter. The middle of your palm is cupped lightly over the horse's body as  you maintain contact with the outside of the thumb. This *TTouch* spreads contact over a larger area and is therefore calming; improves attention and focus; and reduces pain and prevents swelling in acute injury. Use pressures 1 or 2. (See photo 9.3 G.)

MANE AND FORELOCK SLIDES These *TTouches* are useful preparation for pulling or braiding the mane. They also help relax the horse's neck, shoulders, and back, increasing blood flow and circulation (especially good for horses doing collected work, which can restrict circulation). There are two ways to perform *Mane Slides*: Separate the mane into 1-inch sections, and taking one section at a time, slide your fingers from crest to the end, pulling straight upward. Or, do the same thing except pull downward as you tip the crest over slightly, then take one section toward the left and the next section to the right. The *Forelock Slide*—sliding your fingers from the base of the forelock downward to the end—is one of the most rewarding means of relating to your horse, deepening trust, and achieving a relaxed, peaceful state in both of you.

MOUTH AND NOSTRIL TTOUCH Stand facing the same direction as your horse, holding the halter firmly with one hand. Begin with a few flat-hand circles (*Lying Leopard TTouch*—see p. 269) around the mouth. Loosen the chin with circles and gentle kneading to relax your horse and overcome tension. Next work the tongue and lips. Slide three fingers into the mouth over the tongue, and use your middle and index fingers to tap the tongue as if you are playing a piano. Tapping on the tongue can help resensitize a dull or hard mouth, and a horse with an oversensitive mouth will learn to accept contact and respond more willingly to the bit. Gently knead the lower lip between your thumb (inside the horse's mouth) and your fingers (hooked behind in the groove of his chin). Stretch the edges of the nostrils in every direction; gently reach inside and do little circles as far as your thumb or fingers will reach. Use a 1 to 3 pressure to make a resistant horse more accepting and calm and stabilize the overreactive, skittish, or "willful" horse, to name just a few benefits. (See photos 3.4 A, 8.2, 9.3 H, 9.10 C, 9.12 B, 10.12 A & B.)

NECK BENDING With your horse standing squarely, place the fingers of the hand closest to him in *Bear TTouch* (p. 265) in the middle of his neck, about 8 inches back from his ears. With your other hand on the halter or his nose, ask him to turn the head to the side just a few degrees while pressing into the neck and keeping the centerline of his nose perpendicular to the ground. Repeat, then try the *Neck Bend* the other way. This *TTouch* improves balance and straightness, and releases tight shoulder and back muscles.

NECK RELEASE This neck "stretch" gently opens the throatlatch area. Place one hand on the top of the horse's neck or between his ears (when you're standing in front of him) and the other in his chin groove. Invite the horse to bring his chin forward, while encouraging the head to lower through the neck. This *TTouch* helps horses who come behind the vertical or ones who are regularly required to carry themselves in a collected frame.

NECK ROCKING This *TTouch* frees and lengthens the neck. Begin at the top of the neck and work toward the chest, rocking the crest away from you with one hand while rocking the windpipe toward you with the other. Use a 2 to 4 pressure. (See photos 3.6 D, 8.10 F.)

NECKLINE AND GROUND DRIVING A two-person exercise using four 21-foot driving lines. To begin, the lines are looped around the horse's neck, and the horse is introduced to the lines by his sides and signals on his neck as one person leads the horse by the halter and the other "drives." The exercise progresses to the "driver" using four lines, with two attached to the halter and two to the neck, which teaches the horse to stop in balance and improves lightness and responsiveness. It also calms horses who are spooky. (See photo 9.4 F.)

NOAH'S MARCH This is the term for long connecting strokes of your flat, relaxed hand all over the horse's body, which complete a *TTouch* session; refresh the horse between *TTouches*; or help introduce you to a new horse. Use a 1 to 3 pressure.

OBSERVATION As noted in this book, it is the rider's responsibility to observe the horse's posture, carriage, degree of tension (negative or positive), response to environment, as well as the expression reflected in the horse's eyes and the movement of his ears.

OCTOPUS TTOUCH This *TTouch* is complicated but quite wonderful to do once you have the rhythm. It grounds the horse, helps revitalize tired legs, increases circulation, proprioception, and confidence. Polarity therapists have suggested that the inexplicably powerful effect of this *TTouch* may be due to the unique figure-eight pattern created by the crossing of the hands in the stroke down the leg. Place your hands a few inches below the horse's elbow on the front and back of the leg. Slide your thumbs upward and outward in an arc across the hair to activate circulation. Continue sliding your hands around to the inside of the leg and place the heel of one hand lightly on the top of the other with the back of both hands facing the horse's leg. Then, slide your hands lightly down the inside of the leg to mid cannon, pause, and slide your hands upward against the hair to the top of the inside of the leg, where you then slide them back to the outside of the leg (closer to you). Turn your hands inward and place one hand *above* the other on the leg (*not* one hand on top of the other). Slide both hands around the leg, one around the front and the other around the back, until your own forearms are crossed. Slide down the leg with your hands wrapped around the front and back of the leg, down over the hoof, until the sides of your thumbs actually touch the ground. Repeat all the way down the leg, on both fore- and hind legs.

OWL TTOUCH   Curve the fingers of one hand and touch the tip of the index finger with the tip of the thumb, creating a circle with your thumb and index finger. Use the side of the thumb and forefinger to make contact with the horse's body and perform circular *TTouches*. This less threatening *TTouch* is like *Chimp* or *Llama TTouch* (pp. 266 and 269).

PEACOCK   This exercise teaches the horse to respect your space in hand. When on the near side, hold the lead with your right hand and the *Tellington Wand* with the button end in your left hand. Sweep the *Wand* like a windshield wiper back and forth between you and the horse, slowly and rhythmically.

PELVIC TILT   Stand behind your horse facing his tail. Place one foot ahead of the other and your fists just below your horse's buttock bones. Push slightly forward, pause and hold, then slowly release. This helps relieve tension and increases the horse's sense of connection through his body. (See photo 9.4 D.)

PLAYGROUND OF HIGHER LEARNING   Working your horse over, through, and around obstacles, and "chunking" the steps down to do so, provides a positive alternative to teaching your horse via repetition and pressure. Obstacles in my "Playground" include: barrels; ground poles; cavalletti; plastic tarps/sheets; wooden platforms; teeter-totters; tires; and more. (See photos 7.3 A & B, 7.5 A & B, 9.1 D & E, 9.6 A–J, 9.11 C–F, 9.13 A & B, 9.14 A & B.)

PROMISE WRAP AND PROMISE ROPE   These *Tellington Tools* are so named because they "promise engagement" of the horse's hindquarters. Use an Ace bandage or elastic wrap, or a half-inch rope, fasten it to the horse's saddle on either side and fit it around the hindquarters. These *Tools* give spooky horses a feeling of containment, encourage lazy or short-striding horses to move out, and help those with a dropped back or ewe neck. (See photos 6.5 A & B, 9.1 B & C.)

RACCOON TTOUCH   These are very small, light *TTouches* done with the fingertips, but without contact with the fingernails. Curve your fingers so the distal phalange is vertical and your fingers are lightly apart. The heel of the hand and your wrist are held well off the body and the side of the thumb should not be in contact with the rest of the hand. Use this *TTouch* with a 1 to 3 pressure around areas of injury, swelling, or arthritis. (See photos 6.3, 9.1 A.)

RAINBOW TTOUCH   Stand facing your horse, slightly to one side, and move both hands at the same time in opposite directions on the inside and outside of each leg. Begin at the top and work down to the fetlock. This *TTouch* promotes circulation and energizes the horse prior to performance. (See photos 9.3 C & D.)

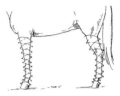

RHINO TTOUCH   Snug your thumb tightly against your curled fingers and make a 3 pressure circle-and-a-quarter on the horse's neck, *spongeing in* with your thumbnail (see below). At the same time, pull the crest toward you with the other hand, or turn the horse's head toward you, allowing the *TTouch* to go deeper. (See photo 3.6 C.)

RIB RELEASE   Place one hand on the horse's ribs with the thumb anchored in a groove between two ribs. Use the other hand to hold the horse's tail firmly down as you put pressure between the ribs, using your pelvis to create a slight torque between your hands and a 3 to 4 pressure. Use *Rib Release* to increase flexibility, improve lateral movement, and enhance the quality of the horse's gaits.

SHOULDER RELEASE   Run the side of your hand down the front of the horse's shoulder, feeling for the ridge of the scapula. When the shoulder is free you can fit your fingers under the front of the shoulder. If the shoulder is tight, turn the horse's head toward the side you are working, curl your fingers lightly and slip them into the groove between the scapula and the neck. This allows the horse to immediately lower and lengthen the head and neck, lengthen stride, and relax tense muscles in the shoulder, chest, neck, and back. (See photos 3.4 B, 9.9 G, 9.10 D.)

SNAIL'S PACE   This *TTouch* is like a mini *Coiled Python Lift* (p. 266) but done only with the first two phalanges of your fingers on one hand. Support the horse's skin bringing it up, pause, and then "carry" it back down. *Snail's Pace* helps release tension along the neck, just below the spine, or in the forearms.

SPONGE TTOUCH   Push the horse's skin in a circle-and-a-quarter and spiral into the center of the circle, as though depressing a wet sponge. Withdraw your fingers straight out and slide an inch or two to the next spot. Use a 2 to 3 pressure. This *TTouch* releases tight neck muscles.

SPRINGBOK TTOUCH   Place the tips of your fingers and thumb on the body, with your thumb about 2 inches away from fingers. Bring your fingers and thumb up, off the horse's body in a light "snapping," lifting motion that actually makes a snapping, thumping sound. This *TTouch* is generally used over the loin area to activate areas that are tight or shut down and to increase energy output.

STATUE   With your horse standing squarely, back away until you've reached the end of the lead. As he stands quietly, move to the right and then to the left, keeping the arm holding the *Tellington Wand* stretched out toward the horse to maintain his distance. Concentrate on your breathing and body posture, holding the *intent* that he stands absolutely still. This exercise teaches the horse patience, obedience, and trust.

SWISH OF THE ZEBRA'S TAIL   This exercise is a traditional method of teaching the horse to come forward at the walk and trot. The handler stands facing the same direction as the horse, holding the lead in both hands. The *Tellington Wand* should be held at the button end in the outside hand, along with the end of the lead. The inside hand should be on the lead about 14 inches from the halter. Use the tip of the *Wand* behind you on the horse's side or hindquarters, "bouncing" it while making certain you aren't pulling forward with the hand position close to the halter.

TAIL TTOUCH   This is actually a "suite" of *TTouches* that are especially beneficial for horses who fear movement or noise behind or around them, who kick at other horses or in the trailer. Tail work also helps relax tight back and neck muscles and stops tail wringing/switching. Begin by standing safely to one side of your horse's hindquarters. Hold the tail in one hand and with your other hand separate a small clump of hair and stroke slowly to the end of the hair. Then, with one hand on the croup, make 3 pressure *Raccoon TTouches* (p. 271) all around the area before placing both hands under the sides of the tail and doing small circles with the tail until you feel your horse release it. Lift the tail by grasping a clump of hair and circle it in both directions, then hold the tail firmly between both hands, tipping the vertebrae back and forth down the tail-bone (called "pearling"). Put one hand under the tail about 6 inches from the top, place the other hand on top of the tailbone a few inches below the first hand, and push the tail inward with your bottom hand as you lift up with your other hand, creating an arch as you rotate the tail several times in each direction. Finally, hold the tail firmly in both hands and shift your weight back and from the left foot to the right, pausing a few seconds and slowly releasing the traction by shifting your weight slowly forward again. Repeat two or three times. (See photos 3.4 D, 8.5, 8.11 A, 9.4 E, 9.12 E, 10.2 C.)

TAMING THE TIGER   This "half-cross-tie position" is a safe way to tie or retrain a horse to tie. It controls pawing, prevents kicking or biting, and encourages the horse to stand quietly. It is best used in space with a boundary on one side and behind, such as a fence or wall. With the horse parallel to the fence or wall on one side, fasten the *Chain* or *Zephyr Lead* (pp. 266 and 273) up the left side of the halter (when you are on the near side), and thread a 15- to 20-foot rope through the halter ring under the horse's chin, through a safe tie ring on the fence or wall, then clip it to the right- (off-) side halter ring. Hold the rope and lead line, separated by your index finger, in your left hand, and use your right hand to stroke the horse and/or position him with the *Tellington Wand*. (See photo 10.4.)

TARANTULAS PULLING THE PLOW   This is actually similar to an ancient form of "skin rolling," called *chua'ka* in human therapy. It is thought to break habitual emotional patterns in humans by releasing skin that has become "stuck" to muscles due to longstanding holding patterns. *Chua'ka* can be painful and invasive, but the *TTouch* version is pleasant. It releases fear and instills confidence. "Walk" the fingertips of both hands positioned side by side, pulling the thumbs behind them like a plow, along the horse's body in lines running parallel to the spine from neck to hindquarters, and down both front and hind legs. It should, at most, create only a small furrow; in the case of very tight skin, slide over it.

TELLINGTON TRAINING BIT   This bit is stainless steel with a copper roller and port, with curved, loose shanks and two sets of reins. It has the effect of softening the mouth, jaw, poll, back, and pelvis of the horse, and is an effective tool for horses who are on the forehand, strung out, ewe-necked, stiff in the back or hindquarters, uneven in their gait or spooky, to name just a few benefits. (See photos 6.1, 9.14 D, 10.9 A & B.)

TELLINGTON WAND   The *Wand* is a 4-foot (120-centimeter) stiff white dressage whip with a hard plastic "button" on the end, which I import from Germany and have specially constructed for optimum balance and effect. It is called a "Wand" because most people think of a "whip" as something used for punishment. Instead, the *Wand* is used as an extension of the handler's arm to stroke, and give reassurance and light signals. (See photos 9.4 G, 10.2 B, 10.3.)

TIGER TTOUCH   Place your hand on the horse's body in a claw-like position, the first phalange perpendicular to the body, with fingers spread apart and your wrist raised several inches off the body. Maintain a steady connection with your thumb and move your four fingers simultaneously in four circle-and-a-quarters. *Tiger TTouch* stimulates areas of the body lacking feeling or awareness. Use pressure 2 to 5.

TROIKA TTOUCH   This is a two-part move, using the side of your thumb and all four fingers opening and closing as they circle over the skin. With your fingers curved and your thumb near your index finger, start by sliding your nails across the skin in a circular, scratching motion, with a bigger circle-and-a-quarter, then a smaller one. Your thumb also makes a circle-and-a-quarter. This *TTouch* can be done with a 1 pressure with the fingernails, or with a firmer more activating 2 to 3 pressure, depending on what is acceptable to the horse. It can be a great way to get acquainted with a horse and establishes trust in horses who are fearful or wary of people.

TTEAM   This was the original acronym for the Tellington Touch Equine Awareness Method and the Tellington Touch Every Animal Method. Although you may still see reference to it in my older books and videos, in the last decade the work I and my practitioners do has become the Tellington Method or Tellington TTouch Training.

TTOUCH PRESSURE SCALE   My *TTouches* are applied on a special scale developed to ensure the horse experiences them without discomfort while allowing them to remain effective. You can read details about the Pressure Scale on p. 262.

TURTLE TTOUCH   With open hands on opposite sides of the horse's body, such as on each side of his neck or jaw, place one hand at "twelve o'clock" and the other at "six o'clock" (so one is high and one is low). Move the skin on each side in a circle-and-a-half to bring the opposite hand to twelve o'clock and six o'clock, pause, and with the hand at twelve, support the tissue in an upward motion, and with the hand at six, take it slightly downward. Pause again and go back to the starting point. You can also lift with both hands, or do not lift and simply pause before the circle.

ZEPHYR LEAD   A nylon lead with a quarter-inch-thick, soft rope on one end instead of a chain; ideal for use with sensitive or young horses.

ZIGZAG TTOUCH   This *TTouch* consists of diagonal strokes, primarily along the horse's back, but it can also be used on the neck, croup, or under the belly. Curve the fingers of your hand and hold it against the horse's skin with a 2 to 3 pressure. Move your hand upward across the hair while "opening" your fingers and thumb. Reverse the motion as you then move your hand downward and repeat the motion along the body in a zigzag line. Move about 12 inches up or down with each stroke. You can use both hands to perform this *TTouch* over the loins or under the belly. *Zigzag TTouch* can "break the freeze" when your horse is blocked and shut down and is excellent for encouraging rapid cooling when applied under your saddle pad before removing your tack.

**FOR MORE INFORMATION ABOUT THE TELLINGTON METHOD,
VISIT MY WEBSITE WWW.TTOUCH.COM.**

LINDA TELLINGTON-JONES HIGHLY RECOMMENDS THE FOLLOWING TITLES REFERENCED IN THIS BOOK

The Bond by Lynne McTaggart (Free Press, 2011)

Centered Riding by Sally Swift (Trafalgar Square Books, 1985)

The Divine Matrix by Gregg Braden (Hay House, 2008)

The Field by Lynne McTaggart (Harper Perennial, 2008)

Gallop to Freedom by Magali Delgado and Frédéric Pignon (Trafalgar Square Books, 2009)

The Heartmath Solution by Doc Childre and Howard Martin (HarperOne, 2000)

The Hidden Messages in Water by Masaru Emoto (Atria Books, 2005)

The High Performance Mind by Anna Wise (Tarcher, 1997)

The Horse's Pain-Free Back and Saddle-Fit Book by Joyce Harman, DVM (Trafalgar Square Books, 2004)

The Intention Experiment by Lynne McTaggart (Free Press, 2008)

Klaus Balkenhol: The Man and His Training Methods by Britta Schöffmann (Trafalgar Square Books, 2007)

The New Basic Training of the Young Horse by Ingrid and Reiner Klimke (Trafalgar Square Books, 2010)

The Secret of the Lost Mode of Prayer by Gregg Braden (Hay House, 2006)

Zero Limits by Joe Vitale and Ihaleakala Hew Len (Wiley, 2008)

FURTHER READING AND SELECTED BIBLIOGRAPHY

Bee, Vanessa. *The Horse Agility Handbook*: *A Step-by-Step Introduction to the Sport.* North Pomfret, Vermont: Trafalgar Square Books, 2012.

Cayce, Edgar. *Auras: An Essay on the Meaning of Colors.* Virginia Beach, Virginia: A.R.E. Press, 1973.

Cooper, J.J., McDonald, L., and Millis, D.S. "The effect of increasing visual horizons on stereotypic weaving: implications for the social housing of stabled horses." *Applied Behavior Science.* 69 (1) 67–83, 2000.

Fillis, James. *Breaking & Riding.* Guilford, Connecticut: The Lyons Press, 2005.

Getty, Juliet. *Feed Your Horse Like a Horse: Optimize Your Horse's Nutrition for a Lifetime of Vibrant Health.* Indianapolis, Indiana: Dog Ear Publishing, 2009.

Hamilton, Allan. *Zen Mind, Zen Horse: The Science and Spirituality of Working with Horses.* North Adams, Massachusetts: Storey Publishing, 2011.

Harman, Joyce. *English Saddles: How to Fit—Pain-Free.* North Pomfret, Vermont: Trafalgar Square Books, 2006.

Klimke, Ingrid and Reiner. *Cavalletti: Schooling of Horse and Rider Over Ground Poles.* North Pomfret, Vermont: Trafalgar Square Books, 2008.

Loving, Nancy S. *All Horse Systems Go: The Horse Owner's Full-Color Veterinary Care and Conditioning Resource for Modern Performance, Sport, and Pleasure Horses.* North Pomfret, Vermont: Trafalgar Square Books, 2006.

McGreevy, P., Warren-Smith, A., and Guisard, Yann. "The effect of double bridles and jaw-clamping crank nosebands on temperature of eyes and facial skin of horses." *Journal of Veterinary Behavior.* Volume 7, Issue 3, pp. 142-148, May 2012.

Meyners, Eckart. *Rider Fitness: Body & Brain.* North Pomfret, Vermont: Trafalgar Square Books, 2011.

Mistral, Kip. "Heart to Heart." *Horse Connection Magazine.* August 2007.

Podhajsky, Alois. *My Horses, My Teachers*. North Pomfret, Vermont: Trafalgar Square Books, 1997.

Reed, Robertson, and Addison. "Heart rate variability measurements and the prediction of ventricular arrhythmias." *QJM: An International Journal of Medicine*. Volume 98, Issue 2, pp. 87–95.

Retallack, Dorothy L. *The Sound of Music and Plants*. Camarillo, California: Devorss & Co, 1973.

Sapolsky, Robert M. *Why Zebras Don't Get Ulcers*. New York: Holt Paperbacks, 2004.

Savoie, Jane. *It's Not Just About the Ribbons: It's About Enriching Riding (and Life) with a Winning Attitude*. North Pomfret, Vermont: Trafalgar Square Books, 2008.

Savoie, Jane. *That Winning Feeling! Program Your Mind for Peak Performance*. North Pomfret, Vermont: Trafalgar Square Books, 1997.

Shideler, R.K. *Management of the Pregnant Mare and Newborn Foal*. Colorado State University, Experimental Station,1984.

Steiner, Betsy, and Bryant, Jennifer. *A Gymnastic Riding System Using Mind, Body & Spirit*. North Pomfret, Vermont: Trafalgar Square Books, 2003.

Tucker, Renee. *Where Does My Horse Hurt: A Hands-On Guide to Evaluating Pain and Dysfunction Using Chiropractic Methods*. North Pomfret, Vermont: Trafalgar Square Books, 2011.

Wendler, M. Cecilia. *The HeART of Nursing: Expressions of Creative Art in Nursing*. Indianapolis, Indiana: Sigma Theta Tau International, 2005.

PHOTO AND ILLUSTRATION CREDITS

Barbara Schnell: Part One, 1.2, 1.3 A & B, 2.5, 2.6, 3.1 A–C, 6.2 A & B, Part Two, 7.3 A & B, 8.2, 8.11 A–C, 9.6 A–J, 10.2 E & I, 10.3

Gabriele Metz: Foreword, 2.1, 2.2, 2.3, 3.3 A & B, 3.4 A–D, 3.5, 6.4 A & B, 7.2, 7.5 A & B, 7.7, 8.12, 9.1 A–F, 11.1 A–C, 11.2

Gabrielle Boiselle: 3.6 A–F, 6.3, 8.13, 10.10 A–G, 10.11 A & B, 10.12 A–C

©Annalena Kuhn: 4.2, 7.4, 7.6, 7.8 A–C, 8.3, 8.4, 8.5, 8.6, 8.7, 8.8, 9.2 A & B, 9.6 K, 10.2 A–D, 10.2 F–H

Ingvil Ann Schirling: 8.9 A & B, 8.10 A–F

AshalaTylor.com: 6.1, 9.12 A–F, 9.14 A–D

Ella Bittel, Holistic Veterinarian, www.spiritsintransition.org: 9.10 A–E, 9.11 A–F, 9.13 A & B

Eric G. Jones: 9.4 A–N

Kate Riordan: 6.5 A & B

Susan Harding: 9.9 A–H

Courtesy of Dodo Laugks: 9.5 A & B

Ingo Grammel: 9.5 C

Courtesy of Kristen McDonald: 10.5

Rebecca Didier: 10.7 A & B, 10.9 A & B

Ellen van Lloewven: 1.4 A & B, 1.5

Courtesy of Joyce Harman (by Susan Harris): 10.8 A & B

Courtesy of Frédéric Pignon and Magali Delgado: 10.13 A & B

Courtesy of Linda Tellington-Jones: 1.1, 2.4, 5.1, 9.3 A–I, 9.7, 9.8, 10.4

Carrie Fradkin: 3.2, 4.1, 4.3, 4.4, 4.5, 4.6 A–D, 7.1, 8.1, 10.1, 12.1 A–D, 12.2, 12.3

All illustrations appearing on pp. 262–273 are from *The Ultimate Horse Behavior and Training Book*: Laura Maestro (pp. 262; 267 top right); Jeanne Kloepfer (pp. 264 top left, bottom right; 267 middle left, bottom right); and Cornelia Koller (pp. 264 middle right; 265; 266; 267 top left, bottom; 268; 269; 271; 272; 273).

ACKNOWLEDGMENTS

....••.From Linda Tellington-Jones:

While strolling along a path with my dog Rayne, I started to develop a mental list of people and horses to acknowledge in this book. It was a task I welcomed, and as I started adding up the names and years, my heart swelled with gratitude.

Later that afternoon as I sat in front of my computer typing the list, a wave of humbleness overcame me as I stared at the compilation of names: some of the top riders and trainers in the dressage world, and in the horse world in general. In addition to accruing medal-winning accolades, they are caring and compassionate horse people whom I believe acknowledge horses as gifts of spirit and companionship like I do.

Many of these experienced and talented riders and trainers shared their wisdom and techniques with me over the years, and indeed you may have already read about my experiences with them in the pages of this book. I revel in the memories and my connections with them and with the marvelous horses I have been priviliged to work with. In creating a title and theme for this book, it is these experiences that gave me the courage to "color outside the box."

And so it is with a respectful heart that I acknowledge these people and horses.

My sincere thanks goes to my brilliant and infinitely patient publisher, Caroline Robbins, for her insistence that I must bring the Tellington Method to a broader audience in the world of dressage. Her attention to the smallest detail is legendary, and I am so grateful for her support and enthusiasm for my work.

Caroline insisted I write this book because Klaus Balkenhol praised the work I did on his gold-medal-winning horse Goldstern in *Klaus Balkenhol: The Man and His Training Methods* by Britta Schoffmann (see p. 153 for details). I have so very much enjoyed sharing my work with Klaus and Judith Balkenhol, and their daughter Anabel, for almost two decades. My heartfelt thanks goes to Klaus for the fair and kind methods with which he so skillfully trains both horses and riders. I treasure the lessons he gave me on the brilliant stallion, Garcon, pictured on the cover of this book and for his openness to my work when he was first approached by my German publisher, Kosmos Verlag in 1995 and asked to participate in the making of my *TTouch for Dressage* video. In the ensuing years I've been back many times to the Balkenhol stable to work with their horses and twice to give seminars for the Xenophon Society, which is actively supporting the maintenance and support of classical riding principles and training of dressage horses.

Finding adequate words to thank my co-author, Rebecca Didier, senior editor of Trafalgar Square Books, is a daunting challenge. Although she has been the editor of many excellent horse books, this is the first time she has been listed as a co-author. It is my privilege to make her name public. I'm often asked how I manage to write so many books with my teaching schedule. With this book I followed my usual procedure. I sat down for three days with Rebecca and "downloaded" concepts and stories for many hours onto her trusty tape recorder. She spent more than three years putting the book together and digging deeper to research some of my basic concepts. It has been such a pleasure to work with her, and I am thrilled with what we've created in this book.

It is such an great honor to have the foreword written by Ingrid Klimke. She is an inspiring trainer, teacher, and rider, and I loved the days I spent sharing *TTouch* and the magic of the *Liberty Neck Ring* with Ingrid and her mother, Ruth. Although Dr. Reiner Klimke is no longer with us, I believe his influence is carried on by all who experienced his clarity of teaching and generosity of heart toward horses and riders. I first met Dr. Klimke and his family at his private stable in 1989 and gave them a mini-seminar before visiting with them in their home. Before sitting down to lunch, Dr. Klimke gave me a tour of his cabinet full of trophies. He pulled out two Olympic gold medals and with his playful charm, hung them around my neck! I could never have guessed that years later he would invite me to actively participate with him in his last four-day dressage seminar in California. At the end of the seminar, as we were getting ready to leave for the airport, he said, "Next year we'll do another seminar together and film it so riders will get to know the value of your work." His support and enthusiasm for my work was incredibly influential in my decision to write this book.

I want to thank the many photographers (all horse lovers) who contributed to this project. My dear friend, Gabriele Boiselle, is almost like my "personal" photographer because we have done so many photo shoots together in so many countries. Here her photos of Frédéric Pignon and Magali Delgado and their horses lend a special flavor to the book. The two days I spent with Gabriele Metz photographing my work with Ingrid Klimke were particularly memorable. I am grateful to Gabriele's extraordinary skills and her friendship with Ingrid, which helped make this shoot so special.

The cover photo of me riding Klaus Balkenhol's stallion Garçon by Ellen Van Lloewven holds a special place in my heart because I have such poignant memories of our photo shoot in Paris with the French Olympic jumping team and chief veterinarian, Dr. Sylvi Guigan. And I'm so thankful to have the priceless photos of my lessons with Klaus Balkenhol. Thank you also to Barbara Schnell, Ashala Tylor, Ella Bittel, Annalena Kuhn, Ingvil Schirling, Eric Jones, Susan Harding, and Kate Riordan for the use of their photographs in illustrating my work.

Frédéric Pignon and Magali Delgado are next on my list. I want to thank them for their generosity of heart—toward me and the horses and peope who surround them. I first had the pleasure of meeting them and working with their horses when they were on tour with *Cavalia* in California seven years ago. I have since enjoyed numerous visits to their home in southern France. I have the delightful honor of being referred to in their book *Gallop to Freedom* as their "fairy godmother," because they say I always seem to turn up when they need me! I've known many really brilliant horsemen and horsewomen over the years, but I've never seen anyone work with horses at liberty like Frédéric or with the grace that Magali teaches her riding students. These two are the quintessential role models for how to develop meaningful relationships with horses.

One of my most inspiring Easter Sundays was spent with Tony and Marina Meggle and Dodo and Dieter Laugks. The support of Dodo and Dieter has been a highlight, and working with Weltall, and many of their other horses, has kept me energized throughout the writing of this book.

I'm very impressed by and grateful to Dodo's groom, Kathy Raft, for the dedication she displayed in skillfully learning and applying *TTouch* to Weltall almost every day for over a year. Her work contributed greatly to the success that Weltall experienced in his comeback in the German dressage world, winning 10 Grand Prix in three months.

Thank you to Anke Recktenwald. It's doubtful that this book could have made the publishing deadline without the assistance of Anke, who while visiting me in Hawaii spent many generous hours reading the manuscript and pointing out missing pieces when she could have been out surfing or swimming with the wild dolphins off the shore.

I've so enjoyed knowing Barbi Breen-Gurley, who I first met more than 30 years ago. In the last few years, I've spent many hours in the arena working with her horses on the ground, in addition to riding her Grand Prix horse Octango. I thank Barbi for the many happy hours I've spent at Sea Horse Ranch.

Annegret Ast was the only woman who served on the Austrian Equine Education Committee chaired by Brigadier General Albright. She was also an alternate rider on the Austrian dressage team and our first Tellington Instructor in Europe. It was Annegret who in 1984 organized a day-long seminar for riders of the Spanish Riding School to be held at the stable of dressage trainer Arthur Kottas, with whom I have stayed in contact all these years, and she assisted me during the filming of my *TTouch for Dressage* video featuring Klaus Balkenhol riding Goldstern and Gracioso, and Nicole Uphoff on Rembrandt. Annegret left us more than a decade ago, but her contributions to the horse world are still felt by all who knew her. It's a rare day that goes by that I don't feel thankful that she was such an important participant in my life.

The time I spent with Nicole Uphoff and Rembrandt rates among my fondest memories. I thank Nicole for trusting me to work with her incredible horse although at the time my work was new to her

I met Colonel Alois Podhajsky in 1969 in Woodside, California, when he was coaching Kyra Downton. I, like tens of thousands of others, love his book *My Horses, My Teachers*, and I thank him for his inspiration and his open heart.

In 1997 I had the pleasure of working with Rafael La Vista and his Andalusian stallion, Garboso, in preparation for the National Andalusian Dressage Championships in Mexico City. I thank Rafael for the three days we spent together, which helped (much to all of our delight) Garboso win his class.

I'm very grateful for the experience I gained working with American dressage riders Sandy Howard and Gwen Stockebrand at the World Championships in Goodwin, England, in the late 1970s. That's when I sat with Gwen in the stall with her $300 horse, visualizing and sensualizing the ride that would ultimately win her the bronze medal.

Thank you to Jennifer Oldham and Carl Hester who had me work with the fabulous horse Gershwin in 1995. Thanks to Christine Stuckelberger for the time we spent together in 1984, including our week at the Aachen Dressage Championships. I've always been grateful for the recognition she gave me.

Thank you to Robert Dover and Marnie Reeder for inviting me to work on Fledermaus and Romantico. And to Claus Earhorn and his gold-medal-winning event horse "Justyn Thyme" for agreeing to be a case study in my German video on jumping and event horses.

Even though many people may not know Fredy Knie, Sr., I consider his visit to one of my trainings in southern Germany among the many special highlights of my life. Although he was head of the famous Knie Circus, he was also highly respected among leading European dressage trainers for his ability to teach horses to piaffe and passage without stress. I was fortunate to observe him at work in Switzerland a number of times. He was a friend of Dr. Reiner Klimke, and I have a feeling that the two of them are sitting together in Heaven, sending sparks of advice to dressage riders all over the world.

I thank Kyra Kyrklund and Matador for the time we worked together.

A number of years ago, Ella Bittel, who had just graduated from veterinary school in Germany, had the courage to trust me and my training methods in order to transform a special dressage horse. She then spent the summer driving me to clinics around Europe, "soaking up" my work. In the past five years Ella has assisted me at week-long trainings throughout the United States. I thank her for her time and devotion to the Tellington Method.

When I watched Elena Petushkova and her horse Pepo win the Olympic silver in Mexico City in 1968, I never dreamed that 16 years later I would have the great pleasure of working with her in Moscow, Russia. I thank her and the other Russian Olympic dressage riders and veterinarians who I worked with on five separate occasions as a Citizen Ambassador.

Many, many thanks go to Caroline Larrouilh, French dressage connoisseur, equine massage therapist, and Tellington Method Practitioner. I so appreciate Caroline's endless encouragement in sharing Tellington TTouch with the dressage world. I also want to thank Caroline's marketing partner, Kim Carneal. The two of them have made me aware of the value of passing this work along to dressage riders.

Thank you to veterinarians Dr. Joyce Harman and Dr. Renee Tucker, and to Juliet Getty for their contributions to this book. Thank you to US Dressage Team Technical Advisor Anne Gribbons and her groom, Kristen McDonald.

Any book I write has to include my gratitude for the ongoing partnership I have with my sister, Robyn Hood, and the beautiful way she has contributed to the Tellington Method over these years—not to mention the fact that she helps keep me on track!

I can't imagine being able to continuously function at full-tilt without the support of Kirsten Henry. Kirsten came from Germany 17 years ago to spend a month with me, and ever since has held a primary place in the *TTouch* organization, heading my office in Santa Fe, New Mexico. Her dedication, talent, and skill at keeping the connections going between Santa Fe and the rest of the world make a significant contribution to my life.

Words cannot express my gratitude for the love and support that my husband Roland Kleger has brought to my life since our marriage in 2000. His skill in editing is something I tap into every day. The fact that he is willing to accompany me on my twice-yearly teaching trips to Europe brings more joy than can be imagined. My intense life is only possible because of Roland's love for me and for the work that I do.

And thank YOU for reading this book and forming a clear intention to create a better world for dressage horses everywhere.

......From Rebecca M. Didier:

I would like to thank Linda Tellington-Jones for the amazing opportunity to work with her, and for enabling me to, I hope, play a small part in helping make the world a better place for horses, whatever their breed or discipline.

Thank you to Caroline Robbins and Martha Cook at Trafalgar Square Books for all they have taught me during my tenure there, for their support of my writing, and for their friendship.

Thank you to my parents, Ronald and Francesca Schmidt, who gave me horses against the odds. I appreciate all they sacrificed through the years to make my dreams come true.

Thanks to my brother, Erik, for inspiring me with his own creativity and supporting me with his constant friendship.

And to my husband, Brian, and my son, Augustin, who put up with my working into the wee hours and on weekends to get my words right. I love my boys—their presence in my life is the source of the smile and infinite hope I bring to each new day.

INDEX

Page numbers in *italics* indicate illustrations.